ENGAGING
DISCOURSE
2.0

A 21st Century Composition Reader & Curriculum

Bradley Summerhill
Truckee Meadows Community College

Kendall Hunt
publishing company

Cover image © Shutterstock.com

Kendall Hunt
publishing company

www.kendallhunt.com
Send all inquiries to:
4050 Westmark Drive
Dubuque, IA 52004-1840

ISBN 978-1-7924-3192-0

Published in the United States of America

WELCOME TO *ENGAGING DISCOURSE 2.0*

Welcome to the most important conversations of our time: literacy, social (dis)connection, neuroplasticity, appropriation, love, AI, Gen Z, and happiness. New discourses define a new era of human experience. Yet these same discourses remain timeless, as relevant as medicine and mindfulness, love and literacy, the latest technology, generational discontent, and the pursuit of happiness. (Not to mention that a computer will soon be doing my job for me.) And all of these discourses, the new and the timeless alike, are crucially important to the first generation to be born in the new millennium. We welcome you to discover, and later in life rediscover, these vital conversations.

BRIEF CONTENTS

CONTENTS

Author's Note

Unlike most textbooks, this one has a personality—namely, me. Over the years, I have developed my own perspective, of course, but I feel no need to force the world to inhabit my viewpoint. In fact, when this course functions according to plan, students are forced to develop their own independent perspectives. Yet we live in a time and in a cultural moment where we, at least we so-called adults, are suspicious of each other's social and political motives. So, let me make it clear: I have no agenda.

Wait. That's not true. I do have one item on my agenda, actually. I would like us to avoid binary modes of thinking: *either/or, yes/no, us/them*. Complexity is embedded in the textbook's title. "Engaging Discourse" can be understood as an adjective modifying a noun, as in, *we appreciate this engaging discourse*. "Engaging Discourse" can also be understood as a verb acting upon a direct object, as in, *we are engaging this discourse*. Maybe that's not as clever or complex as I would like it to be, but it's the best I've got right now. *Engaging Discourse 2.0* reflects my belief that college students must, for a wide variety of sound reasons, learn how to engage in complex and respectful modes of discourse.

Any claims that I make in my unit introductions I substantiate with good evidence, cited in a "Further Inquiry" bibliography at the end of each unit. I am not, however, attempting to persuade anyone of anything. As writing instructors, we want students to develop their own views based on sound principles of critical reasoning and mutual respect for the views of others. I am more likely to ask open-ended questions than to attempt to sway anyone toward a particular viewpoint. The fancy term for this effort is "dialectic." I prefer "dialogue" or "conversation." It should be a normal mode of discourse in America, not the rarity it has become.

These are apolitical discourses, the most important conversations of our time. Some—love, literacy, happiness—seem ancient, while others—AI, neuroplasticity, appropriation—seem new.

Most, if not all, of these discourses are science-based. Although concepts of "love" and "happiness" speak to the core of the human experience and humanistic scholarship, we approach the topics mainly from an angle of scientific evidence, often incorporating cutting-edge studies. These are the most timely topics of our age, yet—as with any good liberal arts curriculum—the topics remain as timeless as our need for love and happiness.

Bradley Summerhill
Reno, Nevada

The Definition of "Discourse"

1. verbal <u>interchange</u> of ideas; *especially* : <u>conversation</u>
2. **a**: formal and orderly and usually extended expression of thought on a subject
   b: connected speech or writing
   c: a <u>linguistic</u> unit (such as a conversation or a story) larger than a sentence
3. a mode of organizing knowledge, ideas, or experience that is rooted in language and its concrete contexts (such as history or institutions)
   - critical *discourse*
4. *archaic*: the capacity of orderly thought or procedure: <u>rationality</u>
5. *obsolete*: social familiarity

First Known Use: Fifteenth century
Examples of "discourse" in a sentence:

He likes to engage in lively *discourse* with his visitors.
She delivered an entertaining *discourse* on the current state of the film industry.

—Merriam-Webster Dictionary, *www.merriam-webster.com*

Discourse as Dinner Conversation

American literary theorist Kenneth Burke (1897–1993) famously describes "discourse" as an ongoing conversation. He creates the following metaphor to describe the process of literary discourse and academic scholarship: Imagine that you arrive at a dinner party. A lively conversation has been going on for some time. You must listen for a moment to figure out what the conversation is all about. Before you jump in, you want to make sure that you have heard from several voices in order to determine not only the subject matter but also the tone and the manner of the conversation—in other words, in order to determine how these people are communicating. Once you feel familiar enough with the subject matter, and once you are confident in how you will approach the subject, you offer your own insights and contributions.

It's a useful metaphor. In composition, we often paraphrase the main points of one or more authoritative sources in order to familiarize ourselves (and our audience) with the subject matter, and in order to establish a proper tone and context into which we can set forth our own insights, our own contributions.

We use the term "public discourse" because the conversation is not really taking place at a private dinner party. These conversations take place in all kinds of public venues. For example, public discourse takes place in many forms via social media. Public discourse takes place on news broadcasts, in podcasts, in TED Talks, in blogs and vlogs, and in college classrooms. Open public discourse enjoys a rich history that predates the founding of the United States and reaches back to the ancient Greek and Roman civilizations.

We want to learn how to write college essays. That's an immediate goal. At the same time, we strive to maintain a rich legacy of meaningful public conversation in order to carry these traditions into the twenty-first century and beyond.

READ THIS NOW! *A Preface for Students and Instructors*

This textbook is designed to honor your time, your money, your curiosity, and your well-being. That sentence—neatly italicized—is intended for students and instructors alike.

The students I teach tend to have jobs. My colleagues manage 15 credits per semester, often five classes of composition. We all deserve the most and the best that we can get from a textbook, a textbook that simplifies and clarifies the complex tasks of research and composition, a textbook that demands authentic engagement and high levels of critical thinking.

"How many of you work a job at least 20 hours per week?" I ask a late afternoon class of 28 students. Every hand in the room goes up. For how many years, decades now, have I been counseling students to prioritize the abstract concept of education over the concrete reality of a paycheck? I also counsel my students to avoid clichés, but this one comes to mind: Money doesn't grow on trees.

The Millennials (born circa 1985 to 2000) and Gen Z (born 1995-2010) have been criticized in academia, in media, and in popular culture for "having no grit," for being entitled whiners, for lacking a work ethic and a learning ethic. Maybe so. Maybe that's true of twenty-first century Americans in general. I have a hard time seeing it, though, especially when all those hands go up in the classroom. I see the latest generation—usually called Gen Z—struggling with a new world and a tough economy. As unemployment rates hit historic lows, college and high school students, who aspired beyond the service sector, already faced a tough economy. Then the Covid-19 pandemic made the job situation much worse. We suddenly faced an uncertain economic future, at least in the short term. Even before the pandemic, though, we were witnessing a twenty-first century that welcomed part-time service sector employment, a world where an elite four-year university degree costs a quarter of a million dollars. And the saddest notion is that few of my students seem to possess the wherewithal to question the validity of the cultural criticism that rains down on them. Various and sundry measures reveal that the latest generation is ignorant and unknowledgeable. Yet that hardly distinguishes them from the youth of prior ages. What's unprecedented is the global spread and flow of information. Information of all sorts, factual and otherwise, spreads across our world at light speed, while knowledge (that is, understanding how to make use of the information) becomes scarce.

We are not born with knowledge. We have to learn. In an age where literature retreats to the realm of fantasy and mythology (*Harry Potter, Hunger Games, A Song of Fire and Ice* i.e. *Game of Thrones,* all kinds and manners of super hero, etc.) we continue to believe in a human creature who is and remains exactly who he or she is at birth—chosen boy, girl of destiny, call it what you will. (The Disney iterations of *Star Wars* have turned "The Force" into a magical birthright rather than a discipline that requires training under wise masters.)

Science tells us that we *become.* Myth and culture tell us that we *are.* Our environment ("nurture," training, practice, learning) allows us to maximize our innate qualities ("nature"). In the twenty-first century, as scientists uncover evidence substantiating the importance of *context* and *environment,* popular culture and mainstream media seem stuck in a twentieth century paradigm.

Engaging Discourse 2.0 touches on a *nature/nurture* dynamic only indirectly. The reading guides encourage students to perceive and to formulate such connections. For example, our brain is inherently plastic (nature), yet whether that plasticity turns in a positive or negative direction largely depends on external input (nurture).

As you explore each unit discourse, please also discover the many connections *between* the units. Make it a fun brain puzzle to put together each unit with every other one: Where does romance meet AI? (Hmm. Online dating?)

Engaging Discourse 2.0 operates in the inquiring spirit that used to be called the Socratic method and now seems to be called a "flipped classroom." ("Hold on," I tell my students, "you want me to *teach* you something? That's so twentieth century!")

Engaging Discourse 2.0 provides scaffolding and a multitude of progressive composition assignments appropriate for first year college composition, following best practices and pedagogical guidelines. The variety of readings and topics honors an instructor's academic freedom.

Engaging Discourse 2.0 is not a cumbersome anthology devoid of guidance, and it is not an empty shell of a resource guide. We offer something that is not readily available in the bookstore or on the Internet—an all-in-one reader, content-specific exercise guide, and comprehensive research curriculum that honors the needs and interests of both students and instructor.

Three Levels of Essay

Engaging Discourse 2.0 features three fundamental levels of essay assignment. **Level I, II, and III essay prompts appear in each unit.** Students and instructor alike will naturally strive to personalize these topics.

The parameters outlined below are suggestions *which must be adjusted to fit student and instructor needs.*

Level I: Analysis-Response

1. Introduce the Text
2. Define a Discourse
3. Analyze the Evidence as Presented in the Article
4. Respond to the Article

Typical length requirements range from 500 to 1000 words, plus bibliography.

First and foremost, analyze the reading material. Offer a global introduction to an outside audience, including relevant thesis interpretation, relevant background or context information, and identification of a significant public discourse or matter of public concern (*Why do experts care about this topic? Why should anyone care?*). Offer **detailed analysis** of the author's language, evidence, techniques, and argument. Conclude with an appropriate, thoughtful personal **response** to the author's argument and the overall discourse.

Level I writing involves critical exposition and reflection. Level I writing assignments might include comprehension reports, article or book reviews, argument response, field reports, personal narrations, or reader responses.

Typical Level I Evaluation Criteria:

Holistic Assessment: Student demonstrates the global capacity to analyze the source article, including thesis and supporting evidence; on deadline; meets word count.	20%
Student introduces the source text to readers not familiar with the source material; general interest audience, academic audience, or other audience as specified by instructor.	10%
Student places the analysis-response within the context of a significant public discourse; the essay indicates why this is important subject matter.	10%

Student examines and illuminates the author's most significant supporting evidence. Student's commentary clarifies and contextualizes the source text.	20%
Student quotes meaningfully and insightfully multiple times from the source text; proper handling of quotations; appropriate integration and punctuation.	20%
Student follows proper MLA or APA format, or another standard format as specified by the instructor.	10%
Student's ability to draft and revise for clear standard usage and syntax.	10%

See alternate Suggested Level I Analysis-Response Evaluation Criteria *in unit one Resources.*

Level II: Making Connections

1. Identify a Public Discourse
2. Analyze Thesis and Evidence in Two (or more) Texts
3. Demonstrate Interaction of Language and Ideas Between the Texts
   - *Synthesis of Unrelated Texts:*
     - What new ideas arise from discourse between these separate texts?
   - *Synthesis of Related Texts:*
     - What insights or additional knowledge arise from discourse between texts that address similar subject matter?

Typical length requirements range anywhere from 600 to 1800 words, plus bibliography.

Offer a global introduction of a relevant, significant public discourse, demonstrating how the themes and evidence in two (or more) separate texts speak within this discourse or form a new discourse or a new understanding. The goal is "synthesis," that is, bringing together words and ideas to form a coherent whole. In writing, *synthesis* means to form a connection, or to create a new idea by combining separate or even disparate ideas. *Address an outside audience, or address a specific audience as identified by your instructor* (for example, you may be required to speak to a particular discourse community, an audience of psychologists or biologists, for example). Identify and analyze the thesis, context, and rhetorical situation of each article, including relevant background or publication information. Offer detailed analysis of language, concepts, evidence, methodologies, techniques, and/or arguments.

Level II involves critical exposition of multiple source articles. Level II assignments might include comparative analysis, argument analysis, problem identification, or trend identification.

Typical Level II Evaluation Criteria:

Holistic Assessment: Student demonstrates the global capacity to establish a clear synthetic connection(s) between source articles; on deadline; meets word count.	20%
Student introduces source texts to readers not familiar with the source material; general interest audience, academic audience, or other audience as specified by instructor.	10%
Student synthesizes source materials within the context of a significant public discourse; the essay indicates why the subject matter and discourse is important and timely.	10%
Student examines and illuminates the authors' most significant concepts and supporting evidence. Student commentary clarifies, connects, and contextualizes the source texts.	20%

Student quotes meaningfully and insightfully multiple times from the source texts; proper handling of quotations; appropriate integration and punctuation.	20%
Student follows proper MLA or APA format, or another standard format as specified by the instructor.	10%
Student's ability to draft and revise for clear standard usage and syntax.	10%

See alternate Suggested Level II Making Connections Evaluation Criteria *in unit two Resources.*

Level III: Research

1. Develop a Significant "Major Research Question"
   - *Your inquiry responds to or is inspired by a significant twenty-first century public discourse.*
2. Produce a Focused Annotated Bibliography or Works Cited Page on the Topic You Have Identified
   - *Seek high quality sources and use various research methods.*
3. Your Purpose Is More Than Informational
   - *You must define and direct the discourse.*
4. Your Paper must be Claim-Based, Featuring a Significant Claim, Thesis or Argument
   - *You must present credible evidence to support your claim or thesis.*

Typical length requirements range from 2500 to 7500 words, plus bibliography.

Level III research writing might include problem identification/proposed solution, trend analysis/future forecast, exposition/argument paper, or feature journal/magazine article.

See unit nine for detailed information on the composition and research process.

How to Use *Engaging Discourse 2.0*

- Study the unit introduction
- Read "Questions to Consider" **before** you read the feature article
- Annotate while you read
- Check yourself with the "Questions for Comprehension" **after** you read
- Investigate the "Finding Connections" articles
- Review unit resources and essay prompts
- Look over the "Further Inquiry" unit bibliography

Consider Playing a Research Game

See Start Playing Games: Using a Fictional Scenario to "Make It Real" *in unit nine.*

In order to produce a particular type of research paper (an academic paper aimed at a sophisticated popular interest audience), students may benefit from using a "fictional scenario" in order to imagine a certain audience of readers. In this scenario, the instructor plays the role of journal editor. *See* "The Scenario" *and* "Write the Editor a Pitch Letter: The *Timely Topics* Research Prospectus" *in Unit Nine Research in the Twenty-First Century.*

ABOUT THE AUTHOR

Bradley Summerhill is a tenured English professor at Truckee Meadows Community College in Reno, Nevada. He graduated with Highest Distinction in English Language and Literature from the University of Virginia and obtained a Master of Fine Arts degree in writing from the University of Arkansas. He has worked as a journalist and paperboy (Google it). He is the author of many short stories and a novel, *Gambler's Quartet*. He is a songwriter and guitarist for the most excellent garage band, Adapter. He is father to one daughter and dreams of leading a full reggae orchestra on sold-out world tours.

© Judy Prutzman

Bradley Summerhill stands at the graveside of Jim Morrison, the Lizard King (Google it).

UNIT ONE

Literacy in the Twenty-First Century

Experts in fields as diverse as economics, communications, anthropology, and other branches of human studies agree that we have entered a new era of human history in the twenty-first century. The Internet era ranks in importance, say these experts, alongside the pre-historic Agricultural Revolution and the Industrial Revolution of the eighteenth and nineteenth centuries. It may be difficult to understand—or is it easy for young minds to understand?—that you are coming of age in an era that is separate and distinct from the one in which your parents and grandparents came of age.

Many facets of society have experienced profound transformation since the late twentieth century. Economists tell us that the United States operates in a post-industrial economy. Communications experts describe the vast transformations that have taken place in the distribution of information and electronic data. Psychologists describe the intense effects of digitalization on the human experience.

Is it possible that the way in which we humans "read" the world is, quite literally, changing? In other words, does the Internet have such a subtle, profound effect on the ways in which we intake data, including words and sentences, that it can alter neural pathways? The provocative title of the article that follows in this unit—"Does the Internet Make You Dumber?"— may strike you as pretty dumb in and of itself. Does the article title imply that the entirety of Gen Z, which doubtless obtains most of its reading materials in electronic formats, is more dumb than prior generations? Are Gen Z brains somehow neurologically "different" from the brains of Baby Boomers, Gen Xers, and Millennials?

Newspaper and magazine writers, in fact, do not oftentimes create their own article titles. That is typically the job of the publication's editorial staff. So, first of all, we need to be careful about blaming free-lance writers for article titles. Nonetheless, the title and the article itself clearly indicate a point of controversy: *whether an overwhelming amount of electronic data can have a negative effect on human cognition.*

In 2008, writer Nicholas Carr authored a cover story for *The Atlantic* magazine entitled "Is Google Making Us Stupid?" This article delves into the same concerns. Carr shares data as well as personal perceptions regarding the way in which he is processing literature, i.e. reading online instead of reading traditional physical books. Has e-reading fundamentally affected the way that we process language? "Once I was a scuba diver in the sea or words," he laments. "Now, I zip along the surface like a guy on a Jet Ski."

In fact, Carr acknowledges, young people appear to be reading more than older generations did as kids. The core of the matter, he argues, is that the *quality* of that reading has changed. Read "quality" here

1

to mean *characteristics* or *attributes*. In other words, we're not focusing on the actual quality of the content that is being read, rather on how that content, or any content, is being processed in the brain. Essentially, e-reading is different from traditional reading. Basically, he claims that the reading process itself has changed in the twenty-first century. In fact, early and subsequent studies of "e-reading" versus "paper reading" demonstrate some advantages to traditional reading, including increased memory retention that may result from tactile stimulation. *Scientific American* noted in 2013:

> The matter is by no means settled. Before 1992, most studies concluded that people read slower, less accurately and less comprehensively on screens than on paper. Studies published since the early 1990s, however, have produced more inconsistent results: a slight majority has confirmed earlier conclusions, but almost as many have found few significant differences in reading speed or comprehension between paper and screens. And recent surveys suggest that although most people still prefer paper—especially when reading intensively—attitudes are changing as tablets and e-reading technology improve and reading digital books for facts and fun becomes more common.

Carr quotes researchers who determine that "It is clear that [computer] users are not reading online in the traditional sense ... there are signs that new forms of 'reading' are emerging as users 'power browse'" rather than read in the traditional sense.

I imagine that we are all guilty of power browsing too frequently in the digital era.

We look for quick hit items that we can bend to our own uses and prejudices, meanwhile dismissing items that do not fit into our inherited worldviews. This is not reading, nor is it research or scholarship. Psychologists warn us of *confirmation bias,* the all-too-human tendency to accept facts and stories that we like and to reject facts and stories that we don't like. It is an important concept to acknowledge when we consider the ramifications of so much of our important public discourse taking place online. How we process the world in the digital age is a crucial matter.

A more immediate concern, when it comes to Carr's text, involves *how* we read in the Internet era. Deep reading is neurologically indistinguishable from deep thinking, claim Carr and other experts. It is easy to conclude that superficial reading—that is, power browsing—means shallow thinking.

I heard famous American writer Kurt Vonnegut speak one time, back in the old pre-Internet world. He was speaking of the 1960s and how transcendental meditation came into vogue. All of a sudden everyone was meditating. But he wasn't meditating. Was he missing something? Then he realized: *he read books.* He read lots and lots of books, melding his consciousness into the text that he was reading. "Reading was my form of meditation," he said. "I was doing the same thing." I heard him say that thirty years ago, and it stuck with me.

In his *Atlantic* article, Carr writes, "In the quiet spaces opened up by the sustained, undistracted reading of a book, or by any other act of contemplation, for that matter, we make our own associations, draw our own inferences and analogies, foster our own ideas." For Carr, deep reading provides a contemplative state of being.

Should young minds balk at Carr's hopelessly outdated worldview? Or is it possible to achieve deep reading while e-reading? Carr himself tells us to be skeptical of his claims. Remember, he tells us, that Socrates opposed the new information technology of writing because writing things down would deteriorate memory. Socrates was correct, of course. Our mnemonic abilities almost certainly degrade in literary culture versus oral culture. Yet writing is still a useful medium, allowing ideas to be widely distributed and preserved for future generations. Culturally speaking, it was probably a good trade-off.

Should young minds lament a new world of endless hyperlinks and glittery distractions? The topic of "distractions" is different from, if related to, the distinct topics of "cognitive processing" or "online versus paper reading abilities." We need to be precise in order to produce meaningful discourse. It is a worthwhile question: Do ads, hyperlinks, and pop-ups pose a bigger problem than the electronic screen on which they reside?

Is it possible to capture Vonnegut's meditative reading state in the twenty-first century? How so?

What do the experts tell us? What does your experience tell you?

In the reading that follows, note references to the concept of "brain plasticity" or "neuroplasticity" which we will approach in a subsequent unit. Always be sure to scan the source materials listed in the Further Inquiry unit bibliography. For example, you could find there a citation for a 2018 *Scientific American* article indicating that the Internet may affect cognitive processes but likely does not radically alter brain organization.

- *How do you respond to the concept that we are becoming scattered, shallow, and superficial thinkers in the twenty-first century?*

Questions to Consider

Answer these questions as you read and annotate the text:

- Consider the Seneca quotation that Carr invokes. Does it apply to the twenty-first century? How so?
- What are some examples of online distractions that might occur while a person reads?
- What sorts of associative or connective processes are essential to mastering complex concepts?
- What possible benefits and detriments did the psychologist Greenfield find in regard to how media technologies influence cognitive abilities?
- What is a possible downside to a person strengthening his or her visual-spatial intelligence?
- What does the article have to say about "multitasking?" What is your opinion on multitasking?
- What is Carr's hypothesis? What is his thesis or main argument?
- How do we develop "a rare kind of mental discipline," according to the author?

Nicholas Carr, "Does the Internet Make You Dumber?" (2010)

The Roman philosopher Seneca may have put it best 2,000 years ago: "To be everywhere is to be nowhere." Today, the Internet grants us easy access to unprecedented amounts of information. But a growing body of scientific evidence suggests that the Net, with its constant distractions and interruptions, is also turning us into scattered and superficial thinkers.

The picture emerging from the research is deeply troubling, at least to anyone who values the depth, rather than just the velocity, of human thought. People who read text studded with links, the studies show, comprehend less than those who read traditional linear text. People who watch busy multimedia presentations remember less than those who take in information in a more sedate and focused manner. People who are continually distracted by emails, alerts and other messages understand less than those who are able to concentrate. And people who juggle many tasks are less creative and less productive than those who do one thing at a time.

The common thread in these disabilities is the division of attention. The richness of our thoughts, our memories and even our personalities hinges on our ability to focus the mind and sustain concentration. Only when we pay deep attention to a new piece of information are we able to associate it "meaningfully and systematically with knowledge already well established in memory," writes the Nobel Prize-winning neuroscientist Eric Kandel. Such associations are essential to mastering complex concepts.

When we're constantly distracted and interrupted, as we tend to be online, our brains are unable to forge the strong and expansive neural connections that give depth and distinctiveness to our thinking. We become mere signal-processing units, quickly shepherding disjointed bits of information into and then out of short-term memory.

In an article published in Science last year, Patricia Greenfield, a leading developmental psychologist, reviewed dozens of studies on how different media technologies influence our cognitive abilities. Some of the studies indicated that certain computer tasks, like playing video games, can enhance "visual literacy skills," increasing the speed at which people can shift their focus among icons and other images on screens. Other studies, however, found that such rapid shifts in focus, even if performed adeptly, result in less rigorous and "more automatic" thinking.

In one experiment conducted at Cornell University, for example, half a class of students was allowed to use Internet-connected laptops during a lecture, while the other had to keep their computers shut. Those who browsed the Web performed much worse on a subsequent test of how well they retained the lecture's content. While it's hardly surprising that Web surfing would distract students, it should be a note of caution to schools that are wiring their classrooms in hopes of improving learning.

Ms. Greenfield concluded that "every medium develops some cognitive skills at the expense of others." Our growing use of screen-based media, she said, has strengthened visual-spatial intelligence, which can improve the ability to do jobs that involve keeping track of lots of simultaneous signals, like air traffic control. But that has been accompanied by "new weaknesses in higher-order cognitive processes," including "abstract vocabulary, mindfulness, reflection, inductive problem solving, critical thinking, and imagination." We're becoming, in a word, shallower.

> In your view, what does it mean to be a "shallow" thinker or a "deep" thinker? What are Carr's views on these definitions?

In another experiment, recently conducted at Stanford University's Communication Between Humans and Interactive Media Lab, a team of researchers gave various cognitive tests to 49 people who do a lot of media multitasking and 52 people who multitask much less frequently. The heavy multitaskers performed poorly on all the tests. They were more easily distracted, had less control over their attention, and were much less able to distinguish important information from trivia.

The researchers were surprised by the results. They had expected that the intensive multitaskers would have gained some unique mental advantages from all their on-screen juggling. But that wasn't the case. In fact, the heavy multitaskers weren't even good at multitasking. They were considerably less adept at switching between tasks than the more infrequent multitaskers. "Everything distracts them," observed Clifford Nass, the professor who heads the Stanford lab.

It would be one thing if the ill effects went away as soon as we turned off our computers and cell-phones. But they don't. The cellular structure of the human brain, scientists have discovered, adapts readily to the tools we use, including those for finding, storing and sharing information. By changing our habits of mind, each new technology strengthens certain neural pathways and weakens others. The cellular alterations continue to shape the way we think even when we're not using the technology.

The pioneering neuroscientist Michael Merzenich believes our brains are being "massively remodeled" by our ever-intensifying use of the Web and related media. In the 1970s and 1980s, Mr. Merzenich, now a professor emeritus at the University of California in San Francisco, conducted a famous series of experiments on primate brains that revealed how extensively and quickly neural circuits change in response to experience. When, for example, Mr. Merzenich rearranged the nerves in a monkey's hand, the nerve cells in the animal's sensory cortex quickly reorganized themselves to create a new "mental map" of the hand. In a conversation late last year, he said that he was profoundly worried about the cognitive consequences of the constant distractions and interruptions the Internet bombards us with. The long-term effect on the quality of our intellectual lives, he said, could be "deadly."

What we seem to be sacrificing in all our surfing and searching is our capacity to engage in the quieter, attentive modes of thought that underpin contemplation, reflection and introspection. The Web never encourages us to slow down. It keeps us in a state of perpetual mental locomotion.

It is revealing, and distressing, to compare the cognitive effects of the Internet with those of an earlier information technology, the printed book. Whereas the Internet scatters our attention, the book focuses it. Unlike the screen, the page promotes contemplativeness.

Reading a long sequence of pages helps us develop a rare kind of mental discipline. The innate bias of the human brain, after all, is to be distracted. Our predisposition is to be aware of as much of what's going on around us as possible. Our fast-paced, reflexive shifts in focus were once crucial to our survival. They reduced the odds that a predator would take us by surprise or that we'd overlook a nearby source of food.

To read a book is to practice an unnatural process of thought. It requires us to place ourselves at what T. S. Eliot, in his poem "Four Quartets," called "the still point of the turning world." We have to forge or strengthen the neural links needed to counter our instinctive distractedness, thereby gaining greater control over our attention and our mind.

It is this control, this mental discipline, that we are at risk of losing as we spend ever more time scanning and skimming online. If the slow progression of words across printed pages damped our craving to be inundated by mental stimulation, the Internet indulges it. It returns us to our native state of distractedness, while presenting us with far more distractions than our ancestors ever had to contend with.

> The ability of the brain to remodel itself on a neural level in response to environmental stimuli is called "brain plasticity" or "neuroplasticity." How does the concept of "neuroplasticity" tie into Carr's hypothesis?

Questions for Comprehension

Answer these questions as a comprehension gauge and/or for further clarification on the text:

1. True or False. According to one study at Cornell University, students who used Internet-connected laptops were at an advantage in terms of retaining course content.

   F

2. Describe the benefits of multitasking, according to this article.

3. The Internet encourages: a) introspection, or b) perpetual mental locomotion.

Literacy in the 21st century means more than simply reading texts. It means being able to access, filter, process, and understand a variety of media sources. Review the National Council of Teachers of English (NCTE) statement entitled "Definition of Literacy in a Digial Age" (2019) found at https://ncte.org/statement/nctes-definition-literacy-digital-age/. Also review Unit Nine Research in the 21st Century in this textbook.

According to the National Council of Teachers of English, "As society and technology change, so does literacy." Clearly, a major component of literacy in the twenty-first century involves your ability to decode good information and bad information. Put another way, you must be able to detect and resist "fake news."

"Fake news" is not a twenty-first century phenomenon. As writer Yuval Noah Harari points out in his book *21 Lessons for the 21st Century*, "Humans have always lived in the age of post-truth. *Homo sapiens* is a post-truth species, whose power depends on creating and believing fictions" (238). Humans, prior to the Internet era, dealt with untruthful political speech, incendiary literary tracts, and propaganda films. Nevertheless, the speed with which news, and fake news, spreads represents something new. And the promulgation of tools of deception such as "deep fake" videos may present new challenges to those who want to remain informed and literate in the twenty-first century.

As humans, we are susceptible to *confirmation bias*, that is, the tendency to believe information that reinforces our own value systems and to reject information that challenges our value systems. For example, in our newsfeed, we tend to believe a story that casts a political opponent in a bad light, while we tend to reject a story that casts our own political champion in a negative light.

The first step to sound *political literacy* in the twenty-first century may be, quite simply, to recognize and overcome our own psychologies.

Harari contends, "It is the responsibility of all of us to invest time and effort in uncovering our biases and in verifying our sources of information" (248). He provides two tips for procuring good information:

1. *If you want reliable information, pay for it.* This may not be as bad as it seems. For example, you can go to a library or a database. Or subscribe to a reliable news source rather than being propagandized by ads and content (Harari calls it "brainwashing").
2. *Read and trust scientific, peer-reviewed literature.* Scientists do not have all the answers, but they are humanity's best guide when it comes to matters of fact and objectivity (248-9).

A fun sidenote for nerds like me: Harari extols the virtue of art in public discourse and advocates an increased role for "science fiction" in helping to shape people's worldviews. In this context, I think of Gene Roddenberry's *Star Trek* shaping an entire generation's positive outlook for the future of the human race.

Blame It On the Other

U.S. Senator Ben Sasse (R-Nebraska) believes that one result of the Internet era has been **political alienation**. In his book *Them: Why We Hate Each Other and How to Heal* (2018), Sasse argues that we have lost a sense of place and purpose; therefore, although we are the wealthiest population in the history of the world, we are among the least content. The problem, he finds, is loneliness. We are experiencing the lowest "friend ratio" in the nation's history, according to Sasse. Thirty years ago, each American reported about 3.5 friends. Today, the figure stands at 1.8 friends ("Sen. Ben Sasse").

"Politics didn't cause this," says Sasse. But people erroneously look to politics to fill the void. He believes that work creates happiness and that we must go back to focusing on place, city, and neighborhood.

Note the possibilities for developing Level II synthesis with Social (Dis)connection, Happiness Studies, or another unit discourses.

The average duration at a work firm today is 4.2 years and getting shorter. In the 1970s, a family "breadwinner" averaged 25 years at the same firm. "We've never prepared to become a people that are lifelong learners," notes Sasse. When it comes to making policy, we should be focused on *past vs. future* instead of *left vs. right*.

See Finding Connections: The Workforce of the Twenty-First Century in unit six for further ideas on workforce development and the impact of AI and robotics.

Instead of national solidarity to face the future, the opposite appears to be happening. Political commentators note the deep divisions in the American electorate. Years ago, studies indicated that about 14 percent of citizens thought that people in the "other Party" were "evil." Nowadays, the figure stands at 40 percent (Cornish).

A destructive bifurcation in American politics is taking place. Political rancor and an inability to engage in civil public dialogue may explain a growing tendency for Gen Z to retreat from political discourse altogether.

© Cienpies Design/Shutterstock.com

If your online experiences match my own, then you are familiar with the destructive social disconnection that can take place when partisan politics and social media mix.

- Is the solution to disengage from political discourse altogether?
- Is the solution to take political discussions offline and only engage in face-to-face political discourse?
- In what ways can Gen Z achieve healthy civic discourse in order to disrupt the current rancor?

Finding Connections Works Cited

Cornish, Audie. Interview with Ben Sasse. "In 'Them,' Sen. Ben Sasse Says Politics Are Not What's Dividing Americans." *NPR, All Things Considered*, 15 Oct. 2018, https://www.npr.org/2018/10/15/657588629/in-them-sen-ben-sasse-says-politics-are-not-what-s-dividing-americans.

Goldberg, Jonah. *Suicide of the West: How the Rebirth of Nationalism, Populism, and Identity Politics Is Destroying American Democracy*. Crown Publishing, 2018.

Harari, Yuval Noah. *21 Lessons for the 21st Century*. Spiegel & Grau, 2018.

Inskeep, Steve. Interview with Jonah Goldberg. "Goldberg's 'Suicide Of The West' Tackles Ills Of Identity Politics." *NPR, Morning Edition*, 23 Apr. 2018, https://www.npr.org/2018/04/23/604854281/goldbergs-suicide-of-the-west-tackles-ills-of-identity-politics.

MacDougald, Park. "The Idea-Free Book That Has the Right Excited About Ideas." *New York Magazine*, 1 June 2018, http://nymag.com/intelligencer/2018/06/review-jonah-goldbergs-suicide-of-the-west.html.

"Sen. Ben Sasse on America's Cultural Divide." *CBS This Morning*, 15 Oct. 2018, https://www.cbsnews.com/video/sen-ben-sasse-on-his-new-book-about-americas-cultural-divide/.

Resources

Introducing Texts or Sources for the Benefit of the "Outside" Audience

The purpose of a "text introduction" is to introduce source material to an "outside" audience who is not already familiar with that source material. Why is it an "outside" audience? Let's say that your readers are not "inside" our classroom. Imagine writing your composition to an audience filled with your other instructors or to an assembly of college faculty. You are writing to instructors of math, sociology, psychology, anthropology, engineering, graphic design, etc. Your reader is knowledgeable and educated but does not know your source materials or your topic. So, you need to "introduce" your main texts or sources to your audience. Sometimes in composition we can simply acknowledge sources of information with citations. However, when your writing topic revolves around one or two central texts or sources, then you want to introduce those texts to your audience so that they can enjoy a full understanding of your discourse or discussion. Keep in mind that even though your audience is pretty sharp they don't know what you know about the topic at hand. They need basic information in order to follow your interpretations and analysis of the material.

Do the following when you "introduce" a text:

- **Identify the author's full name and the full title of the source material.**
  - Use the author's full name on first reference; thereafter, use last name only.
  - In MLA format, an "Article Title" receives quotation marks while a *Book Title* receives italics. Other formats call for different title punctuation. Check your style guide and consult your instructor.
- **Clarify the authority of the author.**
  - Sometimes this can be done with a simple adjective: author X, journalist Y, or social psychologist Z.
  - Consider: Is the person an expert? Why is the person interested in the topic at hand? What does your outside audience need to know? What information can you share that will help with your interpretation, analysis, or argument?
- **Identify the author's thesis or main point.**
  - Give a brief overview of the main point of the text or *your* main focal point (that is, your interpretation of the author's thesis).
  - It is often helpful or necessary to provide historical or publication "context" or background information in order for your audience to understand your interpretation, analysis, or argument.
  - Sometimes you will want to clarify the author's tone and purpose. Sometimes it is helpful to provide some rhetorical analysis of the author's literary technique—for example, you might need to inform your audience that the author employs irony in order to make a point. Your audience does not have the benefit of the full original context. Your audience has only what you provide.
- **Whenever possible, incorporate significant language from the author in the form of an integrated quotation.**
- **You may need to touch upon the "Rhetorical Situation" of the text.**
  - See "Rhetorical Situation" in Unit Five Resources for further information.
- **Depending on the depth and complexity of your introduction and your composition assignment, the entire process can be done in one or two sentences or in one or two paragraphs.**
  - Good writing is clear and efficient. Aim for "clean copy" (error-free prose).
  - It is often useful for you to spend an entire paragraph introducing the text. Besides, it's an easy way to boost your word count!
  - Keep in mind **the needs of your outside audience** who has not read the source material.

EXAMPLE: Text Introduction

In his autobiographical essay, "I Just Wanna Be Average," which is an excerpt from the author's book *Lives on the Boundary* (1989), educator Mike Rose reflects upon his school experiences. Rose describes disengaged students who were "bobbing in pretty shallow water" (11). The author advocates a liberal arts education. He writes in praise of a demanding humanities teacher named Jack MacFarland. Rose believes that students "will float to the mark [that teachers] set" (11). If a teacher sets a high bar, the students will achieve more than if the teacher is comfortable with low expectations. For Rose, Jack MacFarland was an inspirational teacher who set high standards.

The MLA-style bibliographical citation that would accompany this paragraph appears below. *Consult your online style guide for directions on MLA, APA, and other formats.*

Works Cited

Rose, Mike. "I Just Wanna Be Average." *Engaging Discourse: A 21st Century Composition Reader & Curriculum* by Bradley Summerhill, Kendall Hunt, 2020, pp. 10-7.

Level I Analysis-Response Guidelines

Level I essays are brief, formal compositions that aim to analyze and reflect upon the textbook readings and discourses therein. Use annotations, discussion notes, and sentence or paragraph exercises to form draft material. One recommended structure for an analysis-response essay is as follows:

Paragraph One: Introduce your source material to your audience. Introduce the reading to an educated "outside the classroom" audience who is not familiar with the reading and has not read the essay or article in question. See "Introducing Texts" above for further information. Typically, you will offer your interpretation of the author's main point or thesis. Provide an overview of the material without summarizing the article's content. *Summary* is point-by-point and sequential, whereas *analysis* deals with global content and meaning.

Paragraph Two: Analyze the reading by quoting important language. Select and appropriately integrate significant language in order to highlight important subject matter from the reading. Your quotation selections help you to focus your audience on whatever you view as the most significant and most relevant topic or discourse that appears in the reading. See "Quotation Integration" below. See further information on quotation integration in Unit Two Resources.

Paragraph Three: Offer a personal response to the reading. Why is this reading selection important, and how is it relevant to our world? What prevalent public discourse do you see operating within the text? One ideal in composition involves coherence, meaning that your composition features one common theme from start to finish. This central focus or idea is often referred to as your "thesis."

Check with your instructor on actual requirements and recommendations for Level I, Level II, and Level III compositions.

Suggested Level I Analysis-Response Evaluation Criteria:

Text Introduction: *The student demonstrates competence in formally introducing the text to an outside audience.*	30%
Quotation Integration: *The student demonstrates competence in appropriately integrating meaningful quotation selections using signal phrases and/or by other means.*	30%
Response: *The student offers a thoughtful response to the text.*	30%
Format and Voice: *The student follows proper MLA format or another standard as specified by the instructor. The student composes in standard written English.*	10%

Quotation Integration

Use your writer's handbook and online resources to study **signal phrases** *and* **quotation integration**.

✓ Visit the Purdue Online Writing Lab (OWL) at *https://owl.english.purdue.edu/owl/*.

Your ability to "integrate" an author's language into your own prose is extremely important. You must be able to analyze an author's argument at the same time that you clarify the argument for the benefit of your reader. Incorporating quotations into your own writing is the best way to simultaneously analyze and explain the author's work. Your ability to paraphrase appropriately and to properly integrate quotations demonstrates your capacity to analyze and to process the text material. To *analyze* means to *break down* the text—that is, to interpret the text accurately and with appropriate detail.

Attribution

Look up the term "signal phrase." Be careful of where you find your definitions, of course. At the same time, take advantage of the amazing technology that is at your disposal. In composition, we want to **signal** or **attribute** ideas and actions to the text's author. It is important to do so for many reasons—to be accurate, to be fair, and to be clear in meaning. Moreover, stylistically, it is important to attribute ideas and actions to the author. For example, it is always better to write *Carr observes* rather than to write *It is observed in the article that....* Compare the concise attribution of "He observes" to the plodding, passive, wordy, and vague "It is observed that."

You will note that suggested evaluation rubrics in *Engaging Discourse 2.0* place a heavy emphasis on "Quotation Integration" and the ability to handle quotations.

- **See "Three Effective Ways to Integrate Quotations" in Unit Two Resources.**

Writing Assignments

Sentence Exercises

Write three fluid, error-free sentences that could serve to introduce the article and the author's thesis or main idea to an outside audience.

1. In an article published in *The Wall Street Journal* in 2010, writer Nicholas Carr argues that _despite the many benefits, the Internet is turning us in to shallow thinkers._

2. Carr questions the notion that _the Net benefits the classroom_; instead, he claims that _the Internet is often more distracting._

3. Carr's most convincing evidence comes in the form of _research findings._

Essay Prompts

Level I: Analysis-Response

1. Analyze Carr's arguments and evidence. What is his most convincing evidence and where do gaps in his argument exist? Do you find his article convincing? Why or why not?
2. What does Carr's article say specifically about the ability or inability to "read deeply" in the twenty-first century? Analyze and respond.

Level II: Making Connections

1. Explore source materials that speak with authority on the issue of on-screen reading versus physical text reading. What are the major distinctions and effects, according to scientific evidence? Note whether your view of Carr's article changes based on a quick survey of online, database, and/or popular science literature.
2. What does Carr's article say about political literacy in the twenty-first century? How do e-reading, neuroplasticity, or other topics mentioned in Carr's article contribute to the political alienation as noted by Sasse in the Finding Connections article?
3. Explore the connections between reading on screen (e-reading), reading on paper, and human neuroplasticity. Connect Carr's concerns with expert source material on "brain plasticity."
4. To what extent can you develop a connection between Carr's article and the concerns expressed in the unit on Social (Dis)connection? In what ways does Carr's article speak to the same or similar concerns that exist regarding the psychological effects of social media?
5. According to Carr, the Roman philosopher Seneca said it best: "To be everywhere is to be nowhere." Develop a connection between Carr's article and credible source material concerning positive psychology or the science of happiness.

Level III: Research

1. What scientific evidence exists to justify Carr's concerns regarding the cognitive processing of electronic data (text as well as other media) in the Internet era? How can the human brain's capacity for "plasticity" affect cognitive processes in both positive and negative ways? What specific brain processes and mechanisms are involved in the cognitive processing of text, electronic text, and/or other media?
2. Conduct a study of "fake news" on the Internet. What scientific evidence exists concerning the spread and effect of "false information" in the Internet era? What are the main concerns or major general effects of false information spreading in a democratic society?
3. What sorts of "political literacies" are required in the Internet era? Relying on sound evidence and expert authorities, investigate how political messaging has changed in the Internet era. In what ways has political participation increased in the Internet era, and in what ways has political participation decreased? Why so? Account for these trends.
4. Research the medical benefits of meditation and/or "deep thinking." (Deep thinking and meditation are distinct activities; do not treat them as the same thing.) In what ways can meditation or meditative activities affect human biology or neurobiology? What physical and cognitive processes and mechanisms are involved? Does research validate Carr's claim regarding the cognitive benefits of the "rare kind of mental discipline" provided by reading pages?

Further Inquiry

"15 Big Ways The Internet Is Changing Our Brain." *OnlineCollege.org*, 10 Apr. 2017, https://www.onlinecollege.org/15-big-ways-the-internet-is-changing-our-brain/.

Carr, Nicholas. "Author Nicholas Carr: The Web Shatters Focus, Rewires Brains." *Wired*, Mar. 7, 2018, https://www.wired.com/2010/05/ff-nicholas-carr/.

Carr, Nicholas. "Is Google Making You Stupid? What the Internet is Doing to Our Brains." *The Atlantic*, July/Aug. 2008, https://www.theatlantic.com/magazine/archive/2008/07/is-google-making-us-stupid/306868/.

"Cognitive Offloading: How the Internet Is Increasingly Taking Over Human Memory." *ScienceDaily*, 16 Aug. 2016, https://www.sciencedaily.com/releases/2016/08/160816085029.htm.

"Cognitive Overload and e-Learning." *Your Digital Learning Expert*, 19 June 2017, https://www.ispringsolutions.com/blog/cognitive-overload-and-e-learning.

Davidson, Cathy. *Now You See It: How Technology and Brain Science Will Transform Schools and Business for the 21st Century.* Penguin, 2011.

Delgado Suárez, Jennifer. "Cognitive Offloading: Memory and Internet." *Psychology Spot*, 3 Sept. 2018, https://psychology-spot.com/cognitive-offloading-memory-internet/.

Harari, Yuval Noah. *21 Lessons for the 21st Century.* Spiegel & Grau, 2018.

Howard, Jacqueline. "FREAKY: Five Ways The Internet Is Rewiring Your Brain." *Huffington Post*, 7 Dec. 2017, https://www.huffpost.com/entry/shocking-ways-internet-rewires-brain_n_4136942.

Jabr, Ferris. "The Reading Brain in the Digital Age: The Science of Paper versus Screens." *Scientific American*, 11 Apr. 2013, https://www.scientificamerican.com/article/reading-paper-screens/.

McLeod, S. A. "Information Processing." *Simply Psychology*, 24 Oct. 2008, https://www.simplypsychology.org/information-processing.html

Pasquinelli, Elena. "Are Digital Devices Altering Our Brains?" *Scientific American*, 11 Sept. 2018, https://www.scientificamerican.com/article/are-digital-devices-altering-our-brains/.

Perry, Philip. "Cognitive Offloading: How the Internet Is Changing the Human Brain." *Big Think*, 17 Sept. 2018, https://bigthink.com/philip-perry/cognitive-offloading-how-the-internet-is-changing-the-human-brain.

"Speaking Freely: The Future of the First Amendment." *NPR, The1A.org*, 6 Dec. 2018, https://the1a.org/shows/2018-12-06/where-is-free-speech-headed.

Tengler, Dorothy L. "Cognitive Offloading: Help or Hindrance?" *MultiBriefs*, 26 Aug. 2016, http://exclusive.multibriefs.com/content/cognitive-offloading-help-or-hindrance/science-technology.

"Using the Outside World to Save on Brainpower." *Neuroscience News*, 16 Aug. 2016, https://neurosciencenews.com/metacognition-technology-4857/.

UNIT TWO

Social (Dis)Connection

In the introduction to her 2011 book *Alone Together*, sociologist Sherry Turkle quotes Winston Churchill: "We shape our buildings and then they shape us." For Turkle, it is clear that the most fundamental "architectures" of the twenty-first century—in particular, robotics and networking—have shaped the new human condition. In much the same way that political scientist Langdon Winner argued in the late twentieth century that we were creating networking and computer technologies without any forethought regarding outcomes or consequences, Turkle argues that we typically adopt and welcome new technologies into our personal lives with little understanding of the profound impact these technologies have on the human experience.

Turkle urges us to ask of every new technology, "Does it serve our human purposes? —a question that causes us to reconsider what these purposes are." Turkle has studied human interactions with "sociable robots"—and, it seems, in almost all cases these studies left her feeling pessimistic when it comes to technology's ability to fill the role of a fellow human being or to replace human touch or genuine human interactions. Yet, she fears, younger generations are learning to live with less when it comes to their relationships in the twenth-first century.

The psychological effects of social distancing in the wake of the Covid-19 pandemic remain unclear, but Turkle would likely speculate that online communications are not an adequate substitute for human touch and physical interaction.

Instead of interactions with handheld digital pets such as the Tamagotchi of the late 1990s, children and teenagers of the new century are more likely to develop relationships both *with* and *through* their handheld smartphones. It is a truism, of course, to point out that our smartphones have become our everything—a constant digital companion that brings us entertainment, connects us with friends, forecasts the weather, tells the time, predicts traffic patterns, recommends eateries, retrieves information from the web, serves as a newspaper, a magazine, a book … maybe even a friend? To what extent do we carry out our relationships *through* our phones, and to what extent is our relationship in reality *with* our phone?

Turkle suspects that Gen Z digital natives have come of age in an era that has prepared them to expect less, and to make do with less, from human relationships. She uses the term "growing up tethered" to describe a new reality—or, we might say, an alternative reality—facing Gen Z. In discussing people's willingness to engage in "relationships with less," Turkle observes, "These are the unsettling isolations of the tethered self.... For a start, it presumes certain entitlements: It can absent itself from its physical surround—including the people in it. It can experience the physical and virtual in near simultaneity." These are the things we *presume* we can do: be there and not be there all at once. Multi-tasking is perhaps a physical manifestation of our new belief that we don't need to be here in order to be here. Clutching my dear handheld friend, I can listen to the lecturer at the front of the room, chat with my boyfriend re: lunch plans, look up a word online that I don't understand (never mind that the entire point of the lecture is to *explain* the word I don't understand), snapchat, and take notes all at once.

Never mind that I can't really do any those things simultaneously. Perception creates reality.

I call the disease "multi-distracting" (*now you are able to perform several tasks inadequately all at once!*) but the condition goes deeper than simple manual and organizational inefficiency. The idea of *being present* becomes a foreign concept to the brain that is always seeking to be elsewhere. The concept of *mindfulness*—so key to so many artistic, scientific and entrepreneurial endeavors—becomes a near impossibility. The plastic human mind learns to be elsewhere and maps its neural networks accordingly. That is one hypothesis, at least. (A *hypo* or "under" *thesis* is a theory or idea that has yet to be proven.)

For many of us, striving for authentic human connection in the vastness of cyberspace has come to seem like a barren, hellish endeavor—something like Sisyphus rolling his boulder up the mountain for all eternity only to have it roll back down whenever he reaches the mountaintop. We have put up a front or created an online double that takes the place of our authentic self. Even though many young people have given up (or never had) any expectations of personal privacy in this new world, most people understand nevertheless that only certain topics are acceptable on social media—stay away from politics, for instance. People want to see pictures of puppy dogs and double rainbows (*ooh, let me YouTube that hilarious double-rainbow video while I'm reading*), or maybe a cat video, but no one wants to hear if you feel sad or heartbroken.

The technologies that are supposed to connect us instead cause us anxiety. *How come only five people like my cat video? Did someone misunderstand my comment on a friend's post? I was trying to be funny, but maybe they thought I was being stupid or offensive. I better post something happy. Time for a smiley snapchat!*

Maybe it's me. My online social skills are not sharp. Smartphones and social media do allow me to do some things simultaneously. For example, social media makes me feel simultaneously like an insecure teenager and a gray-haired curmudgeon.

I am not alone when it comes to feelings of anxiety related to social media. In a 2018 *Psychology Today* post, graduate student Annemarie Kelleghan notes, "Researchers have found that people who use multiple social media platforms report more symptoms of anxiety and depression. Longer or more frequent use of social media also appears to predict depressive symptoms." In other words, according to recent studies, more social media usage corresponds to more feelings of anxiety and depression. People who use social media in small or modest slots of time to strengthen existing relationships can, however, enjoy healthy outcomes.

- **Finding Connections:** How do Gen Z, Millennials, Gen X, and Baby Boomers tend to differ in their use of social media? To what platforms do these generations gravitate, and why? How much time do various demographics spend on social media? How do experts account for the distinctions in how various demographics use social media?
- **Finding Connections:** To what degree, if any, does social media either cause or correlate to social isolation? To what degree, if any, can social media stimulate social connection? What expert source materials are available to investigate these questions?
- **Finding Connections:** In his article, "Does the Internet Make You Dumber?" writer Nicholas Carr reports that neuroscientist Michael Merzenich believes that our brains are being "massively remodeled" by our increasing use of Internet technologies. What scientific evidence exists to validate this concern?

Kelleghan reports some unsurprising research results: "Face-to-face communication increased subjective well-being by both increasing connectedness and decreasing social isolation." On the other hand, social media use "only increased subjective well-being through increasing connectedness, but not through decreasing social isolation." Social media, in other words, cannot cure feelings of isolation or loneliness. People who are feeling isolated or lonely are most likely to find an increased sense of isolation or loneliness by going online. Psychologist Jean Twenge reports that the number of teens who get together with friends nearly every day dropped by more than 40 percent from 2000 to 2015. Twenge attributes this anti-social change to the growing presence of smartphones and social media. Although it is "difficult to trace the precise paths of causation" in a scientific sense, Gen Z, she maintains, is "a generation shaped by the smartphone and by the concomitant rise of social media." (She terms Gen Z "iGen," but I suspect that her neologism, or new word, will not catch on.) She notes an alarming rise in teen suicide and depression since smartphones have come into our lives.

There is a tricky calculus here: When we are feeling sad or lonely—those times when we might feel a real need to connect—we ought to stay away, it appears, from our smartphones and social media. On the other hand, if we are feeling good about ourselves and our lives, a small amount of online connectivity may do no harm and could possibly do some good. The long-standing Monitoring the Future survey, which began asking teens questions in 1975, confirms that teenagers who spend more time than average on screen activities are more likely to report feelings of unhappiness, while those who spend more time on non-screen activities are more likely to report feelings of happiness (Twenge, "Have Smartphones Destroyed a Generation?").

There are more than "feelings" at stake here. Social isolation can correlate to long-term negative health consequences. A healthy mind and a healthy body go together. Scientists in various fields are uncovering the truth of this spiritual axiom. In fact, lively social connections correspond to positive health outcomes. Yet digital natives who have been raised, so to speak, on their smartphones may not always understand how to cultivate real human connections. "Instead of retreating into the perceived comfort of our phones," Kelleghan writes, "we need to put down our devices and engage with those in the world around us (and not the world wide web around us)."

Strange as it sounds, your plastic brain can reap important benefits from awkward social banter, from training your eyes to make contact with another human being, from putting aside your memes and gifs to peer onto the horizon—where one day you may discover a real double rainbow of your own.

Questions to Consider

Answer these questions as you read and annotate the text:

- Walton draws an analogy between "scrolling" and what dangerous public health activity (or inactivity)?
- What is your personal response to the scientific evidence that tends to validate the existence of social media addiction?
- What do you know about or imagine to be the physiological changes associated with withdrawal?
- What are the affective differences between "online" and "offline" social networks?
- This article is largely a list of psychological ills surrounding social media. Chances are you have some experience with social media. How do your own experiences and the concerns expressed by experts coincide or intersect?
- What does social media do well? What does social media not do well?

Health experts love to say that sitting is the new smoking. Given the number of diseases to which sitting is linked, and the number of people it apparently kills every year, sitting is one of the worst things we can do for health. But possibly as concerning is the thing that we often do while we're sitting: Mindlessly scrolling through our social media feeds when we have a few spare minutes (or for some, hours). And as we probably know intuitively, and as the research is confirming, it's not the best habit when it comes to our collective psychology.

The American Academy of Pediatrics **has warned** about the potential for negative effects of social media in young kids and teens, including cyber-bullying and "Facebook depression." But the same risks may be true for adults, across generations. Here's a quick run-down of the studies that have shown that social media isn't very good for mental well-being, and in some ways, it can be pretty damaging.

It's Addictive

Experts have not been in total agreement on whether internet addiction is a real thing, let alone social media addiction, but there's some good evidence that both may exist. A **review study** from Nottingham Trent University looked back over earlier research on the psychological characteristics, personality and social media use. The authors conclude that "it may be plausible to speak specifically of 'Facebook Addiction Disorder'…because addiction criteria, such as neglect of personal life, mental preoccupation, escapism, mood modifying experiences, tolerance and concealing the addictive behavior, appear to be present in some people who use [social networks] excessively." (They also found that the motivation for people's excessive use of social networks differs depending on certain traits—introverts and extroverts use it for different reasons, as do people with narcissistic traits. But that deserves a piece of its own.)

And studies have confirmed that people tend to undergo a kind of withdrawal: A study a few years ago from Swansea University found that people experienced the psychological symptoms of withdrawal when they stopped using (this went for all internet use, not just social media). Their recent follow-up study **found** that when people stop using, they also undergo small but measurable physiological effects. Study author Phil Reed said, "We have known for some time that people who are over-dependent on digital devices report feelings of anxiety when they are stopped from using them, but now we can see that these psychological effects are accompanied by actual physiological changes." Whether this is true of social media per se is unclear right now, but anecdotal evidence suggests it may be.

It Triggers More Sadness, Less Well-being

The more we use social media, the less happy we seem to be. One **study** a few years ago found that Facebook use was linked to both less moment-to-moment happiness and less life satisfaction—the more people used Facebook in a day, the more these two variables dropped off. The authors suggest this may have to do with the fact that Facebook conjures up a perception of social isolation, in a way that other solitary activities don't. "On the surface," the authors write, "Facebook provides an invaluable resource for fulfilling such needs by such

> One of the four basic "levels" of happiness involves comparison. What does social media experience and study have to say regarding happiness by comparison?

allowing people to instantly connect. Rather than enhancing well-being, as frequent interactions with supportive 'offline' social networks powerfully do, the current findings demonstrate that interacting with Facebook may predict the opposite result for young adults—it may undermine it."

In fact, another **study** found that social media use is linked to greater feelings of social isolation. The team looked at how much people used 11 social media sites, including Facebook, Twitter, Google+, YouTube, LinkedIn, Instagram, Pinterest, Tumblr, Vine, Snapchat and Reddit, and correlated this with their "perceived social isolation." Not surprisingly, it turned out that the more time people spent on these sites, the more socially isolated they *perceived* themselves to be. And perceived social isolation is one of the **worst things** for us, mentally and physically.

Comparing Our Lives with Others is Mentally Unhealthy

Part of the reason Facebook makes people *feel* socially isolated (even though they may not actually be) is the comparison factor. We fall into the trap of comparing ourselves to others as we scroll through our feeds, and make judgements about how we measure up. One **study** looked at how we make comparisons to others' posts, in "upward" or "downward" directions—that is, feeling that we're either better or worse off than our friends. It turned out that both types of comparisons made people feel worse, which is surprising, since in real life, only upward comparisons (feeling another person has it better than you) make people feel bad. But in the social network world, it seems that any kind of comparison is linked to depressive symptoms.

It Can Lead to Jealousy—and a Vicious Cycle

It's no secret that the comparison factor in social media leads to jealousy—most people will admit that seeing other people's tropical vacations and perfectly behaved kids is envy-inducing. Studies have certainly shown that social media use **triggers feelings of jealousy**. The authors of one study, looking at jealousy and other negative feelings while using Facebook, wrote that "This magnitude of envy incidents taking place on FB alone is astounding, providing evidence that FB offers a breeding ground for invidious feelings." They add that it can become a vicious cycle: feeling jealous can make a person want to make his or her own life look better, and post jealousy-inducing posts of their own, in an endless circle of one-upping and feeling jealous.

Another **study** looked at the connection between envy and depression in Facebook use and, interestingly, discovered that envy mediates the Facebook-depression link. That is, when envy is controlled for, Facebook isn't so depressing. So it may be the envy that's largely to blame in the depression-Facebook connection.

We Get Caught in the Delusion of Thinking it Will Help

Part of the unhealthy cycle is that we keep coming back to social media, even though it doesn't make us feel very good. This is probably because of what's known as a forecasting error: Like a drug, we think getting a fix will help, but it actually makes us feel worse, which comes down to an error in our ability to predict our own response. One **study** looked at how people feel after using Facebook and how they *think* they'll feel going in. Like other studies suggested, the participants in this one almost always felt worse after using it, compared to people engaging in other activities. But a follow-up experiment showed that people generally believed that they'd feel better after using, not worse. Which of course turns out not to be the case at all, and sounds a lot like the pattern in other types of addiction.

> Are there healthy or beneficial aspects to social media in your view?

More Friends on Social Doesn't Mean You're More Social

A couple of years ago, a **study** found that more friends on social media doesn't necessarily mean you have a better social life—there seems to be a cap on the number of friends a person's brain can handle, and it takes actual social interaction (not virtual) to keep up these friendships. So feeling like you're being social by being on Facebook doesn't work. Since loneliness is linked to myriad health and mental health problems (including early death), getting real social support is important. Virtual friend time doesn't have the therapeutic effect as time with real friends.

* * *

All of this is not to say that there's *no* benefit to social media—obviously it keeps us connected across great distances, and helps us find people we'd lost touch with years ago. But getting on social when you have some time to kill, or, worse, need an emotional lift, is very likely a bad idea. And **studies** have found that taking a break from Facebook helps boost psychological well-being. If you're feeling brave, try taking a little break, and see how it goes. And if you're going to keep "using," then at least try to use in moderation.

URL and DOI references (in order of appearance, indicated by **underlined** text):
has warned: https://doi.org/10.1542/peds.2011-0054
review study: https://www.mdpi.com/1660-4601/8/9/3528
found: https://doi.org/10.1371/journal.pone.0178480
study: https://doi.org/10.1371/journal.pone.0069841
worst things: https://www.psychologytoday.com/us/blog/the-athletes-way/201511/
    loneliness-perceived-social-isolation-is-public-enemy-no-1
study: https://doi.org/10.1521/jscp.2014.33.8.701
triggers feelings of jealousy: https://www.forbes.com/sites/alicegwalton/2013/01/22/
    jealous-of-your-facebook-friends-why-social-media-makes-us-bitter/#62b3c1b135cc
study: https://doi.org/10.1016/j.chb.2014.10.053
study: https://doi.org/10.1016/j.chb.2014.03.003
study: https://doi.org/10.1098/rsos.150292
studies: https://doi.org/10.1089/cyber.2016.0259

© Elena_Goncharova/Shutterstock.com

Questions for Comprehension

Answer these questions as a comprehension gauge and/or for further clarification on the text:

1. True or False. According to this article, "FOMO" or "fear of missing out" is a genuine psychological phenomenon. Briefly explain or justify your response.

   True

2. True or False. Regarding feelings of "social isolation," researchers have only studied the Facebook platform. *False*

3. Name symptoms mentioned in the article which suggest that social media addiction is a genuine disorder. *Anxiety, depression.*

4. What do experts say regarding the link between having more friends on social media and having a better social life? *They aren't the same, not mutually exclusive*

In 2017, psychologist Jean Twenge attempted to give Gen Z a new name: *iGen*. She claims that the smartphone is the distinguishing factor in the life experience of the latest generation. Her book is called *iGen: Why Today's Super-Connected Kids Are Growing Up Less Rebellious, More Tolerant, Less Happy—and Completely Unprepared for Adulthood* *and What That Means for the Rest of Us*. The good news for college composition students is that you'll have fulfilled much of your word count requirement just by including the book's ludicrously-long subtitle in your text introduction. (Beware though: comp instructors never fall for such tricks.)

iGen, Twenge observes, is "a generation shaped by the smartphone and by the concomitant rise of social media" ("Have Smartphones…?"). While teens today are less likely to party and abuse alcohol than Gen X, they are more prone to negative feelings that Twenge and other experts associate with smartphones and social media. "Rates of teen depression and suicide have skyrocketed since 2011," writes Twenge, indicating the seriousness of the situation (*iGen* 3).

Gen Z may be facing the worst mental health crisis in our nation's history.

Teens today, compared to both Gen X and Baby Boomers, are less likely to go out and less likely to date. In 2015, about 56 percent of high school seniors reported going out on dates. Eighty-five percent of the prior generations went out on dates as high school seniors ("Have Smartphones …?").

What accounts for this radical cultural shift?

The obvious culprits, say Twenge and other experts, are smartphones and social media. Why leave your bedroom when you can "socialize" with your friends without ever leaving your comfort zone? Why practice basketball outside when you can watch an endless stream of dribbling and dunking clips from your sofa?

Young people might say they are too stressed out with academic work to play outside, but high schoolers in the 2010s spent less time on homework than high schoolers in the early 1990s (Twenge, "Have Smartphones…?").

According to the evidence, "Teens who spend more time than average on screen activities are more likely to be unhappy, and those who spend more time than average on non-screen activities are more likely to be happy." There are no exceptions, claims Twenge in her 2017 *Atlantic* essay entitled, "Have Smartphones Destroyed a Generation?"

All screen activities are linked to unhappiness. All non-screen activities (in-person socializing, sports, hobbies, volunteering, whatever) are linked to happiness.

Is there a link between smartphones and psychological distress in Gen Z? Although establishing exact scientific connections are difficult, experts point to an increasing amount of anecdotal and data-driven evidence to argue that there are clear links between smartphones, social media, and mental health. On an individual level, you may rightly believe that you are an exception to a generational disorder. Or you may be living in a state of psychological denial regarding your own level of device-dependence. In any case, it's worth asking: What does it mean for Gen Z's future and the future of the nation when so many teens (whose prefrontal cortices, after all, are only partway developed) suffer so much mental distress?

Finding Connections Works Cited

Twenge, Jean M. "Have Smartphones Destroyed a Generation?" *The Atlantic*, Sept. 2017, https://www.theatlantic.
com/magazine/archive/2017/09/has-the-smartphone-destroyed-a-generation/534198/.
*iGen: Why Today's Super-Connected Kids Are Growing Up Less Rebellious, More Tolerant, Less Happy—and
Completely Unprepared for Adulthood (and What That Means for the Rest of Us).* Simon & Schuster, 2017.

Related: See Finding Connections: Generation Stress, version 2.0 in Unit Seven.

Resources

Three Effective Ways to Integrate Quotations

*Here is an original standalone quotation from Nicholas Carr's essay "Is Google Making Us Stupid? What the Internet is Doing to our Brains" (*The Atlantic, *July/Aug. 2008):*

"Over the past few years I've had an uncomfortable sense that someone, or something, has been tinkering with my brain, remapping the neural circuitry, reprogramming the memory."

There are three basic ways to integrate this standalone quotation:

1. **Using a signal phrase and comma:**
   Carr writes, "Over the past few years I've had an uncomfortable sense that someone, or something, has been tinkering with my brain, remapping the neural circuitry, reprogramming the memory."

   Other common signal phrases include **She claims, He argues, Doe suggests,** *and similar phrases. Get in the good habit of attributing information to the correct author or source. See the Purdue Online Writing Lab. Google "owl purdue signal phrases" or go directly to:*

   https://owl.purdue.edu/owl/research_and_citation/using_research/quoting_paraphrasing_and_summarizing/signal_and_lead_in_phrases.html

2. **Using a whole sentence set up with a colon:**
   Carr claims that there may be serious consequences to our twenty-first century reading habits: "Over the past few years I've had an uncomfortable sense that someone, or something, has been tinkering with my brain, remapping the neural circuitry, reprogramming the memory."

   A complete sentence that sets up the quotation is separated from the quotation with a colon. *The colon [:] indicates a logical relationship between the set-up sentence and the quotation.*

3. **Using seamless transition with no punctuation:**
   Carr argues that the Internet may have the extraordinary capacity to "[remap] the neural circuitry."

   The writer changes the verb form of "remapping" to "remap." The writer must indicate any such changes by using [brackets] *within the quotation. Seamless quotation functions just as a normal sentence would, as a single coherent unit of grammar, without interloping or unnecessary punctuation.*

Further on Seamless Quotation Integration

Seamless quotation integration *is an effective composition technique. It is a good tool to have in your toolbox. You can incorporate a phrase or a few words from the source text instead of pulling out a full (often cumbersome) sentence. Often, this form of quotation integration results in improved style.*

Study the example below. *The writer relies on* excerpts *lifted from the text rather than* whole *quotations. This efficient method allows the writer's voice to control the discourse. The sample below uses MLA in-text parenthetical page citation. Note that citations always come at the end of a sentence, even when the quote appears earlier in the sentence. Altered and added words are indicated by* [brackets]:

EXAMPLE: Text Analysis Paragraph that uses Seamless Quotation Integration

Rose describes a self-defense mechanism where students seek to "protect themselves from [the] suffocating madness [of school]" by adopting a mentality that values mediocrity above excellence (12). For Rose, this psychological condition explains why students such as Ken Harvey only want to be "average." The tragedy, Rose states, is that in order to make the defense work "you have to twist the knife in your own gray matter" (13). Some young people deny themselves the chance to succeed by reconciling themselves to failure in a "tremendously disorienting place" like school (12). It's a downward spiral that keeps students from succeeding. They shield themselves from humiliation by not trying, by championing the average, and by rejecting the "confusion and frustration" of academic scrambling, philosophical inquiry, and scientific reasoning (13).

The MLA-style bibliographical citation that would accompany this paragraph appears below. *Consult your online style guide for directions on MLA, APA, and other formats.*

Works Cited

Rose, Mike. "I Just Wanna Be Average." *Engaging Discourse: A 21st Century Composition Reader & Curriculum* by Bradley Summerhill, Kendall Hunt, 2020, pp. 10-7.

Level II Making Connections Guidelines

Throughout *Engaging Discourse 2.0*, you will perceive general, abstract connections between unit topics. For example, Carr's unit one article mentions "neuroplasticity," which is our unit three topic. Additionally, you probably already understand that the effects of social media tie in directly to generation studies and happiness studies, as well as AI and brain plasticity.

These connections are sometimes called **synthetic connections**—not because they are fake or artificial but because you, as the reader and critical thinker, are perceiving and thereby producing the connections. Your goal in a Level II type of composition is to **demonstrate** these connections with sufficient detail, connecting evidence and language across two or more texts.

Goals of a Level II: Making Connections essay:

1. identify a general connection between two texts, and
2. demonstrate a detailed evidentiary connection between the two texts.

In other words, you must **analyze and connect**

a. the language and general principles represented across two or more texts
b. the actual *evidence* that the authors present in each text.

Ideally, it may be possible to identify **fresh concepts** that arise from the discourse between these texts. Your multi-text analysis of ideas and evidence may lead to new ideas distinct from those that appear in any single text.

Always include a **bibliography** in MLA or APA style, or another acceptable style of your instructor's choosing.

The general goal of "synthesis" in composition and the world of arts and letters is to bring together words and ideas from separate and even disparate sources to form a coherent whole. In writing, *synthesis* means to form a connection, or to create a new idea by combining separate ideas. You may need to address an outside audience of general educated readers, or you may need to address a specific audience or "discourse community," for example, an audience or biologists or psychologists or sociologists or other scientists, specialists, or experts.

Composition Tips

✓ It is often useful to identify and analyze the *rhetorical situation* of each text or article. See The Rhetorical Situation in Unit Five Resources.
✓ Whenever we write, we strive to offer our audiences *details* and *specificity*.

Suggested Level II Making Connections Evaluation Criteria:

Holistic Evaluation *The essay features a coherent purpose and addresses an appropriate audience.*	20%
Quotations *The writer properly presents and contextualizes significant language from the source texts and clarifies the rhetorical situations of the source texts as necessary.*	20%
Synthetic Connections *The writer clarifies general principles connecting source texts and identifies relevant public discourse(s) as necessary. The writer analyzes supporting evidence within each source and identifies relevant connections of evidence that exist between the source texts.*	30%
Voice *The writer presents clear, effective prose. The writer follows the conventions of standard written English prose.*	20%
Format *The writer follows MLA, APA, or another acceptable format as specified by the instructor.*	10%

Writing Assignments

Sentence Exercise

Walton cites numerous negative effects that may result from overuse of social media, the most significant of which might be _the evidence provided in reference to social media & Internet addiction._

Paragraph Exercise

Look for logical **transition words or phrases** *to complete the following paragraph:*

Experts disagree on whether Internet addiction is real. In fact, studies do confirm that people may experience anxiety and other symptoms of withdrawal when separated from their digital devices. Depression feelings of social isolation are linked to social media use. As a resu It we ought to use caution when engaging these powerful communication tools.

See Examining Your Draft Essay: Tips for Editing and Revision *in unit nine for a list of useful transition words and phrases.*

© Prostock-studio/Shutterstock.com

Essay Prompts

Level I: Analysis-Response

1. Alice G. Walton's article "6 Ways Social Media Affects Our Mental Health" is a product of journalism. As such, the article cites studies in a more general and less rigorous way than would be required in an academic paper. Track down the studies that Walton cites and rewrite the relevant sentences and/or paragraphs with proper attribution and MLA or APA citation.
2. Review the Further Inquiry unit bibliography and/or a library database. Select a text that focuses on the effects of social media. Analyze the author's main contentions and evidence regarding the effects of social media. Respond to the use of social media *as a social communication tool*.
3. Review the Unit Four Further Inquiry unit bibliography and/or a library database. Select a text that focuses on social media and dating. Analyze the author's main contentions and evidence regarding the effects of social media. Respond to the use of social media *as a tool for dating and romance*.

Level II: Making Connections

1. How do generations differ in their use of social media? How do Gen Z, Millennials, Gen X, and/or Baby Boomers tend to differ in their use of social media? (Focus on two generations, not more.) To what platforms do these generations gravitate, and why? How much time do various demographics spend on social media? How do experts account for the distinctions in how various age groups or demographics use social media?
2. To what degree, if any, does social media either cause or correlate to social isolation? To what degree, if any, can social media stimulate or enhance social connection? What expert source materials are available to investigate these questions?
3. In his article, "Does the Internet Make You Dumber?" writer Nicholas Carr reports that pioneering neuroscientist Michael Merzenich believes that our brains are being "massively remodeled" by our increasing use of Internet technologies. What scientific evidence exists to validate this concern?

Level III: Research

1. Develop a Level III Research topic from one of the topics listed above. Define a meaningful public discourse and a specific MRQ or major research question as you investigate source materials.
2. Research the topic of cyberbullying. How has the issue of bullying changed in the Internet era? Why does the topic of bullying appear to garner more concern in the twenty-first century than in prior eras?
3. How has social media affected romance in the twenty-first century? In other words, how has social media affected the practice of dating and relationships?
4. How has social media affected politics in the twenty-first century? Your purpose is scientific rather than partisan. Lean on scientific and analytical source materials rather than political source materials.

Further Inquiry

Anderson, Monica, and Jingjing Jiang. "1. Teens and Their Experiences on Social Media." *Pew Research Center: Internet & Technology*, 28 Nov. 2018, www.pewinternet.org/2018/11/28/teens-and-their-experiences-on-social-media/.

Bennet, Annmarie, editor. *Social Media: Global Perspectives, Applications and Benefits and Dangers.* Nova Science Publishers, 2014.

Cruz, Carlo. "9 Steps to Disconnect from Social Media and Connect With Life Again." *Lifehack*, 11 Sept. 2015, www.lifehack.org/280613/9-steps-disconnect-from-social-media-and-connect-with-life-again.

Duggan, Maeve, and Aaron Smith. "2. The Tone of Social Media Discussions Around Politics." *Pew Research Center: Internet & Technology*, 25 Oct. 2016, www.pewinternet.org/2016/10/25/the-tone-of-social-media-discussions-around-politics/.

Ehmke, Rachel." How Using Social Media Affects Teenagers." *TheChildMind.org*, 2020. The Child Mind Institute, https://childmind.org/article/how-using-social-media-affects-teenagers/.

Fetters, Ashley. "The 5 Years That Changed Dating." *The Atlantic*, 21 Dec. 2018, www.theatlantic.com/family/archive/2018/12/tinder-changed-dating/578698.

Glaser, Philip, et al. "Is Social Media Use for Networking Positive or Negative? Offline Social Capital and Internet Addiction as Mediators for the Relationship between Social Media Use and Mental Health." *New Zealand Journal of Psychology*, vol. 47, no. 3, Nov. 2019, pp. 12-18, https://www.psychology.org.nz/wp-content/uploads/Is-Social-Media-Use-for-Networking-Positive-or-Negative.pdf.

Greco, Dorothy Littell. "Is Social Media Disconnecting Us? Pt. I." *Biola University Center for Marriage and Relationship*, 8 May 2018, cmr.biola.edu/blog/2018/may/08/social-media-disconnecting-us/.

Horwood, Sharon. "Technology and Relationships: Have We Become Disconnected?" *This.*, July 18, 2018, Horwood, Sharon. "Technology and Relationships: Have We Become Disconnected?" This., 18 July 2018, this.deakin.edu.au/society/technology-and-relationships-have-we-become-disconnected.

Hou, Yubo, et al. "Social Media Addiction: Its Impact, Mediation, and Intervention." *Cyberpsychology,* vol. 13, no. 1, Mar. 2019, https://cyberpsychology.eu/article/view/11562/10373.

Kelleghan, Annemarie. "The Social Media Disconnect: Social Isolation in the Time of Social Media Connection." *Psychology Today*, 26 Feb. 2018, https://www.psychologytoday.com/us/blog/home-base/201802/the-social-media-disconnect.

Meyer, Robinson. "Your Smartphone Reduces Your Brainpower, Even If It's Just Sitting There." *The Atlantic,* 2 Aug. 2017, https://www.theatlantic.com/technology/archive/2017/08/a-sitting-phone-gathers-brain-dross/535476/.

Naughton, John. "Anti-Social Media: How Facebook Disconnects Us and Undermines Democracy by Siva Vaidhyanathan – Review." *The Guardian*, 25 June 2018, www.theguardian.com/books/2018/jun/25/anti-social-media-how-facebook-disconnects-us-undermines-democracy-siva-vaidhyanathan-review.

Onyewuchi, Chiamaka. "Connected Yet Disconnected: Teen Depression and Social Media ." *UMPC Pinnacle*, 18 May 2018, www.pinnaclehealth.org/wellness-library/blog-and-healthwise/blog-home/post/connected-yet-disconnected-teen-depression-and-social-media.

Parnell, Bailey. "Is Social Media Hurting Your Mental Health?" TEDx Talks, *YouTube,* 22 June 2017, https://www.youtube.com/watch?v=Czg_9C7gw0o.

Price, Michael. "Alone In The Crowd: Sherry Turkle Says Social Networking is Eroding our Ability to Live Comfortably Offline." *American Psychological Association*, June 2011, www.apa.org/monitor/2011/06/social-networking.

Sapolsky, Robert. "To Understand Facebook, Study Capgras Syndrome: This Mental Disorder Gives Us a Unique Insight into the Digital Age." *Nautilus,* 16 Nov. 2016, http://nautil.us/issue/42/fakes/to-understand-facebook-study-capgras-syndrome.

Sharot, Tali. "The Optimism Bias." TED Talk, Feb. 2012. *YouTube.com*, https://www.ted.com/talks/tali_sharot_the_optimism_bias?language=en.

Stevenson, Ross. "Disconnection in a Connected World: An Insight to our Relationship with Technology and Each Other." *Thrive Global*, 22 Oct. 2018, thriveglobal.com/stories/disconnection-in-a-connected-world-2/.

Tendler, Alexandra. "The Disconnect: How Social Media Is Making Us Anti-Social." *The Odyssey Online*, 15 Sept. 2015, www.theodysseyonline.com/disconnect-social-media-making-anti-social.

Turkle, Sherry. *Alone Together: Why We Expect More from Technology and Less from Each Other.* Basic Books, 2011.

Twenge, Jean M. "Have Smartphones Destroyed a Generation?" *The Atlantic*, Sept. 2017, https://www.theatlantic.com/magazine/archive/2017/09/has-the-smartphone-destroyed-a-generation/534198/.

— *iGen: Why Today's Super-Connected Kids Are Growing Up Less Rebellious, More Tolerant, Less Happy—and Completely Unprepared for Adulthood (and What That Means for the Rest of Us).* Simon & Schuster, 2017.

Walton, Alice G. "6 Ways Social Media Affects Our Mental Health." *Forbes.com*, 30 June 2017, https://www.forbes.com/sites/alicegwalton/2017/06/30/a-run-down-of-social-medias-effects-on-our-mental-health/#6b663e462e5a.

UNIT THREE

Brain Plasticity

If you have read unit one, some of the significant implications surrounding brain plasticity have already become clear to you: Dr. Michael Merzenich's pioneering work on neuroplasticity is referenced in Nicholas Carr's "Does the Internet Make You Dumber?" Merzenich was one of the first to discover the mammalian brain's incredible capacity for neural mapping and, in effect, rewiring.

In his book *Soft-Wired*, Merzenich claims that we are in the early stages of a "Brain Plasticity Revolution." Throughout the book, he advocates the positive power of brain training. "You have powers of re-strengthening, recovery, and re-normalization," Merzenich writes, "even when your brain has suffered large-scale distortions that accompany developmental or psychiatric disorders, and even when it has been physically damaged in any one of the innumerable ways that can befall you in your life."

Scientists have long understood the immature brain's propensity for neuroplasticity. One of the major discoveries that Merzenich made involves demonstrations of plasticity in the adult brain. Merzenich identified "neurological remodeling" in an adult patient with a severe hand injury, for example, revealing the flexible nature of the adult brain's ongoing neurological processes. The brain, in fact, does not grow into a static maturity. It keeps growing and changing. Or at least a healthy brain does. Our brains are not hard-wired, Merzenich informs us, they are *soft-wired*. Our neurological processes continue to fluctuate even as we reach advanced ages.

In the twentieth century, scientists deduced our DNA's double helix structure and mapped the human genome. Alongside these revolutionary discoveries, the concept of genetic determinism arose. The idea that our genes were largely responsible for intelligence, for disease, for mental conditions, and for sundry crucial facets of our lives was engrained in the popular culture. Yet few twenty-first century scientists hold such deterministic views. Many scientists who study so-called cancer genes, for example, acknowledge that environment seems to be a key factor in whether the disease actually expresses itself. Psychologists, educators, and sociologists typically emphasize *context* rather than character when it comes to behavior and the development of human intelligence. Neuroscientists and experimental philosophers investigate schemes of higher intelligence that stress the importance of stimuli input in human cognition. Modern commentators have taken to computer metaphors: human thinking, in this analogy, becomes the result of data input, the coding of our environment. Clearly, according to twenty-first century understandings, environment is an important factor for consideration in fields of study from education to neuroscience. In our studies of criminology, philosophy, sociology, politics, disease, and even the computer sciences, experts now emphasize the role of environment and contextual factors as they seek insights, assess situations, and draw conclusions.

The computer metaphor has become a widespread analogy to explain brain functions and human cognition. We speak of human hardware, the brain's gray matter, neurons, and electrical impulses. We speak of human software, the mind's capacity for *plasticity*. **Neuroplasticity** can be understood as the brain's inherent capacity for flexibility and adaptability.

In the Industrial Age, we used clock metaphors to describe human cognition, as in, *his mind runs like clockwork*. In the Internet era, we declare our need to *update our brain's software* and, especially in the vulnerable early stages of childhood brain development and in the later stages of elderly cognition, we consider our need to install *anti-viral software* in order to protect ourselves from the ravages of negative influences. Increasingly, scientists use the language of *data input* and *data output* to describe human cognition. In old age, negative inputs include, quite simply, our aging brains and bodies, our slowing senses, for example. New scientific understandings of neurological development now provide insights on the damaging influences of violence, abuse, and financial stress, especially on developing childhood and teenaged brains. By one estimate, for example, the human IQ (intelligence quotient) drops 13 points when an individual experiences severe financial stress. And while the severe negative effects of alcohol and drugs on the developing brain are becoming more obvious to scientists, our understandings of the amygdala's fight-or-flight mechanism also evolves. Children suffering environments of violence or abuse become incapable of real learning as their higher cognitive functions shut down in order to engage in survival mode. Such situations are examples of *negative* neuroplasticity. The fact that the brain is *plastic* is neither positive or negative: **neuroplasticity signifies that the human brain tends to change in positive ways due to positive influences and in negative ways due to negative influences**.

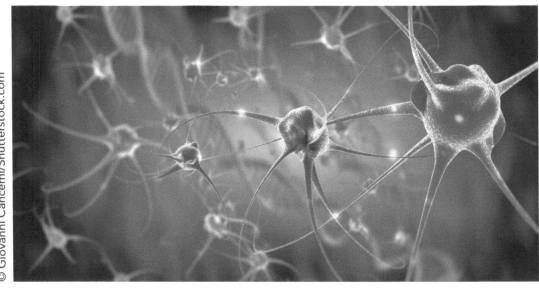

© Giovanni Cancemi/Shutterstock.com

The good news is that the human neural network is capable of amazing feats of *positive* neuroplasticity. For pioneering neuroscientist Dr. Michael Merzenich, the fact of human neuroplasticity, even amidst the stark realities of aging and disease, implies empowerment. We can consciously train the brain, bending our cognitive functions toward positive plasticity while circumventing the consequences of negative plasticity.

One of the sources of negative brain plasticity may surprise you: our increasing reliance on AI (artificial intelligence) to do tasks such as road navigation. Merzenich implores his readers to take on the task of mapping and routing the streets and highways oneself instead of relying on GPS (global positioning systems) to tell you how to get from point A to point B. Why might this small change prove important when it comes to the effects of neuroplasticity on cognition? Merzenich addresses his book, *Soft-Wired*, to mainly an audience of older readers. As we age, issues of cognition and dementia obviously become more immediate; yet it stands to reason that the earlier we concern ourselves with brain plasticity, the better off we can be as we age. The benefits of building a strong physical foundation in youth are well acknowledged. It does not seem to be a stretch for us to tout the benefits of building a strong mental foundation as well.

Millennials and Gen Z could face hidden danger from our increasing reliance on AI and computers to perform everyday mental functions. Such a claim is far from scientifically proven, and it doesn't appear to represent accepted wisdom at this point. Rather, the effects of interactions between human cognition and computers is an emerging twenty-first century discourse. What important questions stand unanswered? What would the experts like to know? What "major research questions" can you develop as you investigate this discourse?

Questions to Consider

Answer these questions as you read and annotate the text:

- The original article opens up with an anecdote, or story. What happened? What is the conclusion to the story?
- What is unusual about Michael Merzenich's election to the Institute of Medicine?
- What human brain capacity allowed Ryan, the accident victim, to recover?
- What scientific dogma or belief did Merzenich overturn or cast doubt on? In other words, what did scientists used to believe about human mental capacities?
- What is neurological "micromapping"?
- How does the example of dyslexia illustrate the new way that neuroscientists think about cognitive disorders?
- How are Posit Science's methods for treating schizophrenia different from traditional methods for treating the symptoms of schizophrenia?
- What is the purpose of the video game, *NeuroRacer*?

How to 'Game Your Brain': The Benefits of Neuroplasticity

The science of neuroplasticity illuminates the dynamic evolution of our brains throughout life
By JOÃO MEDEIROS

Update: 10.04.2017: On 5 April, Akili Interactive Labs announced the results of a study demonstrating its cognitive-training computer game, Project: EVO, improves the symptoms of children with cognitive deficits.

In the clinical study, 57 children with sensory processing disorder, a condition that affects how the brain receives and responds to sensorial information, played Project: EVO for four weeks.

After the treatment, the symptoms in 33 per cent of the patients had improved to the extent that they no longer met the criteria for the disorder.

"These findings are quite exciting given that they both reproduce critical elements of the study of this technology in older adults and suggest that this treatment approach can have powerful effects across the lifespan and in distinct populations with specific cognitive deficits," said Joaquin Anguera, from the Departments of Neurology and Psychiatry at UCSF and lead author of the study.

Akili's Project: EVO is currently still under evaluation in a large clinical trial with ADHD patients, a study that aims to get the game FDA approved as a medical treatment.

Original story

One day in January 2007, a US federal government construction contractor called Doug Reitmeyer arrived at the offices of a brain-fitness software company called Posit Science, in downtown San Francisco. Reitmeyer's son, Ryan, had had a devastating boat accident two years earlier. At about 9.45pm, four of Ryan's friends had asked him to take them back to their car across the lake. Ryan, 29, was driving the small Sea Ray boat across lake Travis, a reservoir on the Colorado River in Texas, when it collided with a ten-metre black Carver cabin cruiser that had no lights on. The Sea Ray's five occupants went overboard and Ryan's head was crushed between the two boats. Surgery to remove the shattered bone that had pierced his brain lasted several hours and he was in a coma for two weeks. Surgeons had to remove part of his brain's frontal lobes, leaving him with an indentation in his head, where parts of his brain and skull were missing. When Doug Reitmeyer asked the surgeon if he could save his son's life, the surgeon said that he could, but that Ryan would probably never be able to speak or live independently again. Reitmeyer was willing to prove the medics wrong, so he took early retirement and dedicated his life to helping his son make a full recovery. He researched brain-damage therapies and attended conferences and seminars, until he came upon the work of Michael Merzenich, a neuroscientist at the University of California, San Francisco, and founder of Posit Science, a company pioneering brain-fitness software to improve memory and processing speed in older adults. Reitmeyer scheduled a meeting.

Merzenich has silver hair and exudes bonhomie. He talks with the confidence of someone who believes he's usually right. One of his mantras is to hear, feel and taste as if he were a child again.

Every day he goes for walks and, comically, he varies his pace and the length of his stride, as a way of exercising his brain. He drives a Fiat 500 and refuses to use a GPS, or indeed any other technology that may act as a substitute for his brain. At the weekend he usually repairs to his villa in Santa Rosa, a 60-minute car journey north of San Francisco, where he tends to a small vegetable garden and vineyards. (His wife calls him "the farmer *and* the farmer's wife".) He is a member of the US National Academy of Sciences and, despite not being a medical doctor, is also a member of the Institute of Medicine, making him one of the few to have been elected to both academies.

Merzenich listened as Reitmeyer described the challenges facing his son Ryan, whose daily schedule at the time included sessions of neurofeedback, speech, physical and occupational therapies. Ryan had made some progress recovering his speech and movement but his memory and cognitive control remained deficient: Reitmeyer could take Ryan to a restaurant and his son would ask him when they were going to eat right after they'd had a meal. Merzenich reviewed Ryan's brain scans and medical records. Ryan was highly cognitively impaired, "down in the first few percentiles in cognitive ability".

He had very restricted syntactic ability. He couldn't hold much of a conversation. He couldn't sustain attention and couldn't memorise something for more than a couple of minutes. Merzenich's software had been tested on patients with traumatic brain injury, but this case was so severe that Merzenich didn't even know if Ryan would be able to initiate the exercises. But when Reitmeyer asked Merzenich if he could help his son, the doctor said of course he could.

Merzenich tailored a programme of regimented brain-fitness training for Ryan. It was heavily focused on redeveloping language and auditory abilities, with further emphasis on other skills, such as cognitive control and visual-processing. Ryan had spent more than 50 hours completing Posit Science's brain-fitness exercises when he came to see Merzenich some months later. "They came to thank us and to show how well Ryan was doing," Merzenich recalls. Ryan had recovered his memory and had made astonishing progress with his language and ability to control his attention. He could also hold a conversation and even use wit in his responses. Merzenich recalls Reitmeyer asking Ryan to pick something from a local drug store a couple of blocks away, a neighbourhood where Ryan had never been before. "And he did it. That would have been impossible a few months ago. They were so thankful. They knew that Ryan had come back into real life from such a deep hole," Merzenich says.

Merzenich keeps in touch with the Reitmeyers. Last time he spoke to Ryan, he was driving again, playing the guitar, had a job and was talking about getting married. "I choose not to talk about these things publicly because I don't want people to think that if you have 30 per cent of your frontal lobes removed you can expect this kind of recovery," Merzenich says. "One thing is clear though. Ryan would have never have recovered from such an injury if the human brain didn't have a remarkable capacity to change."

Merzenich is one of the few scientists and doctors who, in the past 30 years, have transformed the field of neurology by overturning the dogma that our mental abilities are immutable and fixed early in life. Cognitive impairment associated with neurological maladies, such as schizophrenia, strokes, autism and traumatic brain injury, were considered largely untreatable. Normal age-related cognitive decline was considered unavoidable. The capacity to train and improve the diverse mental abilities that make up our intelligence was not considered possible. But Merzenich and other researchers have shown that the brain is what they call "plastic"—it can physically remodel itself. The notion that the brain we are born with is not a fixed structure with a set of weaknesses and strengths, but a mutable organ that is adaptable and can be trained to overcome its deficiencies, has profound implications for how we perceive our brain and its associated capacities. Not only can brain plasticity be manipulated in ways that treat and prevent neuronal disease that was deemed permanent, but it can also keep our brains fit and resilient. "It means you're not stuck with it," Merzenich says. "We can improve and often fix it, whether you're 90 or when you're nine."

> In real biological terms, what does it mean that the human brain is "plastic"?

In 1968, Merzenich made his first breakthrough. He was a recent neuroscience graduate, studying at the University of Wisconsin-Madison under the supervision of a neurophysiologist called Clinton Woolsey. Merzenich was an expert in a technique called "micromapping", a precise but time-consuming way of finding which parts of the brain responded to external stimuli, using extremely small electrodes that measure the electrical activity of a single neuron. Merzenich used macaque monkeys, measuring neuronal activity as he tapped different parts of the monkey's hand, in order to see which areas of it stimulated electrical activity in the monitored part of the brain. Mapping a whole hand using this method could take between 20 and 40 hours.

When he arrived at Madison, Woolsey asked Merzenich to supervise two young neurosurgeons, Ron Paul and Herbert Goodman, and the three set out to find what happened in the brain of adult macaque monkeys after a severe hand injury. The mainstream view at the time was that the brain reached a fixed state after just one year of existence. If, for instance, one of the main nerves in the hand were cut, then the corresponding area in the brain was supposed to be rendered silent and unused from the lack of sensorial input.

Merzenich, Paul and Goodman, however, found that this wasn't the case. After the injury, neighbouring areas in the brain would expand into the vacant territory. Later, as the nerve regenerated, its corresponding brain connections would reclaim much of its original neurological real estate. This dynamic remodelling of the brain that Merzenich and his colleagues observed was completely at odds with the conventional view that the structure of a brain was immutable. In their scientific report, they wrote a lengthy discussion section about what these observations implied. Woolsey thought it was too conjectural and deleted it.

When, in 1971, Merzenich moved to the University of California, San Francisco, he continued his experiments at the department of otolaryngology, and showed again and again that adult brains remained plastic. The scientific establishment, however, was slow to accept it. Early reviews of his scientific papers often came back with sarcastic comments, and at conferences he was subjected to insults. That didn't bother him. He was sure that the scientific truth always wins in the end. "What irritated me is that I was

also arguing that this discovery could be used for all sorts of therapies," Merzenich says. "I became a sort of missionary going to people and saying, 'Listen, you should take this research seriously, it can help people.'" It took a couple of decades. In the late 80s, he met a neuroscientist from Rutgers University in New Jersey, called Paula Tallal. Tallal was interested in children who had difficulties reading and speaking, such as dyslex-

Why was the concept of "dynamic remodeling of the brain" so difficult for scientists to accept?

ics. Her studies showed that children with dyslexia had something wrong with their brains. At the time, scientists believed that dyslexics had a deficiency with their eyes, but Tallal suspected that instead their brains were too slow in processing sound. "People thought dyslexia had something to do with seeing letters backwards," says Tallal. "However, words are made of smaller units of sound represented by letters. It was becoming clear that the majority of dyslexic children find it difficult to be aware that words can be broken down into sounds. This in turn will affect their reading ability, because reading stands on the shoulders of spoken language. And because learning to read requires matching symbols to sounds, the child will be affected in understanding words and speech."

At the time, Merzenich had been conducting experiments with adult macaque monkeys that showed how radically their brains rewired after they learned new skills, such as being able to distinguish sounds in shorter and shorter periods of time. "We would progressively train them to an extent that their initially sluggish brains were fast and accurate," Merzenich says. When Tallal told him about her findings, Merzenich wondered if he could train these kids who lacked the necessary neurological circuitry to process sounds at speed. "Paula, if these kids were monkeys, I'm almost certain I could fix them," he told her.

Tallal and Merzenich decided to collaborate. In six months, with the help of a team of language specialists, neuroscientists and computer scientists, they developed language-training software called Fast ForWord. Fast ForWord consisted of games that used acoustically enhanced speech, which initially made very rapid acoustic changes longer and louder and then would slowly revert back into a normal speech range. For a month during the summer of 1994, seven dyslexic children came to Tallal's lab in Newark, New Jersey, to exercise their brains with the software. "At the time, the software was still very limited," Merzenich says. "The difference it made on the children, however, was amazing."

He remembers a quiet five-year-old boy who had the language abilities of a 30-month-old. "He was very limited, but when we returned to Newark after the tests he was a confident chatterbox. His tests indicated that his language ability was now normal after a month," Merzenich says.

Tallal and Merzenich decided to conduct a larger-scale controlled trial with improved software and more children, the results of which were later published in the journal *Science*. Within days of the report coming out, Merzenich and Tallal received thousands of messages from parents and therapists desperate to try the new treatment on their children. In 1996, Tallal and Merzenich, along with two other neuroscientists, founded the Scientific Learning Corporation, a company that produces Fast ForWord today. It was the first company to provide a brain-fitness programme online. To date, according to Tallal, Fast ForWord has helped more than two million children overcome learning disabilities.

Merzenich was CEO of Scientific Learning Corporation for only 18 months. He returned to the lab to continue to file patents for brain-plasticity-based methods that could help adults with normal, age-related cognitive decline and clinical impairments such as schizophrenia, autism and brain trauma. At board meetings he would insist the company needed to invest in plasticity therapies for adults, but the board wanted to keep the focus on treating children with learning disabilities. He was proud that they could help children to read and write, but that wasn't enough. So in 2003, he cofounded Posit Science with the goal of using the science of brain plasticity to help everybody else.

Merzenich runs Posit Science from a suite of offices in downtown San Francisco. He has a team of 36 people, including neurologists, computer scientists and game designers. Using the same brain-plasticity principles that he and Tallal used to treat children with Fast ForWord, Posit has developed an online software package called BrainHQ, a set of brain-training exercises aimed not only at treating neurological conditions, but also to arrest the normal cognitive decline that comes with age, and to improve the cognitive abilities of normal individuals. "I've looked at old brains, brains of animals we'd expected would die within months," Merzenich says. "And you look at the various capabilities of these brains and everything that disadvantages them. And which of these capabilities can we reverse by intensive, progressive training? All of them. Their decline is inherently reversible. As far as we can see, the same is true for humans."

To understand how Posit Science tackles neurological diseases, let's consider schizophrenia. Schizophrenics typically suffer from hallucinations, delusion and disorganised reasoning. These symptoms result from an excess of dopamine and noradrenaline, the neurotransmitters that modulate the reward feedback-loop control-arousal levels in the brain. Underlying this chemical reaction are what Merzenich calls "failure modes of the plastic brain": weaknesses in the neurological apparatus, specifically in working memory—a cognitive skill that indicates a person's capacity to manipulate information, such as computing sums—and the ability to make predictions. Antipsychotic medication, which suppresses these neurotransmitters, is effective in mitigating symptoms such as hallucinations but doesn't fix the cognitive structure.

"Drugs are an extremely primitive method to treat the neurology," Merzenich says. "We're manipulating machinery that is controlled by dozens of variables, by powerfully distorting one particular chemical. What we're doing instead is replacing that chemical approach with strategies that actually correct the neurological underpinnings of these problems. And the only way is to have the brain correct itself." Using BrainHQ, monitored schizophrenic patients can work on computer exercises that specifically target those cognitive weaknesses. Two recent studies led by Sophia Vinogradov, vice chair of psychiatry at the UCSF, have shown that 50 to 80 hours of using BrainHQ significantly improved not only patients' working memory and learning, but also their social functioning and ability to distinguish reality. Posit Science is currently conducting studies to gain US Food and Drug Administration approval to treat schizophrenia, brain injury and stroke. "We're transforming neuroscience-based software into medicine," Merzenich says.

To show how BrainHQ's exercises work, Merzenich instructs Wired to take a 36-part cognitive assessment that lasts three hours and purports to measure everything about cognitive abilities. "It allows us to tailor a programme to someone's specific needs," says Merzenich. In all, there were more than 40 exercises. One, called Hawk Eye, aims to sharpen visual perception and expand one's field of view. A set of identical birds flashes briefly on-screen, except for one of a different colour that needs to be identified. A simpler exercise is Sound Sweeps, which tests auditory accuracy by requiring subjects to identify whether a sound, which might last only milliseconds, is going up or down in frequency. Even harder is Mixed Signals, which requires subjects to watch a string of symbols, listen to a piece of information and react when they match. As new levels are unlocked, colourful fireworks explode on-screen. The exercises in Merzenich's brain gym are simple but strangely compelling.

On average, cognitive decline in humans starts when we're between the ages of 20 and 30. At the onset of this steady downfall, the brain slows down and its reliability deteriorates. Listening becomes less accurate. Peripheral vision narrows. Attention and memory begins to falter. To make matters worse, this gradual decline is usually accompanied by social withdrawal, egocentrism and a loss of confidence. As Merzenich likes to put it, everything is going to hell.

This problem is compounded by our laziness. When we get older, we rest on our laurels, auto-piloting our behaviours, operating effectively throughout the day using skills that we learned when we were younger. The problem with that approach is that our brain can be maintained only by a life of continual learning—but, as older people effectively decide to stop challenging the brain, like an unused car, the learning machinery slowly seizes up. "Like every organ in our bodies, the brain undergoes changes in how it performs. You see it in your muscles, your bones, your hair—and you feel it in your brain," says Adam Gazzaley, a neuroscientist at the University of California, San Francisco. "That is not helped by people seeking comfort and a less demanding life when they are older. The fact is that the brain is still plastic even when they are 70 or 80 years old. It can still be optimised—but instead, many people unwittingly accelerate its deterioration."

Gazzaley is best known for demonstrating some of the mechanisms behind cognitive decline. He showed, for instance, that as we get older we are more susceptible to interference—be that in the form of distractions, irrelevant information or multitasking. The problem with older adults is that they don't filter information, and consequently they overprocess irrelevant information that they can't seem to ignore. One of the consequences of interference is poor memory: it's difficult to recall something that was never properly imprinted in the brain in the first place.

One evening in 2008, Gazzaley had a strange, vivid dream about a video game. In that game, the player was driving a car along a winding road in the mountains and, at random intervals, a sign would pop up on the screen. If the sign had the right shape and colour, the player had to shoot it down while steering the car.

Gazzaley realised that he could design a video game to induce improvements in the brain. Later that day, Gazzaley called Matt Omernick, a friend who worked at the now-defunct games company LucasArts Entertainment, and recounted his dream. Omernick liked the idea and spoke to Eric Johnston, the legendary games developer who created the classicMonkeyIslandseries, and Noah Falstein, who had been one of LucasArts' first game designers and was now Google's chief game designer. "I explained to them the concept and Matt drew it out," Gazzaley says. "I didn't have any funding, but they wanted to work on it anyway. They said to me, 'We spent our whole careers teaching teenagers how to kill aliens. We're ready to use our skills to do something of impact.'"

Like Fast ForWord, Gazzaley's game, called *NeuroRacer*, was designed according to the rules of how plasticity is induced in the brain. Gazzaley's team used an "adaptive staircase algorithm" that constantly matched the difficulty of the game to the player's skill. "Adaptivity is at the core of our game mechanics because that's how you tap into plasticity," Gazzaley says. "Between 70 to 80 per cent difficulty is the sweet spot. That's where the player gets into a flow state and plasticity is maximal." When the game was completed, Gazzaley recruited 174 people, with ages ranging from 20 to 80. In the first phase of the study, they tested the multitasking skills of their participants, confirming that older players had more multitasking deficiencies than younger ones. They then recruited 46 participants aged 60 to 85 and put them through a four-week training period with *NeuroRacer*, "After the training period, the multitasking skill levels of the older guys exceeded even the levels of the 20-year-olds who had played the game once," says Gazzaley, "Those levels were sustained six months later." Also, Gazzaley found that the older players not only improved their ability to multitask, which the game explicitly trained, but other abilities, such as working memory and sustained attention.

Last year, Gazzaley cofounded a company called Akili Interactive Labs, which is developing an upgrade of *NeuroRacer* called *EVO*. Like Posit Science, Akili is seeking FDA approval for EVO as a possible software-based treatment for ADHD. "Most people associate medicine with drugs, and that's the result of a big, successful brainwashing campaign by pharma companies," Gazzaley says. "But when it comes to brain health, drugs don't work very well—and the drug companies know that. If you look across the world's top-ten pharma companies, four have withdrawn research from neuroscience. That's not because we've cured any of these diseases. Hopefully now we'll start thinking of software and hardware as a form of medicine."

Gazzaley has been preparing to open a new neuroscience laboratory at the University of California, San Francisco. "We're going to be able to record real-time EEG data as you play one of our games," Gazzaley says.

> How does the idea that "we can take control of such [neurological] transformation" run contrary to concepts of genetic determinism?

"The challenge won't just be correlated to your performance, but also directly by neural processes in your brain." He gives Wired a copy of the November 2013 issue of the scientific journal *Nature*. The cover headline is "Game Changer" and the image shows the cartoon of an old balding man driving a car through *NeuroRacer*'s mountainous roads. "Before I'd developed *NeuroRacer*, I used to give talks to groups of colleagues and present my data on cognitive decline and its mechanisms, and they would love it, find it fascinating.

But when I gave a talk about it to a public audience of older people, like the American Association of Retired Persons, it was horrifying. If you give a lot of talks you get good at reading subtle signs in the audience. Every year at the AGM, I had over a thousand people in the audience, all grey, and at the end of my talk, I could just see them asking "Is this it? Is this the end of the movie?" There was this feeling like that was not really the right ending." He points to the *Nature* cover. "That is the right ending."

Older adults are often advised to keep their minds sharp, but such advice is so general as to be useless. "It's true that we lose abilities as we get older, but I believe that most of that loss is driven by a lack of effort to sustain brain fitness," says Alvaro Pascual-Leone, a neurologist at Harvard Medical School and one of the most-cited scientists in the field of brain plasticity. "We're lazy, we don't get out of our comfort zones, we stop learning new things. The fact is that whatever you do, from activities to relationships to thoughts, ultimately enters the brain and affects it. But we can harness that property of the brain for our own benefit. Ultimately, it's a message of hope for people."

The science of neuroplasticity illuminates the dynamic evolution of our brains throughout life, documenting how different experiences can dramatically change it. Its most pertinent insight, however, is that we can take control of such transformation.

Merzenich's and Gazzaley's brain-training exercises provide us with a tool to do it. They are a gym for the brain, a place where we can go to strengthen and expand our cognitive capabilities, which, to a very large extent, define who we are and determine what we are capable of.

This article was original published in May 2014 and has been updated to include the clinical trial.

Questions for Comprehension

Answer these questions as a comprehension gauge and/or for further clarification on the text:

1. Michael Merzenich's work proved which of the following: 1) the brain is a fixed structure, or 2) the brain is a mutable, adaptable structure.

2. True or False. Dyslexia results when there is a problem with the eyes.

3. On average, when does cognitive decline begin in humans, according to this article?

4. What are the symptoms of cognitive decline, and what characteristic traits accompany cognitive decline?

5. Instead of pharmaceutical drugs, researcher Adam Gazzaley advocates what as a form of medicine?

Finding Connections: Aging and the Plastic Brain

Mark Twain said it best: "There are many advantages to aging … it's just that no one has discovered them yet." Like all great jokes, this one contains a profound truth. To one degree or another, most of us fear aging.

© Lightspring/Shutterstock.com

Scientists in the ancient world believed that the brain was a useless lump of matter. They felt that all of the important functions of the mind were contained in the heart rather than in the head. Enlightenment era philosophers and scientists still had little understanding of the brain's importance, but once scientists did discover some of the most important functions of the brain the belief quickly developed that the brain, much like the heart or any other organ, was a fixed entity. In 1890, American philosopher and psychologist William James suggested that the brain was perhaps not so unchanging as previously thought (or "hard-wired," in our contemporary parlance). James' observations on the brain's "extraordinary degree of plasticity" were largely ignored. Well into the twentieth century, the concept of "neuroplasticity" was an unrecognized phenomenon. The dominant conceptions when it came to brain functions involved unchangeability and permanence. Even when scientists later recognized the amazing plasticity of the human child's brain, scientific dogma presumed that the adult brain was incapable of such changeability.

Our brain, it turns out, is shaped by environment to an extent heretofore unknown and misunderstood. For example, babies raised under conditions of constant white noise or droning are limited in their later ability to process spoken and written language. Their "language intelligence" is not genetic in origin. Instead, the brain never learns how to process auditory input in any meaningful way, so later attempts to make meaning from auditory input are difficult. This example represents a profound example of brain plasticity. Recent discoveries regarding adult brain plasticity are equally profound. In the twenty-first century, we are beginning to understand that "nurture" is sometimes more important than "nature." Nowadays, we understand computer metaphors, so let's put it this way: our software must be continually reset and updated.

The reality is that a 70-year-old brain usually takes twice as long to "know" things compared to a 30-year-old brain. Nonetheless, in his book, *Soft-Wired*, neuroscientist Michael Merzenich insists, "Every person has the capacity to control positive plastic brain change in their own brain" (129).

What do you imagine are the best ways to carry out Merzenich's mantra of positive control of the plastic mind? *(See Unit Three Notes at the end of the textbook.)*

What would you tell older relatives that they must do in order to remain on the positive side of cognition as they age? *(ibid.=See Unit Three Notes at the end of the textbook.)*

In what crucial ways do the physical body and the thinking mind interact? *("ibid" is Latin for "ibīdem" meaning literally "in the same place" and used to indicate "same as the preceding reference or citation.")*

Finding Connections Works Cited

Merzenich, Michael. *Soft-Wired: How the New Science of Brain Plasticity Can Change Your Life.* Parnassus Publishing, 2013.

"In this world," Benjamin Franklin wrote in 1789, "nothing can be … certain, except death and taxes."

Although they are anything but certain, there are two other constants in life that virtually all humans pursue: love and happiness.

True, some folks might think love nothing more than a distraction or a weakness of character, and some might be too embittered or psychologically damaged to embrace it as a real possibility. Despite such sad instances, a desire to love and be loved is at the core of human experience. One other certainty, as sure as death and taxes, is the certainty that humans want to be happy. Aristotle determined more than two millennia ago that humans seek happiness above all else.

Definitions of what actually constitute "love" and "happiness" seem as wide-ranging as humanity itself. Are these emotions completely subjective and relativistic in nature, as varied as the individuals who experience these abstract concepts?

Can love and happiness be studied scientifically?

Naturally, we would have to sort through the types of love we mean to study, and we would need to agree upon the type of happiness that we wish to explore. *Engaging Discourse 2.0* provides opportunities for you to learn more about these fields of study. *See Unit Four Romance in the Twenty-First Century and Unit Eight Happiness Studies.*

Before jumping into research, it can be useful to develop synthetic connections with other fields of study in order to sort out what you already know and what you would like to know.

Love, Happiness, and Plasticity

Experts inform us that *brain plasticity* can lead to either positive or negative outcomes. The brain's neural network responds to both positive and negative external stimuli. The fact of *neuroplasticity* is not good or bad, positive or negative; it is a process, a capacity for change. That change can result in positive or negative outcomes. Strong human emotions and experiences (such as surprise or trauma) impact the "plastic" human brain.

In unit eight, we read psychologist Daniel Gilbert's description of what he labels the "psychological immune system." Look for connections that indicate the role which "neuroplasticity" plays in our so-called mental immune system. Most of what Gilbert describes takes place in the subconscious mind. *To what extent, if any, can the conscious mind affect happiness due to our positive capacities for mental plasticity?*

In unit four, we read psychologist Barbara Fredrickson's account of "positivity resonance" associated with the biology of love. Look for connections that indicate the role of human brain plasticity in this so-called *positivity resonance. To what extent, if any, can the conscious mind affect feelings associated with love due to our capacities for mental plasticity?*

Make You Do Right, Make You Do Wrong

Love as a research topic isn't all fun and games. In his song "Love and Happiness," the Reverend Al Green sings, "Power of love … Make you do right, love'll make you do wrong." Anthropologist Helen Fisher explores the emotional connection between romantic love and abandonment rage in her book *Why We Love* (2004). Love and hate can appear, on a biological level, to be a single emotion. "The basic brain network for rage is closely connected to centers in the pre-frontal cortex that process reward-assessment and reward expectation," she writes (164). And when the "reward" of love is withdrawn or discovered to be unattainable, these centers in the prefrontal cortex "signal the amygdala and trigger rage."

Neuroplasticity, we might say (riffing on Shakespeare's *Hamlet*), is neither good nor bad, but thinking makes it so.

Finding Connections Works Cited

Fisher, Helen. *Why We Love: The Nature and Chemistry of Romantic Love.* Henry Holt & Co, 2004.

Fredrickson, Barbara. *Love 2.0: How Our Supreme Emotion Affects Everything We Feel, Think, Do, and Become.* Hudson Street Press, 2013.

Gilbert, Daniel. *Stumbling on Happiness.* Alfred A. Knopf, 2006.

Merzenich, Michael. *Soft-Wired: How the New Science of Brain Plasticity Can Change Your Life.* Parnassus Publishing, 2013.

Resources

Identifying a Public Discourse

21st C. Literary * Social (Dis)Connection * Brain Plasticity * Love's Biology * Appropriation * AI Robotics * Generation Studies * Happiness Studies

Finding Connections : In order to specify and narrow your topic and research scope, you may want to d evelop synthetic connections and areas of concern that span two discourse topics.

Identify a Discourse That Is Significant to You and Others

What concerns do experts express in regard to this discourse?

What concerns do you share in regard to this discourse?

What audiences are aware of these concerns?

What audiences exist who would be interested but are not yet aware of these concerns?

What do these audiences know or not know in regard to these concerns? What would they want to find out? What problems require examination, contemplation, or solutions? What specific questions would interest your readers?

Develop a Major Research Question

See Unit Nine Research in the Twenty-First Century for detailed information on the research paper composition process.

Writing Assignments

Sentence Exercises

Use information from the unit article to complete clear, coherent sentences. You might think of these as topic sentences *to open a middle or body paragraph.*

Merzenich believes that _____ allows a person to _____.

Cognitive decline in humans can _____ and can _____.

Neuroscientist Adam Gazzaley developed _____ in order to _____.

Paragraph Exercise

Use information from the unit article to complete a coherent paragraph using the following template.

Merzenich and other scientists believe that the human brain is _____. Some of the most significant implications of _____ can be seen when _____. As a result of _____, people who have suffered from _____ now find that _____.

Making Connections Template Exercise

Draw a connection between different unit topics. For example, consider using the Carr article from unit one to complete the first sentence of the template exercise below.

In the essay "_____," writer _____ expresses concerns about our declining attention spans. Similarly, neuroscientist Michael Merzenich expresses concerns that the human brain _____.

Essay Prompts

Level I: Analysis-Response

1. New clinical training methods indicate the promise of neurological recovery and modification throughout a lifetime. Explain the science behind some of these clinical training methods. Respond to the concept of "brain training."

Level II: Making Connections

1. According to experts, frequent, lengthy social media use can correlate to increased anxiety and depression. Analyze the role of neuroplasticity in this process.
2. Use one or both of the Finding Connections articles in this unit to develop a Level II topic of your own.
3. It is important to recognize that neuroplasticity, in and of itself, is neither positive or negative. Neuroplasticity can be either positive or negative. Another way of stating this concept would be to say that the plastic brain, to some extent, responds to outside stimuli. A computer coding analogy for this process might be: *garbage in, garbage out*. Considering the realities of neuroplasticity, take a fresh look at Nicholas Carr's articles dealing with twenty-first century literacies ("Does the Internet Make You Dumber?" and "Is Google Making Us Stupid?"). Develop connections between Carr's main ideas and the phenomenon of neuroplasticity.

Level III: Research

1. Expand the Level II topic listed above. Research the connection between neuroplasticity and Internet era literacies. Research the science that exists on the effects of electronic information on the human brain. Neurologically speaking, what are the primary differences between traditional physical book reading and e-reading, for example? Distracting Internet ads and hyperlinks is its own distinct topic. Be specific and try not to conflate issues. The key point of investigation involves how electronic information and screen time effects the plastic human brain.
2. For pioneering neuroscientist Michael Merzenich, neuroplasticity means continual neural revision throughout a person's lifetime. Neuroplasticity offers the hope of recovery from traumatic brain injuries and cognitive disorders. Research the science of cognitive recovery.
3. Around the age of 60, the average adult brain begins to shrink in volume. Frequently, cognitive decline accompanies this loss of volume in the cerebral cortex. Neuroscientist Michael Merzenich believes that continual neural revision occurs throughout a person's lifetime, even in old age. Research how the human brain ages and how positive neuroplasticity may be able to address some of the effects of aging, including cognitive decline due to symptoms associated with dementia.
4. In her book, *The Myth of Sanity*, psychiatrist Martha Stout discusses the phenomenon of dissociation. She observes both normal and extreme forms of *dissociation*, a subconscious process of disconnection or separation from what we usually term reality. Daydreaming is a mild form of dissociation, while the loss of hours or days to a person's conscious awareness may come about as a result of the brain's response to psychological trauma, including childhood trauma. Research the phenomenon of dissociation and the role that neuroplasticity plays in the process of dissociation.

Further Inquiry

Barker, Eric. "Neuroscience Reveals 4 Rituals That Will Make You Happy." *The Week*, 28 Feb. 2016, https://theweek.com/articles/601157/neuroscience-reveals-4-rituals-that-make-happy.

Bergeisen, Michael. "The Neuroscience of Happiness." *Greater Good Magazine*, 22 Sept. 2010, https://greatergood.berkeley.edu/article/item/the_neuroscience_of_happiness.

Bergland, Christopher. "The Neurochemicals of Happiness." *Psychology Today*, 29 Nov. 2012, https://www.psychologytoday.com/us/blog/the-athletes-way/201211/the-neurochemicals-happiness.

Carulli, Daniela. "Perineuronal Nets: A Mechanism to Control Brain Plasticity." *The Scientist*, 1 Apr. 2018, https://www.the-scientist.com/cover-story/perineuronal-nets-a-mechanism-to-control-brain-plasticity-29877.

Cherry, Kendra. "How Experience Changes Brain Plasticity." *Very Well Mind*, 26 Sept. 2019, https://www.verywell-mind.com/what-is-brain-plasticity-2794886.

Corcoran, Kevin. "Happiness on the Brain: The Neuroscience of Happiness, Part 1." Biola University Center for Christian Thought, 21 Oct. 2015, https://cct.biola.edu/happiness-on-the-brain-neuroscience-happiness-part-1/.

Davis, Shirley. "Trauma-Informed Care, Neuroplasticity and Mindfulness." *CPTSDFoundation.org*, 27 Jan. 2019, https://cptsdfoundation.org/2019/01/27/trauma-informed-care-neuroplasticity-and-mindfulness/.

Department of Neurology and Neurosurgery, Montreal Neurological Institute, McGill University. "Dynamic Brains and the Changing Rules of Neuroplasticity: Implications for Learning and Recovery," 4 Oct. 2017, https://www.ncbi.nlm.nih.gov/pmc/articles/PMC5649212/.

Di Pino, Giovanni, et al. "Review Article: Augmentation-Related Brain Plasticity." *Frontiers in Systems Neuroscience*, 11 June 2014, https://doi.org/10.3389/fnsys.2014.00109.

Hampton, Debbie. "How to Heal the Brain with Neuroplasticity After Injury," 13 Jan. 2019, https://thebestbrain-possible.com/healing-brain-neuroplasticity-trauma-injury/.

—. "Neuroplasticity: The 10 Fundamentals Of Rewiring Your Brain," Oct. 2015, https://reset.me/story/neuroplasticity-the-10-fundamentals-of-rewiring-your-brain/.

Hoiland, Erin and Eric H. Chudler "Brain Plasticity: What Is It?" https://faculty.washington.edu/chudler/plast.html.

Medeiros, João. "How to 'Game Your Brain': The Benefits of Neuroplasticity." *Wired*, May 2014, updated 10 Apr. 2017, https://www.wired.co.uk/article/game-your-brain.

Merzenich, Michael. *Soft-Wired: How the New Science of Brain Plasticity Can Change Your Life*. Parnassus Publishing, 2013.

Michelon, Pascale. "Brain Plasticity: How Learning Changes Your Brain," 26 Feb. 2008, https://sharpbrains.com/blog/2008/02/26/brain-plasticity-how-learning-changes-your-brain/.

"Neuroplasticity: How the Brain Can Heal Itself." *Bodywise Physical Therapy*, 14 Oct. 2017. https://www.become-bodywise.net/neuroplasticity-brain-can-heal/.

Newhouse, Eric. "When Plasticity Poses a Problem." *Psychology Today*, 22 Mar. 2012, https://www.psychologyto-day.com/us/blog/invisible-wounds/201203/when-plasticity-poses-problem.

Park, Soyoung Q. et al. "A Neural Link Between Generosity and Happiness." *Nature*, 11 July2017, https://www.nature.com/articles/ncomms15964.

Rosenthal, Michele. "Neuroplasticity: What You Need to Know in PTSD Recovery," 20 Mar.2013, https://www.healthyplace.com/blogs/traumaptsdblog/2013/03/neuroplasticity-what-you-need-to-know-in-ptsd-recovery.

Sapolsky, Robert. "To Understand Facebook, Study Capgras Syndrome: This Mental Disorder Gives Us a Unique Insight into the Digital Age." *Nautilus*, 16 Nov. 2016, http://nautil.us/issue/42/fakes/to-understand-facebook-study-capgras-syndrome.

Shaffer, Joyce. "Neuroplasticity and Clinical Practice: Building Brain Power for Health," *U.S. National Library of Medicine*, 26 July 2016, https://www.ncbi.nlm.nih.gov/pmc/articles/PMC4960264/.

Sharot, Tali. "The Optimism Bias." TED Talk, Feb. 2012. *YouTube.com,* https://www.ted.com/talks/tali_sharot_the_optimism_bias?language=en.

Stout, Martha. *The Myth of Sanity: Divided Consciousness and the Promise of Awareness.* Viking, 2001.

Su, YouRong Sophie, Anand Veeravagu and Gerald Grant. "Neuroplasticity after Traumatic Brain Injury." *Translational Research in Traumatic Brain Injury,* 2016, https://www.ncbi.nlm.nih.gov/books/NBK326735/.

Suzuki, Wendy. "The Brain-Changing Benefits of Exercise." TED Talk, TEDWomen, Nov. 2017, https://www.ted.com/talks/wendy_suzuki_the_brain_changing_benefits_of_exercise.

Wolkin, Jennifer. "The Science of Trauma, Mindfulness, and PTSD." *Mindful.org,* 15 June 2016, https://www.mindful.org/the-science-of-trauma-mindfulness-ptsd/.

UNIT FOUR

Romance in the Twenty-First Century

The meaning of the word "love" in the English language is famously inexact. What kind of love do we mean? The bond between two friends, the love of a parent for a child, and the dizzy ecstasy of two lovers in a new relationship all call forth radically different emotions, yet they are covered under the umbrella of the single noun "love." Naturally, we have other nouns to supplement our meaning—friendship, adoration, romance—but the word we value most remains *love*.

In her book, *Why We Love: The Nature and Chemistry of Romantic Love* (2004), anthropologist Helen Fisher documents poems, songs, and stories from cultures across the globe celebrating and lamenting romantic love. "Romantic love," she concludes, "is a universal human experience." Fisher shares the results of a questionnaire that she and colleagues distributed at two universities, one in America and one in Japan. The results, she writes, remained constant across age, gender, sexual orientation, religious affiliation, and ethnicity. "None of these human variables made much difference in the responses," she reports.

Love, especially the form of ecstatic romantic love Fisher has studied, is equally powerful in emotional, poetic, and transcultural terms.

Arguably, we are raised in American culture to conceive of love as the end goal of existence. Rarely, though, do we pause to consider, "What is love?" Is it an object of desire? Is it a state of being? Is it a feeling that lasts a month, a decade, a lifetime?

© AwayIGI and NASA/Shutterstock.com

If we have not yet experienced it, we yearn to experience it; yet we don't know how to get it. Are we waiting for metaphorical lightning to strike? Are we supposed to download an app? Do we join online dating sites where every profile proclaims the fundamental importance of the search for love?

The fleeting and illusive quality of love may seem apparent in the twenty-first century as online dating sites and mobile dating apps become the norm. In the late twentieth century, work was the most common place to find a partner. Nowadays, online sites have supplanted more traditional avenues for dating.

Nothing sways us from love's allure. Heartbreak represents a profound form of grief, yet not even heartbreak prevents us humans from seeking out love again and again.

More than 60 percent of the "in love" respondents to Fisher's survey agreed with the statement, "I love everything about _____." I haven't studied the matter scientifically, but I would wager that not many spouses in successful marriages would agree, *I love* everything *about my spouse*. Psychologists attest to the distinctions between new love and enduring love. There are, in fact, actual biological differences as well as experiential differences in these forms of love. The sources referenced in this unit provide you an opportunity to discover a great deal about the biology, and maybe even the actual experience, of love.

No is saying that new love cannot transform into enduring love. Clearly, though, on an emotional and a biological level, we can identify differences in these distinct forms of love. Fresh romance burns hot and volatile compared to the love of old friendship. That much is obvious. What is not so obvious is that there are distinct biological mechanisms that determine our love experiences.

Love is more than longing. According to psychologist Barbara Fredrickson, love is "the essential nutrient that your cells crave." In her book, *Love 2.0: How Our Supreme Emotion Affects Everything We Feel, Think, Do, and Become* (2013), Fredrickson urges us to step away from the Romeo and Juliet paradigm. As spiritualists and theologians have done in completely different contexts, Fredrickson urges us to consider "love" as a verb rather than a noun. In other words, she claims that love is a matter of *doing* and *behaving*. It is not simply an object that can be plucked from the sky.

Intriguing possibilities arise when we meditate on the biology of love.

- To what extent does love control us, our thoughts, and our behavior?
- What if you had some level of control over love?
- To what extent can we control love by way of our thoughts and behavior?

Many of us, I would guess, are culturally conditioned to believe in the supreme ecstasy of *love-at-first-sight*, the sort of love experienced by the "star-crossed" teenaged lovers Romeo and Juliet. Theirs is the sort of wild ecstasy that everyone, it seems, wants for him- or herself. It's worth asking ourselves, "How did that love work out for Romeo and Juliet?" It's funny—and (spoiler alert) a bit disturbing—that even though these teens end up dead, we typically envy them the mad love affair they experienced. *I wish something like that would happen to me.*

It's crazy, right?

- What are the biological mechanisms of this kind of "crazy love"?
- What are the biological mechanisms of Fredrickson's so-called "Love 2.0"?
- As always, check out Finding Connections for further insights and inspirations.

Questions to Consider

Answer these questions as you read and annotate the text:

- What are the three main players in love's biological system?
- What is the definition of "positivity resonance"? What are mirror neurons?
- What are the distinctions between what Fredrickson terms a "bond" and what we refer to as "love" or "love connection"?
- What is the significance of the "trust game" study?
- What is the *calm-and-connect* response?
- What is the *vagal tone*? What are the advantages of having a higher vagal tone?
- What are Fredrickson's claims in regard to brain plasticity? How does she extend the concept of plasticity to the body?

THE SOUL MUST ALWAYS STAND AJAR, READY TO WELCOME
THE ECSTATIC EXPERIENCE.

—Emily Dickinson

It's all too tempting, especially in Western culture, to take your body to be a noun, a thing. Sure, it's a living thing, but still, like other concrete things that you can see and touch, you typically describe your body with reference to its stable physical properties, like your height, your weight, your skin tone, your apparent age, and the like. A photo works well to convey these attributes. You recognize, of course, that five years from now, today's photo will seem a bit outdated. By then, your body's physical properties might shift a bit—you might, for instance, become a little shorter, a little heavier, a little paler, or look a little older. Still, you're comfortable with the idea that your body remains pretty much the same from day to day. It has constancy.

Yet constancy, ancient Eastern philosophies warn, is an illusion, a trick of the mind. Impermanence is the rule—constant change, the only constancy. True for all things, this is especially true for living things, which, by definition, change or adapt as needed in response to changes in context. Just as plants turn toward the sun and track its arc from dawn to dusk, your own heart alters its activity with each postural shift, each new emotion, even each breath you take. Seen in this light, your body is more verb than noun: It shifts, cascades, and pulsates; it connects and builds; it erodes and flushes. Mere photographs fail to capture these nonstop and mostly unseen churning dynamics. Instead, you need movies. Increasingly, scientists work to capture these and other dynamic changes as they unfurl within living, breathing, and interacting bodies. True, scientists need to understand form as well as function, anatomy as well as physiology, nouns as well as verbs. Yet when it comes to love, verbs rule. Positivity resonance lies in the action, the doing, the connecting. It wells up, like a wave forming in the ocean, and then dissipates, like that same wave, after its crash. To fully appreciate love's biology, you'll need to train your eye to see this evershifting ebb and flow.

Taking cues from what leading neuroscientist Stephen Porges calls the *social engagement system*, I describe love's biology as a system, a whole comprised of several interacting parts. You can think of love, or positivity resonance, as one of the more complex and recurrent *scenes* nested within the *act* of your day, which is in turn nested within the *play* of your life. As with any scene in a play, the drama of love has its own cast of characters. Here I turn the spotlight on three main biological characters: your brain; one particular hormone, oxytocin, which circulates throughout your brain and body; and your vagus nerve, the tenth cranial nerve that runs from deep within your brain stem down to your heart, lungs, and other internal organs. Other characters step onto the biological stage to deliver their own lines, to be sure, but these three are primary players in love's biology.

Although always on stage, these main characters deliver their lines quietly, most often fully outside of your conscious awareness. As you move through your day, these biological characters—your brain, your oxytocin, and your vagus nerve—are ever responsive to set changes. As you interact with one person after another, they gently nudge you to attend to these others more closely and forge connections when possible. They shape your motives and behaviors in subtle ways, yet ultimately, their actions serve to strengthen your relationships and knit you in closer to the social fabric of life. In the sections that follow, I'll shine the spotlight on each of these three main characters in turn, to help you see how each forges and supports those life-giving moments of positivity resonance for which your body thirsts.

Love on the Brain

When you and another truly connect, love reverberates between you. In the very moment that you experience positivity resonance, your brain syncs up with the other person's brain. Within each moment of love, you and the other are on the same wavelength. As your respective brain waves mirror one another, each of you—moment by moment—changes the other's mind.

> What does Fredrickson mean that "your body is more verb than noun"?

At least this is what I've been telling you. How do you know it really happens? You can't see this brain synchrony surface in real time after all. What you'd need is some way to peer inside two people's heads while they chatted so that you could tell whether their respective brain activity really does march along in time together. This would tell you whether they really "click." Only with this sort of X-ray vision could you decide whether love is better described as a solo act—an emotion contained within the boundaries of the person feeling it—or a duet or ensemble, performed by a duo or group. That sort of X-ray vision sounds like science fiction.

Yet turning science fiction into science fact is what scientists and engineers love most. Breakthrough work by neuroscientist Uri Hasson, of Princeton University, has done just that. He and his team have found ways to measure multiple brains connecting through conversation. The obstacles they faced to do this were large. First, brain scanners are loud machines—no place to carry on actual conversations. Second, they're also extraordinarily expensive, both to buy and to use. Almost all brain imaging studies thus scan just one person's brain at a time. Yet with clever engineering and clever experimental logistics, Hasson's team cleared both obstacles. They created a custom optic microphone that canceled out the noise of the scanner without distorting the delicate brain signals his team sought to capture. The logistics feat was to mimic a natural conversation by pulling it apart in time.

Suppose, for a moment, you were stranded at the airport last week. Your plane to Miami was delayed for hours. Bored with your reading and webbrowsing, you got to talking to another stranded passenger, a lively young college student on her way home for break. You'd been chatting back and forth for a while, every so often, meeting eyes and sharing smiles. The conversation was very natural, like you were friends already. Somehow or another, she got to telling you about her crazy high school prom experience. In great detail, she launched into how she happened to have two dates to the same prom; how she ended up having only five minutes to get dressed and ready for the prom after a full day of scuba diving; how, on her way to after-prom festivities, she crashed her boyfriend's car in the wee hours of the morning; and then how she completely lucked out of getting ticketed (or arrested!) by the officer who witnessed her accident. She's a good storyteller: You hung on her every word. Fifteen minutes melted away as she shared all the twists and turns of her hapless prom night. It's clear, too, that you both enjoyed the chance to connect, rather than read, while you waited for your plane together.

Okay, now it's time for a set change: Instead of in an airport terminal, this conversation actually unfolded in a brain imaging lab at Princeton University. And instead of you sitting side by side with your impromptu friend, Hasson's team actually invited her to visit the lab weeks ago, and they audio-recorded her entire prom story while scanning her brain's activity with functional magnetic resonance imaging (fMRI). You're here lying in the scanner today, listening to her story over fancy headphones, while Hasson's team records your own brain activity. After you get out of the scanner, they ask you to report on what you heard in as much detail as possible. This takes a while; hers was a long, circuitous story after all.

Hasson's team later looked at the extent to which your brain activity mirrored hers. They painstakingly matched up each specific brain area across the two of you, time-locked your respective scans, and looked for "coupling," or the degree to which your brains lit up in synchrony with each other, matched in both space and time.

It turns out that the brain coupling evident between you two is surprisingly widespread. In other words, speaking with and listening to the human voice appear to activate much of the exact same brain activity at pretty much the same time. Keep in mind that—despite your new friend's gift for storytelling—this was still a pretty artificial conversation. Isolated inside the brain scanner across different days, you never actually got to see each other's gestures, meet each other's eyes, or even take turns speaking. You only listened to her voice over headphones. The brain coupling that would emerge in real time with the full and animated dialogue that could well spring up between the two of you if you were in fact seated side by side in the airplane terminal is likely to be far more extensive. Yet hearing someone's voice offers an important channel of sensory and temporal connection, because voice can convey so much emotion. By contrast, consider how little brain coupling would emerge if the connection between the two of you were to be further reduced, for instance, if you only read her story, at your own pacing and presumed intonations, or only heard about her story, as in my thumbnail depiction of it a few paragraphs back.

Forget the idea of a few isolated mirror neurons. So-called mirror neurons refer to a microscopic brain area that Italian neurophysiologists found to "light up" both when a monkey reaches for a banana and when that same monkey sees a person reach for a banana. The discovery of mirror neurons was a huge breakthrough because it told us that taking some action and seeing someone else take that same action are far more alike than previously thought. This means that when you know something—like why that person who just walked into your office is smiling—you know it because your brain and body simulate being in that person's shoes, in their skin. Your knowing is not just abstract and conceptual; it's embodied and physical. Yet it seems now that the concept of isolated mirror neurons was just the tip of the unseen and enormous iceberg. What Hasson and his team uncovered was far more extensive neuronal coupling than previously imagined. Far from being isolated to one or two brain areas, really "clicking" with someone else appears to be a whole brain dance in a fully mirrored room. The reflections between the two of you are that penetrating and widespread.

It turns out that you weren't the only one listening to your new friend's prom story. Hasson's team invited ten other people to have their brains scanned while listening to the very same audio-recording of her story that you heard. Whereas you listened attentively to everything she said, others didn't so much. Those differences showed up clearly when you were each asked to recount her story afterward. By tallying up the matches between her original, impromptu prom story and each listener's retelling of it, Hasson's team rank-ordered the whole set of listeners by how well they understood the story. Those differences in comprehension reflect the success or failure of communication—how thoroughly information from her brain was transferred to your brain, and to the brains of the other listeners. Strikingly, Hasson's team discovered that the degree of success in communication predicted the degree of brain coupling between speaker and listener, and did so in surprising ways.

Most of the time, across most brain areas, listeners' brains mirrored the speaker's brain after a short time lag, around one to three seconds later. It only makes sense, after all, that the speaker leads this dance, since the story is hers and she chooses her words before you and the others hear them. In other cases, though, this neural pas de deux between speaker and listener showed hardly any lag at all—the respective changes in brain activity were virtually synchronized. Your particular case was different, however. Recall that you were the one who grasped your new friend's story better than anybody. You hung on every word and picked up every detail of it, even the seemingly inconsequential ones. Your more complete grasp of her story went hand in hand with something truly remarkable: Your brain activity actually *anticipated* her brain activity by a few seconds in several cortical areas. Excellent communication, it thus seems, doesn't simply involve following along very closely. It also involves forecasting. Once you were in sync and on the same page with your new friend, enjoying her and her story, you could even anticipate what she'd say next, or how she'd say it. Your brain could anticipate her brain's next move.

Brain coupling, Hasson argues, is the means by which we understand each other. He goes even further to claim that communication—a true meeting of the minds—is a single act, performed by two brains. Considering the positivity resonance of love, what I find most fascinating about these findings is that a key brain area that showed coupling in Hasson's speaker-listener study was the insula, an area linked with conscious feeling states. Evidence for synchrony in two people's insulae suggests that in good communication, two individuals come to feel a single, shared emotion as well, one that is distributed across their two brains. Indeed, in other work, Hasson and colleagues have shown that people's brains come particularly into sync during emotional moments. Neural coupling, then—really understanding someone else—becomes all the more likely when you share the same emotion. Even more so than ordinary communication, a micro-moment of love is a single act, performed by two brains. Shared emotions, brain synchrony, and mutual understanding emerge together. And mutual understanding is just steps away from mutual care. Once two people understand each other—really "get" each other in any given moment—the benevolent concerns and actions of mutual care can flow forth unimpeded.

As you move through your day, quite naturally you move in and out of different scenes. Each scene, of course, has its own script. For perhaps most of your day, you're pretty much caught up in your own thoughts and plans, oblivious to the presence or feelings of anyone nearby. Your brain, in such moments, is doing its own thing. But in those rarer moments when you truly connect with someone else over positivity—by sharing a smile, a laugh, a common passion, or an engaging story—you become attuned, with genuine care and concern for the other. You empathize with what they're going through, as your two brains sync up and act as one, as a unified team.

Neural coupling like this is a biological manifestation of oneness. Laboratory studies have already shown that when positive emotions course through you, your awareness expands from your habitual focus on "me" to a more generous focus on "we." When you're feeling bad—afraid, anxious, or angry—even your best friend can seem pretty remote or separate from you. The same goes for when you're feeling nothing in particular. Not so, when you're feeling good. Under the influence of positive emotions, your sense of self actually expands to include others to greater degrees. Your best friend, in these lighthearted moments, simply seems like a bigger part of you.

Hasson's work suggests that when you share your positive emotions with others, when you experience positivity resonance together with this sense of expansion, it's also deeply physical, evident in your brain. The emotional understanding of true empathy recruits coinciding brain activity in both you and the person of your focus. Another telling brain imaging study, this one conducted by scientists in Taipei, Taiwan, illustrates self-other overlap at the neuronal level. Imagine for a moment being a participant in this study. While you are in the fMRI brain scanner, the researchers show you a number of short, animated scenes and ask you to picture yourself in these scenes. Some of these scenes depict painful events, like dropping something heavy on your toe or getting your fingers pinched in a closing door. What the brain images show is that, compared to imagining neutral, nonpainful situations, imagining yourself in these painful situations lights up the well-known network of brain areas associated with pain processing, including the insula, that area linked with conscious feeling states. When you are later asked to imagine these same painful events happening to a loved one—your spouse, your best friend, or your child, for instance—these same brain areas light up. By and large, then, your loved one's pain is your pain. By contrast, when you imagine these painful events happening to complete strangers, a different pattern of activation emerges altogether, one that shows little activation in the insula and more activation in areas linked with distinguishing and distancing yourself from others, and actively inhibiting or regulating emotions, as if to prevent their pain from becoming your pain. At the level of brain activity during imagined pain, you and your beloved are virtually indistinguishable.

Whereas the Taipei research team defined love to be a lasting loving relationship (what, for clarity's sake, I call a bond), the work from Hasson's team at Princeton tells me that neural synchrony and overlap can also unfold between you and a complete stranger—if you let it. Positivity resonance between brains, as it turns out, requires only connection, not the intimacy or shared history that comes with a special bond. Even so, the distinctions revealed in the Taipei study, between imagining your loved one's pain and imagining a stranger's pain, underscore that stifled emotions and guarded personal boundaries, while at times necessary and fully appropriate, can also function as obstacles to positivity resonance. As we'll see in the next section, your attunement to various opportunities for positive connection with others is supported not just by neural synchrony, but by the hormone oxytocin as well.

Biochemistries in Love

Oxytocin, which is nicknamed by some the "cuddle hormone" or the "love hormone," is actually more properly identified as a neuropeptide because it acts not just within your body but also within your brain. Oxytocin has long been known to play a key role in social bonding and attachment. Clear evidence of this first emerged from experiments with a monogamous breed of prairie voles: Oxytocin, when dripped into one animal's brain in the presence of the opposite sex, creates in that animal a long-lasting preference to remain together with the other, cuddled up side by side, behavior taken as evidence that oxytocin sparked the formation of a powerful social bond between them. In humans, oxytocin surges during sexual intercourse for both men and women, and, for women, during childbirth and lactation, pivotal interpersonal moments that stand to forge new social bonds or cement existing ones. The natural blasts of oxytocin during such moments are so large and powerful that for many years they all but blinded scientists to the more subtle ebb and flow of oxytocin during more typical dayto- day activities, like playing with your kids, getting to know your new neighbor, or striking a deal with a new business partner. Technical obstacles also needed to be cleared. Decades after oxytocin's role in monogamous prairie voles had been amply charted, scientists studying human biochemistry still struggled to find ways to reliably and noninvasively measure and manipulate oxytocin during natural behavior. Scientific understanding of oxytocin's role in your everyday social life could not advance without more practical research tools at hand.

Dramatic new evidence of oxytocin's power to shape your social life first surfaced in Europe, where laws permitted the use of a synthetic form of oxytocin, available as a nasal spray, for investigational purposes. Among the first of these studies was one in which 128 men from Zurich played the so-called trust game with real monetary outcomes on the line. At random, these men were assigned to either the role of "investor" or the role of "trustee," and each was given an equivalent pot of starting funds. Investors made the first move in the game. They could give some, all, or none of their allocated funds to the trustee. During the transfer of funds, the experimenter tripled their investment while letting the trustee know how much the investors had originally transferred. Trustees made the next move. They could give some, all, or none of their new allotment of funds (the investors' tripled investment plus their own original allocation) back to investors. The structure of the game puts investors, but not trustees, at risk. If an investor chose to entrust the other guy with his investment, he risked receiving nothing in return if the trustee chose to selfishly keep the entire monetary gain for himself. But if the trustee was fair, they could each double their money.

Prior to playing this trust game, using a double-blind research design, participants received either oxytocin or an inert placebo by nasal spray. The effect of this single intranasal blast of oxytocin on the outcome of the trust game was dramatic: The number of investors who trusted their entire allotment to their trustee more than doubled. Interestingly, related research using this same trust game showed that the mere act of being entrusted with another person's money raises the trustee's naturally occurring levels of oxytocin, and that the greater the trustee's oxytocin rise, the more of his recent windfall he sacrificed back to the investor. The neuropeptide oxytocin, then, steers the actions of both the investor and the trustee, shaping both trust and reciprocity. These findings suggest that through synchronous oxytocin surges, trust and cooperation can quickly become mutual.

> What is brain coupling?

Since the original study on oxytocin and the trust game was published in *Nature* in 2005, variations on it have abounded. We now know, for instance, that oxytocin doesn't simply make people more trusting with money, it also makes them far more trusting—a whopping 44 percent more trusting—with confidential information about themselves. Interestingly, the simple act of sharing an important secret from your life with someone you just met increases your naturally circulating levels of oxytocin, which in turn raises your confidence that you can trust that person to guard your privacy. Thankfully, we also know that oxytocin does not induce trust indiscriminately, making people gullible and therefore open to exploitation. The effects of oxytocin on trust turn out to be quite sensitive to interpersonal cues, like those subtle signs that tip you off that another may be the gambling type or irresponsible in other ways. Rest assured, then, if oxytocin spray were to be aerated through your workplace ventilation system, you'd still maintain your shrewd attunement to subtle signs that suggest whether someone is worthy of your trust or not.

Researchers have since moved on to examine the effects of oxytocin on people's sensitivities to the subtle social cues that signal whether or not trust is warranted. From this work, I can tell you that, under the influence of oxytocin, you attend more to people's eyes and become specifically more attuned to their smiles, especially subtle ones. Perhaps because of the closer attention you pay to peoples' smiles and eyes, you become a better judge of their feelings and view people on the whole as more attractive and trustworthy. You also become particularly sensitized to environmental cues linked to positive social connections—for instance, to words like *love* and *kissing*. Researchers who have combined the use of oxytocin nasal spray (versus placebo) with brain imaging have also learned that oxytocin modulates the activity of your amygdala, the subcortical structure deep within your brain linked to emotional processing. Specifically, under the influence of a single blast of oxytocin nasal spray, the parts of your amygdala that tune in to threats are muted, whereas the parts that tune in to positive social opportunities are amplified. Reflecting these negativitydampening effects, a single shot of oxytocin can also help you glide through stressful social situations, like giving an impromptu speech or discussing a conflict-ridden topic with your spouse. If you were to face these difficulties under the influence of oxytocin, studies suggest, you'd have less cortisol, the socalled stress hormone, coursing through you, and you'd behave more positively, both verbally, by disclosing your feelings, and nonverbally, by making more eye contact and friendly gestures. Related research shows that behaving kindly in these ways also raises your naturally occurring levels of oxytocin, which in turn curbs stress-induced rises in heart rate and blood pressure, reduces feelings of depression, and increases your pain thresholds.

More generally, oxytocin has been cast as a lead character in the mammalian *calm-and-connect* response, a distinct cascade of brain and body responses best contrasted to the far more familiar *fight-or-flight* response. Let's face it, meeting new people can be a little scary at times. Think back to what it was like for you on your first day at a new school or in a new job. You're suddenly thrown in with people you'd never heard of before. Even if a new person seems friendly, it's hard to know his true motives. Will he help you? Or will he instead take advantage of you in one way or another? Human greed, after all, runs rampant and can yield all manner of exploitation. Oxytocin appears both to *calm* fears that might steer you away from interacting with strangers and also to sharpen your skills for *connection*. As I've mentioned, though, oxytocin is far from blind. It indeed heightens your attunement to cues that signal whether others are sincere or not. Through eye contact and close attention to all manner of smiles—and the embodied simulations such visual intake triggers—your gut instincts about whom to trust and whom not to trust become more reliable. Rather than avoid all new people out of fear and suspicion, oxytocin helps you pick up on cues that signal another person's goodwill and guides you to approach them with your own. Because all people need social connections, not just to reproduce, but to survive and thrive in this world, oxytocin has been dubbed "the great facilitator of life."

It, too, can jump the gap between people such that someone else's oxytocin flow can trigger your own. A biochemical synchrony can then emerge that supports mutual engagement, care, and responsiveness.

The clearest evidence that oxytocin rises and falls in synchrony between people comes from studies of infants and their parents. When an infant and a parent—either mom or dad—interact, sometimes they are truly captivated by each other, and other times not. When an infant and parent do click, their coordinated motions and emotions show lots of mutual positive engagement. Picture moms or dads showering their baby with kisses, tickling their baby's tiny fingers and toes, smiling at their baby, and speaking to him or her in that highpitched, singsong tone that scientists call *motherese*. These parents are superattentive. As they tickle and coo they're also closely tracking their baby's face for signs that their delight is mutual. In step with their parent's affectionate antics, these attentive babies babble, coo, smile, and giggle. Positivity resonates back and forth between them. Micro-moments of love blossom.

Of course, not every infant-parent interaction is so rosy. Some pairs show little mutual engagement. Some moms and dads rarely make eye contact with their infants and emit precious little positivity, either verbally or nonverbally. These pairs are simply less attuned to each other, less connected. And in those rare moments when they are engaged, the vibe that joins them is distinctly more negative. They connect over mutual distress or indifference, rather than over mutual affection.

It turns out that positive behavioral synchrony—the degree to which an infant and a parent (through eye contact and affectionate touch) laugh, smile, and coo together—goes hand in hand with oxytocin synchrony. Researchers have measured oxytocin levels in the saliva of dads, moms, and infants both before and after a videotaped, face-to-face parent-infant interaction. For infant-parent pairs who show mutual positive engagement, oxytocin levels also come into sync. Without such engagement, however, no oxytocin synchrony emerges.

Positivity resonance, then, can be viewed as the doorway through which the exquisitely attuned biochemical tendencies of one generation influence those of the next generation to form lasting, often lifelong bonds. Knowing, too, that oxytocin can ebb and flow in unison among non-kin—even among brand-new acquaintances just learning to trust each other—micro-moments of love, of positivity resonance, can also be viewed as the doorways through which caring and compassionate communities are forged. Love, we know, builds lasting resources. Oxytocin, studies show, swings the hammer.

This core tenet of my broaden-and-build theory—that love builds lasting resources—finds support in a fascinating program of research on . . . rodents. It turns out that rat moms and their newborn pups show a form of positive engagement and synchrony analogous to that of human parents with their infants. Sensitive parenting in a rat mom, however, is conveyed by her attentively licking and grooming her newborn pups. When a rat mom licks and grooms her pup, it increases the pup's sensitivity to oxytocin, as indicated, for instance, by the number of oxytocin receptors deep within the pup's amygdala, as well as within other subcortical brain regions. Sure enough, these wellgroomed— or I dare say well-*loved*— rat pups grow up to have calmer demeanors; they're less skittish, more curious. The researchers can be certain that it's the experiences of loving connection that determine the brain and behavioral profiles of the next generation (that is, their oxytocin receptors and calm demeanors)—and not simply shared genes—because cross-fostering studies show the same patterns of results. That is, even when a rat mom raises a newborn pup that is not her own, her maternal attention still forecasts that pup's brain sensitivity to oxytocin and whether it grows up to be anxious or calm.

Touring Vagus

Who you are today is also shaped by the third biological character that I want you to meet: your tenth cranial nerve. This key conduit connects your brain to your body and is also called your vagus nerve (sounds like Vegas, as in Las Vegas). It emerges from your brain stem deep within your skull and, although it makes multiple stops at your various internal organs, perhaps most significantly it connects your brain to your heart. You already know that your heart rate shoots up when you feel insulted or threatened—registering the ancestral fightor- flight response—but you may not know that it's your vagus nerve that eventually soothes your racing heart, by orchestrating (together with oxytocin) the equally ancestral calm-and-connect response.

Keeping in mind that love *is* connection, you should know that your vagus nerve is a biological asset that supports and coordinates your experiences of love. Completely outside of your awareness, your vagus nerve stimulates tiny facial muscles that better enable you to make eye contact and synchronize your facial expressions with another person. It even adjusts the minuscule muscles of your middle ear so you can better track the other person's voice against any background noise. In these exquisitely subtle yet consequential ways, your vagus nerve increases the odds that the two of you will connect, upping your chances for positivity resonance.

Scientists can measure the strength of your vagus nerve—your biological aptitude for love—simply by tracking your heart rate in conjunction with your breathing rate. Specifically, I can look at the degree to which your heart rate, as tracked by sensors placed on your lowest ribs, is patterned by your breathing rate, as revealed by an expandable bellows that encircles your rib cage. This pattern is called *vagal tone*. Like muscle tone, the higher your vagal tone, the better.

In addition to putting the brakes on the big jumps in your heart rate that may be caused by stress, fear, or exertion, your vagus nerve also increases the routine efficiency of your heart, beat by beat, or more precisely, breath by breath. The human heart rate tends to run fairly high, as if we're always on guard for the next danger that might be hidden around the corner. When you're breathing in, a fast heart rate is an efficient heart rate. After all, each successive heartbeat during an in-breath circulates more freshly oxygenated blood throughout your brain and body. Yet when you're breathing out, a fast heart rate is not all that helpful because your supply of freshly oxygenated blood is waning. Here again, your vagus nerve steps in to help out. It can very gently apply the brake on your heart while you exhale, slowing your heart rate down a small degree. In turn your vagus nerve can gently let up on the brake while you inhale, letting your naturally high heart rate resume to grab all the oxygenated blood that it can get. This creates a subtle yet healthy pattern of cardiac arrhythmia: Your heart rate speeds up a bit when you inhale and slows down a bit when you exhale. This is the pattern that reflects your vagal tone, the strength or condition of your vagus nerve. It characterizes the nimbleness with which your primitive, nonconscious brain holds the reins on your galloping heart.

I give you this quick tour of vagus because this conduit within you, between your brain and your heart, has a story to tell about how attuned you are to sources of love in your midst. It even makes a quiet prediction about what illnesses may beset you and how long you're likely to live. Your biological propensities for love and health, as we shall see, are intimately intertwined. Measured at rest, vagal tone also tends to be extraordinarily stable over time. For most people, it remains roughly the same year after year, rhythmically channeling them toward loneliness or social prosperity, sickness or health.

That's because people with higher vagal tone, science has shown, are more flexible across a whole host of domains—physical, mental, and social. They simply adapt better to their ever-shifting circumstances, albeit completely at nonconscious levels. Physically, they regulate their internal bodily processes more efficiently, like their glucose levels and inflammation. Mentally, they're better able to regulate their attention and emotions, even their behavior. Socially, they're especially skillful in navigating interpersonal interactions and in forging positive connections with others. By definition, then, they experience more micro-moments of love. It's as though the agility of the conduit between their brains and hearts—as reflected in their high vagal tone—allows them to be exquisitely agile, attuned, and flexible as they navigate the ups and downs of day-to-day life and social exchanges. High vagal tone, then, can be taken as high loving potential. Indeed, this is what doctoral student Bethany Kok and I have found: Compared to people with lower vagal tone, those with higher vagal tone experience more love in their daily lives, more moments of positivity resonance.

You might now be wondering whether you're one of the lucky ones blessed with high vagal tone. If you are, that's great. Yet even if you're not advantaged with high vagal tone today, the latest science gives plenty of reason for hope. Just as you can build muscle tone through regular physical exercises, you can build vagal tone through regular emotional exercises of the kind I share in part II of this book. The key, once again, is the power of love.

My students and I work together in what I call the PEP Lab, or the Positive Emotions and Psychophysiology Laboratory. Not long ago, we conducted an experiment on the effects of learning the ancient mind-training practice of loving-kindness meditation. Our study participants visited the PEP Lab at the University of North Carolina one by one, and we measured their vagal tone while they sat and relaxed for a few minutes. At the end of this initial laboratory testing session, we instructed participants how to log on to the study website each evening to record their emotions and social connections of the day. A few weeks later, by random assignment, we determined which participants would learn loving-kindness meditation and which would not. All would continue to monitor their day-to-day emotions and social connections using our study website. Months later, weeks after the meditation workshop ended, one by one we invited all participants back to the PEP Lab, where we again measured their vagal tone under the same resting conditions as before.

In May 2010, I had the immense honor of presenting the results of this experiment directly to His Holiness the Fourteenth Dalai Lama. A handful of scientists were invited to a private meeting to brief His Holiness on their latest discoveries about the effects of mind-training. After briefly describing to His Holiness the functions of the vagus nerve and the concept of vagal tone, I shared what my team and I had discovered in this most recent study: that vagal tone— which is commonly taken to be as stable an attribute as your adult height— actually improves significantly with mind-training. Here is your evidence-based reason for hope: No matter what your biological capacity for love is today, you can bolster that capacity by next season.

For it was those study participants who had been assigned at random to learn loving-kindness meditation who changed the most. They devoted scarcely more than an hour of their time each week to the practice. Yet within a matter of months, completely unbeknownst to them, their vagus nerves began to respond more readily to the rhythms of their breathing, emitting more of that healthy arrhythmia that is the fingerprint of high vagal tone. Breath by breath—loving moment by loving moment—their capacity for positivity resonance matured. Moreover, through painstaking statistical analyses, we pinpointed that those who experienced the most frequent positivity resonance in connection with others showed the biggest increases in vagal tone. Love literally made people healthier.

> What are Fredrickson's claims regarding her studies on the effects of mind-training?

Upward Spirals Unleashed

It's time now to step back from isolated scientific findings and take in the big picture. Recall that your body's positivity resonance operates within a much larger system. Along with love and all the other positive emotions, this system also includes your enduring resources—your physical health, your social bonds, your personality traits, and your resilience. Having assets like these certainly makes life easier, and more satisfying. In addition, though, such resources also serve as booster shots that increase the frequency and intensity of your micromoments of positivity resonance. Love built those resources in you, and those resources in turn boost your experiences of love. This is not a simple case of cause and effect. The causal arrow instead runs in both directions at once, creating the dynamic and reciprocal causality that drives self-sustaining trajectories of growth. Through love, you become a better version of yourself. And as your better self, you experience love more readily. It is in this dance between your enduring resources and your micro-moments of love that lifegiving upward spirals are born.

Looking out from this more encompassing vantage point, let's revisit the scientific findings I shared with His Holiness the Dalai Lama. By learning how to self-generate love, you can raise your vagal tone. And with higher vagal tone, your attention and actions become more agile, more attuned to the people in your midst. You become better able to forge the interpersonal connections that give rise to positivity resonance. Through vagal tone, then, love begets love.

Likewise, evidence suggests that positivity resonance raises your oxytocin levels. And under the influence of oxytocin, you grow calmer, more attuned to others, friendlier, and more open. Here, too, your skills for forging connections sharpen, which increases your ability to cultivate positivity resonance. Through oxytocin as well then, love begets love.

Recall, too, that positive connections with others create neural coupling, or synchronous brain activity between people. With repetition, positivity resonance also produces structural changes in the brain, for instance, rendering the threatdetecting amygdala more sensitive to the calming influence of oxytocin. While much of the work on neuroplasticity—the brain's capacity to change with experience—comes from research on nonhuman animals, tantalizing evidence has also recently emerged from studies of humans. Becoming a parent, for instance, not only opens the door for parent-infant positivity resonance but also appears to usher in structural changes in brain regions that facilitate positivity resonance. This research shows how love reroutes the neural wiring of your brain, making it more likely that you'll have healthy habits and healthy social bonds in the future. Through brain plasticity, too, then, love begets love.

Plasticity, or openness to change, characterizes your body's cells as well. New cells are born within you all the time. Even now, as you take time to read this book, new cells are coming online within you, taking their predetermined place within the massive orchestra of communication and mutual influence that you call your body. Yet not everything about the birth of your new cells is scripted in advance by your

DNA. Some aspects are open to contextual influences signaled by the changing biochemicals that course through you. If you feel lonely and disconnected from others, for instance, your circulating levels of the stress hormone cortisol will rise. Your cortisol levels, in turn, signal your immune system to alter the way your genes are expressed in your nextgeneration white blood cells, specifically making them less sensitive to cortisol. When this happens, studies show, your inflammatory response becomes more chronic, less responsive to cues that a crises situation has subsided. This is how, over time, chronic feelings of loneliness can weaken people's immune systems and open the door to inflammation-based chronic illnesses, like cardiovascular disease and arthritis. The data go further to suggest that *feeling* isolated or unconnected to others does more bodily damage than *actual* isolation, suggesting that painful emotions drive the bodily systems that in turn steer you toward dire health outcomes. By tracking how your emotions—and the biochemical changes they trigger—alter gene expression within your immune system, the tools of molecular biology now show how a lack of love compromises your immunity and your health.

Even so, there is ample reason for hope. In countless social exchanges each day, your potential to alleviate loneliness with love is enormous. Your biology, as we have seen in this chapter, enacts your experiences of love. Even so, you have more control over your biology than you realize. Once you grasp the pathways and common obstacles to love, you gain a measure of control over the biochemicals that bathe your cells. To a considerable extent, you orchestrate the messages that your cells hear, the messages that tell your cells whether to grow toward health or toward illness. My collaborators and I are just beginning to chart the ways that oxytocin and other ingredients that make up love's biochemistry trigger healthy changes in gene expression that may foster physical and mental well-being. Also through the plasticity of your cells, we hypothesize, love begets love.

All of love's unseen biological transformations—in your brain rhythms, your blood stream, your vagus nerve, and your cells—in turn ready you to become even more attuned to love, better equipped, biologically, to cultivate moments of positivity resonance with others. This latent biological upward spiral is a powerful force: Love can affect you so deeply that it reshapes you from the inside out and by doing so alters your destiny for further loving moments. With each micro-moment of love, then, as I feature in chapter 4, you climb another rung on the spiraling ladder that lifts you up to your higher ground, to richer and more compassionate social relationships, to greater resilience and wisdom, and to better physical health.

Love 2.0: The View from Here

Put simply, your body was designed for love, and to benefit from loving. Human bodies become healthier when repeatedly nourished by positivity resonance with others, with the result that human communities become more harmonious and loving. This clear win-win arrangement is written into our DNA.

Everyday micro-moments of positivity resonance add up and ultimately transform your life for the better. You become healthier, happier, and more socially integrated. Your wisdom and resilience grow as well. Having more resources like these in turn equips you to experience micro-moments of love more readily and more often, with further broaden-and-build benefits. Your body, as biology has it, energizes and sustains this upward spiral. The unseen and heretofore unsung biology of love affects everything you feel, think, do, and become.

This isn't all about you, though. Love, as we've seen, is not a solo act. The benefits that unfold from love for you, then, also unfold for all those who are party to positivity resonance. Seen from this vantage point, emotional and physical health are contagious. Indeed, studies of actual social networks show that, over time, happiness spreads through whole communities. Your friend's coworker's sister's happiness actually stands to elevate your own happiness.

The new science of love makes it clear that your body acts as a verb. Sure enough, some aspects of your body remain relatively constant day in and day out, like your DNA or your eye color. But your brain continually registers your ever-changing circumstances and in turn orchestrates the flux of biochemicals that reshape your body and brain from the inside out, at the cellular level. Your body takes action. Most notably, it broadcasts everything you feel—your moments of positivity resonance or their lack—to every part of you, readying you for either health or illness and rendering you either more or less equipped for loving connection.

I hope you've found it mind-opening to zoom in on the biology of love in action—the ways positivity resonance can synchronize your brain and oxytocin waves with those of another, and how, over time, it can build the capacity of your vagus nerve, which points you toward physical health, social skill, and overall well-being. Touring love's biology, I've found, can help ground an otherwise nebulous concept, a concept all too often draped in a gauze of rainbows, unicorns, and cupids taking aim at cartoon hearts. Even so, a fully upgraded view of love can't stop with biology. It demands that you zoom out as well, to appreciate the ways that love also infuses all that lies beyond your physical body, its effects on your actions and relationships, your wisdom and your spiritual potential. For it is these more encompassing changes that spring up in love's path that can motivate you to create a better life for yourself. Before moving on to part II, then, in which I offer practical guidance on how to seed love more readily, I want to show you what's new in the bigger picture that is emerging from the science of love—a picture that shows exactly how creating more positivity resonance in your life influences all that you feel, think, do, and become.

Questions for Comprehension

Answer these questions as a comprehension gauge and/or for further clarification on the text:

1. True or False. No matter how well two people communicate, they will never share the same emotion.

2. Oxytocin is nicknamed the _____ hormone. a) cuddle, b) elite, c) worthwhile, or d) angry

3. Explain the role of the synthetic oxytocin nasal spray in the "trust game" study which was published in *Nature* in 2005.

4. As opposed to the stress hormones involved in the *fight-or-flight* response, the hormone oxytocin is involved in the _____ response. a) *run-and-flee,* b) *calm-and-connect,* c) *love-and-linger,* or d) *woo-and-romance*

5. In May 2010, Fredrickson had the honor of presenting her Positive Emotions and Psychophysiology Lab findings to whom?

Finding Connections: Wild Ecstasy and Positivity Resonance

Anthropologist Helen Fisher reflects on the obsessive nature of romantic love. Psychologists describe the phenomenon of "intrusive thinking," one form of which involves an unhealthy fixation on a person's beloved. (Note that turning someone into an "object of desire" dehumanizes the person, making him or her an object rather than a being.) Intrusive thoughts are common to the human experience, yet these involuntary cyclical ideations are often unwelcome. The person experiencing such thoughts has a difficult time controlling them.

Sometimes, in an English department course, we would examine a plethora of literary and cultural references associated with this most precious and coveted human emotion called love. And, in fact, you are welcome to do so. Shakespeare's love sonnets, Walt Whitman's free verse, Emily Dickinson's poetry, Sappho's lyrics, the Chinese *Book of Songs*, and countless other **love poems from around the world** are available in the public domain, easily accessed with a few clicks of the keyboard. When studying poetry, I encourage students to understand the historical and cultural context of the poem in order to gain insights on the meaning of the poem. In fact, **universal human themes** arise as we encounter love poetry throughout the ages from all parts of the globe. An ancient Egyptian love poem written more than thirteen centuries ago reveals a youthful love-obsession still relevant to our twenty-first century experience of love: "I wish I were your mirror so that you looked at me / I wish I were your clothes so that you would wear me / I wish I were the water washing your body." Fisher opens her book *Why We Love* (2004) with a Kwakiutl poem from the Pacific Northwest recorded in 1896 (*Fire runs through my body—the pain of loving you*). She opens her TED Talk "The Brain in Love" with a grand story of love from ancient Mayan culture.

Love is a universal human theme.

In her book, *Love 2.0: How Our Supreme Emotion Affects Everything We Feel, Think, Do, and Become* (2013), psychologist Barbara Fredrickson argues that love is an "essential nutrient" in our lives (4). Far from arguing love's centrality in the way that a therapist or minister might, Fredrickson instead asks us to set aside the cultural concept of love as being "exclusive, lasting, and unconditional" (6). Instead, she views this powerful human emotion as a fleeting micro-moment of warmth between two human beings. Fredrickson focuses on the neurological and biological processes of love. She claims that in a very real and tangible way, "love is connection" (17). The "positivity resonance" of a loving human connection, she informs us, can be scientifically measured.

Experts in general agree on the positive health benefits of love. Humans who live in sustained, loving relationships tend to live longer, for example. And they tend to suffer fewer physical and mental diseases. Love is not a cure-all, obviously. There is even a form of harmful, obsessive "love-hatred" that can develop in scorned lovers (Fisher 155). A growing field of scientific evidence, however, confirms the benefits of positive emotional connections that can be appropriately termed "love."

In *Why We Love*, Fisher explores the neurochemistry involved in romance. She cites one study in which fMRI brain scans show the brains of love-smitten subjects lighting up like fireworks when looking at a photo of their beloved. Meanwhile, no response, positive or negative, comes while looking at a "neutral" photo of an acquaintance. Fisher emphasizes the natural drive behind romance: "*I came to believe that romantic love is a primary motivation system in the brain—in short, a fundamental human mating drive*" (74). Dopamine, she says, plays a key role in this biological imperative. "And like all other drives," Fisher writes, "romantic love is a need, a craving" (75). Fisher invokes Plato's observation from 2,000 years ago that the God of Love lives in a state of need.

© Iryna Kalamurza/Shutterstock.com

The results of Fisher's "Being in Love" survey indicate the obsessive nature of romantic love. As mentioned in the unit introduction, they also appear to indicate that romance is a cross-cultural phenomenon not restricted by age or gender.

Both scientists focus on the **neurochemistry of love**. Fisher, an anthropologist, emphasizes the role of hormones and brain chemistry, while Fredrickson, a psychologist, emphasizes a "positivity resonance" that can be consciously cultivated. Both authors speak of love as an emotional and biological necessity, yet Fisher's "craving" is entirely distinct from Fredrickson's "essential nutrient."

- To what extent is love the result of the wild natural ecstasy of dopamine, the "neurotransmitter of romance" (Fisher 102)?
- To what extent can love be formed through conscious "micro-moments of love" shared with another human being (Fredrickson 18)?
- What role, if any, does the human brain's neuroplasticity play in these sensations and experiences?

The views of these two scientists are not mutually exclusive, of course. No scientist myself, I tend to frame the discourse in philosophical terms. For me, Fisher emphasizes the role of *nature* in the experience of romantic love, while Fredrickson emphasizes the role of *nurture* in the ongoing experience of love.

As you explore love in the twenty-first century, be sure to define your terms. Considering the nebulous meanings of the noun "love," it's important to continually direct your audience toward specific meanings, specific evidence, specific terms, specific claims, and specific definitions.

Finding Connections Works Cited

Fisher, Helen. *Why We Love: The Nature and Chemistry of Romantic Love.* Henry Holt & Co, 2004.

Fredrickson, Barbara. *Love 2.0: How Our Supreme Emotion Affects Everything We Feel, Think, Do, and Become.* Hudson Street Press, 2013.

Resources

MLA or APA? (Or Something Else?): Formatting Your Work

There are many style guides. The Associated Press publishes a guidebook for journalists, for example. If you go to work for the famous magazine *The New Yorker*, you will follow that magazine's own particular formatting guidelines. Popular online websites and journals tend to use style guides that are similar if not exactly the same. Web and print editors of respectable publications favor straightforward prose and clear source attributions. Note, for example, that a newspaper article will mention a source by name and quote the source directly without any in-text citation or bibliography of the sort you would find in an academic paper.

In academia, that is, within colleges and universities:

- Modern Language Association (MLA) style is favored in the liberal arts and humanities.
- American Psychological Association (APA) style is favored in the social and behavioral sciences.
- Each academic discipline or field of study may have its own set of guidelines or preferences.
- Always ask your instructor which style guide to follow.

Style guides exist so that there is consistency nationally and internationally in how scholars present work to peers and to the public. It's also vital that critics and scholars cite their sources of information in a way so that if the reader wants to dig further into the topic or verify an author's claim, he or she can track down the author's source materials. If each person did things his or her own way, it would be difficult to share information and grow our collective knowledge.

Library experts at the Massachusetts Institute of Technology (MIT) offer clear reasons for students to cite research (*https://libguides.mit.edu/c.php?g=176032&p=1159439*):

- To show your reader you've done proper research, listing the sources you used to get your information,
- To be a responsible scholar by giving credit to other researchers and acknowledging their ideas,
- To avoid plagiarism by quoting words and ideas used by other authors, and
- To allow your reader to track down the sources you used by citing them accurately in your paper by way of footnotes, a bibliography, or a reference list.

Demonstrating that you have "done your homework," so to speak, is a fundamental concept underpinning scholarship, journalism, and any sort of quality writing. The implications are clear when it comes to much of what presents itself to us on various Internet platforms: *Where did this information come from? Is this information cited? Has the author of this information been clear and transparent regarding source materials?*

Sentence and paragraph exercises are good opportunities to practice MLA (or APA, or another style as specified by your instructor). Make sure that you are following a specific formatting style whenever you turn in a formal essay assignment. Sample MLA or APA papers can be found online and via the sites listed below.

Online Resources

The Purdue Online Writing Lab (OWL) is an excellent free web resource:
https://owl.purdue.edu/owl/purdue_owl.html
You can study formatting, citation, and other essential composition skills at this site.

This cite features updated links to:

- an "MLA Guide" for Modern Language Association style,
- an "APA Guide" for American Psychological Association style, and
- a "Chicago Guide" for *The Chicago Manual of Style*.

Modern Language Association publishes useful Internet resources:
https://style.mla.org/

Massachusetts Institute of Technology (MIT) Libraries offers a wealth of information:
https://libguides.mit.edu/citing/citestyle

Truckee Meadows Community College Library offers a helpful, user-friendly metapage:
https://libguides.tmcc.edu/researchmethods/style_guides

Writing Assignments

Making Connections Template Exercise

Attempt to connect the concerns of experts from two different unit topics.

_____ are increasingly aware of the connections between positive emotions and health. Therefore, _____ ought to take _____ into account when considering _____.

Essay Prompts

Level I: Analysis-Response

1. Psychologist Barbara Fredrickson describes the mechanisms of synchronous brain activity and what she calls "micromoments of love." Someone might describe such feelings as *romantic love* or *friendship love* or something else. Describe the biological mechanisms as Fredrickson depicts them. Have you experienced any of the described signs or symptoms of the "biology of love" as she depicts them?

2. Anthropologist Helen Fisher describes the cross-cultural, global phenomenon called "love." Review her TED Talk (listed in the Further Inquiry bibliography). She depicts romantic love as having existed in all of recorded human history. What are the main features of this sort of love, according to Fisher? Have you experienced anything along the lines of the ecstasy that she describes?

3. Based on Fredrickson's work, analyze and respond to the concept of *plasticity* in regard to both brain and body. What does she mean that plasticity "characterizes your body's cells as well"?

4. Philosopher John Dewey said, "Mind is primarily a verb." Respond to this concept as you analyze Fredrickson's article.

Level II: Making Connections

1. Psychologist Barbara Fredrickson and anthropologist Helen Fisher both describe the biological mechanisms and the physical effects of "love." To what extent are they depicting the same emotion, experience, or phenomenon? To what extent are they depicting distinct, entirely separate emotions, experiences, or phenomena?

2. Anthropologist Helen Fisher offers a "personality test" that claims to identify the participant within one of four predominant modes associated with hormones (dopamine, serotonin, testosterone, estrogen). Psychologist Barbara Fredrickson emphasizes the role of the "cuddle hormone" oxytocin in the production of what she terms "positivity resonance." Analyze each researcher's description of love and the role of hormones in the biology of love.

3. Fredrickson writes, "No matter what your biological capacity for love is today, you can bolster that capacity by next season." She claims that a person's vagal tone can significantly improve with mind-training. Develop a synthetic connection between the concepts of "brain plasticity" and "the biology of love." How are vagal tone and a capacity for positivity resonance related to neuroplasticity? How does an understanding of neuroplasticity inform your understanding of the biological mechanisms of love operating in the body and brain?

4. Develop connections between Gen Z characteristics and the realities of romance in the twenty-first century. How do generational characteristics play a role in love, dating, and romance? Be sure to develop a connection between generational studies and the work of Fredrickson, Fisher, or another love expert listed in the Further Inquiry bibliography.

5. According to anthropologist Helen Fisher, the experience of romantic love is a global human phenomenon experienced by all peoples in all cultures. Consider the following: In America, where marital partners typically choose their mates, the divorce rate has been 50 percent in recent decades. In India, where marriages are typically arranged, the divorce rate is 1 percent. Clearly, there are profound social and cultural factors involved here; however, for the purposes of this discourse, how does the "biology of love" factor into these marriage practices? Bear in mind that "love" and "marriage" are two completely separate things. (Ideally, they come together at some point.) Biologically speaking, how might "falling in love" differ under a choice marriage or an arranged marriage? This particular

topic is not a sociological discourse on the practices of marriage; instead, how does "falling in love" take place under the choice scenario versus the arranged scenario? To what extent is "falling in love" the same or a different biological and psychological process under each paradigm?

Level III: Research

1. Consider the Level II topic listed above. In addition to considerations of relevant biological and psychological factors, research the social and cultural practices of choice marriage and arranged marriage. Your goal is not to declare one superior to the other. The goal is to discover and analyze the distinctions between them. Your goal must not be to create a "laundry list" of differences. Instead, you want to be able to support a major claim or thesis regarding the sociology, psychology, and/or biology involved in these two distinct marital customs.

2. Research the biological mechanisms involved in what anthropologist Helen Fisher terms "wild ecstasy" or what others have termed "crazy love" or simply "being in love." You might focus on the phenomenon of one person's love obsession or on the early stages of mutual romance. You may want to describe the personal and social aspects of these states of mind; however, your main focus is on the biological mechanisms of these forms of love: what's going on in the mind and the body in biological terms?

3. Americans used to meet their partners or spouses most frequently in the workplace. Sociologists now say that meeting online is the most common method to encounter a future partner or spouse, at least for heterosexual couples. Develop and support a major claim or thesis regarding the connection between online dating in America and the biological mechanisms of love. How, if at all, are the biological processes of falling in love different in the era of online dating? From a sociological and/or psychological stance, how has online dating affected relationships and marriages? Do not focus on anecdotal evidence. Instead, research social trends and discover what experts think.

Further Inquiry

Aron, Arthur et al. "Reward, Motivation, and Emotion Systems Associated With Early-Stage Intense Romantic Love." *Journal of Neurophysiology*, 1 July 2005, https://www.physiology.org/doi/full/10.1152/jn.00838.2004; https://doi.org/10.1152/jn.00838.2004.

Castro, Giovanna. "The Neuroscience of Love." Tufts University, Department of Psychology, 8 Dec. 2014, https://sites.tufts.edu/emotiononthebrain/2014/12/08/the-neuroscience-of-love/.

Clifton, Mark. "Broken Heart, Broken Brain: The Neurology of Breaking up and How to Get Over It." *CBC Radio-Canada*, 6 Apr. 2018, https://www.cbc.ca/life/wellness/broken-heart-broken-brain-the-neurology-of-breaking-up-and-how-to-get-over-it-1.4608785.

DiSalvo, David. "What Neuroscience Tells Us About Being in Love." *Psychology Today*, 12 Feb. 2014, https://www.psychologytoday.com/us/blog/neuronarrative/201402/what-neuroscience-tells-us-about-being-in-love.

Durayappah-Harrison, Adoree. "Brain Study Reveals Secrets of Staying Madly in Love." *Psychology Today*, 3 Feb. 2011, https://www.psychologytoday.com/us/blog/thriving101/201102/brain-study-reveals-secrets-staying-madly-in-love.

Edwards, Scott. "Love and the Brain." Harvard Mahoney Neuroscience Institute, n.d., https://neuro.hms.harvard.edu/harvard-mahoney-neuroscience-institute/brain-newsletter/and-brain-series/love-and-brain.

Fetters, Ashley. "The 5 Years That Changed Dating." *The Atlantic*, 21 Dec. 2018, www.theatlantic.com/family/archive/2018/12/tinder-changed-dating/578698/.

Fisher, Aron A. "Brain Study Reveals Secrets of Staying Madly in Love." *Psychology Today*, 3 Feb. 2011, https://www.psychologytoday.com/us/blog/thriving101/201102/brain-study-reveals-secrets-staying-madly-in-love.

Fisher, Helen. "The Brain in Love." TED Talk, Feb. 2008, https://www.ted.com/talks/helen_fisher_the_brain_in_love.

Fisher, Helen. *Why We Love: The Nature and Chemistry of Romantic Love*. Henry Holt & Co, 2004.

Fisher, Helen et al. "Intense, Passionate, Romantic Love: A Natural Addiction? How the Fields That Investigate Romance and Substance Abuse Can Inform Each Other." *Frontiers in Psychology*, 10 May 2016, https://www.ncbi.nlm.nih.gov/pmc/articles/PMC4861725/.

Fredrickson, Barbara. *Love 2.0: How Our Supreme Emotion Affects Everything We Feel, Think, Do, and Become*. Hudson Street Press, 2013.

Gregoire, Carolyn. "This Is Your Brain On Love." *HuffPost*, 7 Dec. 2017, https://www.huffpost.com/entry/5-things-neuroscience-can_n_4774811.

Harms, William. "Meeting Online Leads to Happier, More Enduring Marriages." *UChicago News*, 3 June 2013, news.uchicago.edu/story/meeting-online-leads-happier-more-enduring-marriages.

"Helen Fisher's Personality Test." *TheAnatomyofLove.com*, 2020, https://theanatomyoflove.com/relationship-quizzes/helen-fishers-personality-test/.

Laino, Debra. "Technology & the Extinction of Romance: Dissecting Love." TEDx Talks, 17 Mar. 2017, https://www.youtube.com/watch?v=k3gkGkQRhT0.

Lenhart, Amanda, et al. "Teens, Technology and Romantic Relationships." Pew Research Center, Internet & Technology, 1 Oct. 2015, www.pewinternet.org/2015/10/01/teens-technology-and-romantic-relationships/.

Mantel, Barbara. "Online Dating." *CQResearcher*, 20 Mar. 2015, http://library.cqpress.com/cqresearcher/cqresrre2015032000.

Marco, Leonti and Laura Casu. "Ethnopharmacology of Love." *Frontiers in Pharmacology*, 3 July 2018, doi: 10.3389/fphar.2018.00567; https://www.ncbi.nlm.nih.gov/pmc/articles/PMC6041438/.

Miller, Jennifer. "Maybe the Best Way to Find Love Is ... Not on an App?" *The New York Times*, 6 Sept. 2019, https://www.nytimes.com/2019/09/06/style/date-my-friend.html?searchResultPosition=5.

Pressman, Peter. "Where Is Love Located in the Brain?" *VeryWellHealth.com*, updated 20 Jan. 2020, https://www.verywellhealth.com/the-brain-in-love-2488713.

"Scientists Uncover Neurobiological Basis For Romantic Love, Trust, And Self." *Science Daily*, 11 Nov. 2003, https://www.sciencedaily.com/releases/2003/11/031111064658.htm.

Sharot, Tali. "The Optimism Bias." TED Talk, Feb. 2012. *YouTube.com,* https://www.ted.com/talks/tali_sharot_the_optimism_bias?language=en.

Song, Hongwen et al. "Improving Relationships by Elevating Positive Illusion and the Underlying Psychological and Neural Mechanisms." *Frontiers in Human Neuroscience,* 11 Jan. 2019, doi: 10.3389/fnhum.2018.00526; https://www.ncbi.nlm.nih.gov/pmc/articles/PMC6336892/.

Song, Sensen et al. "Romantic Love Is Associated with Enhanced Inhibitory Control in an Emotional Stop-Signal Task." *Frontiers in Psychology,* 25 Oct. 2016, doi: 10.3389/fpsyg.2016.01574; https://www.ncbi.nlm.nih.gov/pmc/articles/PMC5078777/.

Stromberg, Joseph. "This is Your Brain on Love." *Vox,* 12 Feb. 2015, https://www.vox.com/2015/2/12/8025525/love-neuroscience.

"World of Weddings: In India, Arranged Marriages are as Strong as Ever." *CBS News,* 2 Dec. 2019, https://www.cbsnews.com/news/world-of-weddings-in-india-arranged-marriages-are-as-strong-as-ever/.

Xu, Xiaomeng and Ariana Tart-Zelvin. "What Goes On in Our Brains When We Are in Love?" *Scientific American,* 19 July 2017, https://www.scientificamerican.com/article/what-goes-on-in-our-brains-when-we-are-in-love/.

Zeki, S. "The Neurobiology of Love." *ScienceDirect, FEBS Letters* 581, 2007, edited by Veli-Pekka Lehto, DOI:10.1016/j.febslet.2007.03.094, https://www.sciencedirect.com/science/article/pii/S0014579307004875.

UNIT FIVE

Appropriation

As a fan of rock music, I recognized issues surrounding appropriation early on. I could listen to a record like Led Zeppelin's "In My Time of Dying" from *Physical Graffiti* (1975) and see that the four British band members were given songwriting credits. What was harder to find out was that the song is essentially an African-American blues song and that many versions of it had been recorded. (*So how could they be credited with writing the song?* I had to wonder.) Blind Willie Johnson recorded "Jesus Make Up My Dying Bed" in 1927 and Josh White recorded a version called "Jesus Gonna Make Up My Dying Bed" in 1933. Bob Dylan included a version called "In My Time of Dyin'" on his 1962 debut album. In one sense, Led Zeppelin was working in a well-established musical tradition, bringing their own noteworthy genius to the task. In another sense, they were ripping off unknown musicians (unknown to me in any case) and making a great deal of money in the process.

The fact that the earlier musicians were Black and that the musicians on the record were white didn't escape me. Was this *appropriation* as a proper part of the creative endeavor, or was it *cultural appropriation* of a less honorable sort?

Such appropriations weren't one-offs for Led Zeppelin. Since the band's 1968 inception, it had done good business appropriating American blues, reprocessing the tunes, and selling the results back to America. Lead Belly's "The Gallows Pole" (1939) seems to reappear, for example, as a lively Led Zeppelin version of "Gallows Pole" (1970). Fans of Led Zeppelin can cite numerous other examples. Rarely were the artists who inspired the rock musicians credited. Songwriter Willy Dixon sued the band in the early 1970s over uncredited appropriation of his lyrics.

---

* In July 2020 (after "copy" for this textbook had been sent to the publisher) the Associated Press (AP) and other news agencies announced a new formatting standard: to capitalize "Black" but not "white." See *Bauder, David. "AP says it will capitalize Black but not white." AP News, July 20, 2020, https://apnews.com/article/7e36c00c5af0436abc09e051261fff1f.* We have attempted to alter the text in accordance with the new standard. Modern Language Association (MLA) and other organizations have not changed "black" and "white" standards. See also *Nguyen, Ann Thuy and Maya Pendleton. "Recognizing Race in Language: Why We Capitalize 'Black' and 'White.'" Center for the Study of Social Policy, Mar. 23, 2020, https://cssp.org/2020/03/recognizing-race-in-language-why-we-capitalize-black-and-white/.*

Led Zeppelin was hardly alone in its mode of operation. On the one hand, these musicians were spreading the gospel of the blues, raising consciousness regarding one of America's most important musical traditions. On the other hand, they were exploiting musicians who worked in a folksong tradition. U.S. copyright law reaches back to the origins of the nation and musical works were explicitly protected in 1831, yet most of American music prior to the early twentieth century exists in the so-called *public domain*.

The entire 1960s musical movement called the British Invasion was strange in the same way. Bands like The Beatles and The Rolling Stones self-consciously imitated American music then sold it back to an appreciative American middle class who seemed largely unaware that these young Brits were imitating Black American music. In the 1950s, according to some accounts, Elvis Presley simply took Black American music mainstream, gaining prestige and wealth through a process that critics now call *cultural appropriation*.

Jonathan Lethem seems to argue, however, that the very process of creation *requires* appropriation.

- *In what ways does Lethem argue in the feature unit article below that borrowing and appropriation are essential to creativity? How does Lethem formulate his argument?*

The Complicated Nature of Appropriation

"Cultural appropriation" means the unacknowledged or inappropriate adoption of the customs and practices of a people, often an ethnic minority. The critique of this form of appropriation involves an ethnic or cultural majority group exploiting the traditions of another group. The history of American music and entertainment is rife with unacknowledged contributions and unapologetic exploitations of African-American performers from the era of slavery onward. Anyone who understands the history of the United States can see why issues of cultural appropriation remain matters of central importance to social commentators in the twenty-first century.

As a kid, listening to unacknowledged lyrical and musical borrowings pervading the recordings of talented musicians whom I admired, the importance of this discourse seemed self-evident. A band of young white musicians, revered as rock gods, became wealthy, while the Black musicians who inspired them played dive bars. I quickly got interested in learning the names and notes of these musicians. It was much easier to find out about The Beatles, The Stones, and The Yardbirds than it was to find out about Blind Willie Johnson, Muddy Waters, and Jimmy Reed.

And then later, as an aspiring artist myself wielding pen and guitar, I had to reprocess the issue of appropriation. My own beloved favorite punk rock group, The Clash, appropriated the sounds of Jamaican reggae. Punk and reggae share a history analogous in many ways to that of rock and blues. Rock musicians searching for authenticity found the blues, and punk musicians seeking authenticity found reggae. I discovered that creativity does not exist in a vacuum. It was pretty hard, for example, to write a short story of my own without starting out by imitating one I liked. How could I write a song devoid of the inspiration I found on records and radio?

The concept of "appropriation" transformed: no longer was it a simple matter of cheating and injustice. Now it seemed like a pretty good idea. My creative efforts had to start somewhere. Obviously, they would start with *stealing*. I stole most directly from Ernest Hemingway and The Clash. The creative process wasn't what I thought. I could wait for *genius* to appear at my back door. A person could wait cradle to grave for that kind of inspiration. Or I could get going: *mimic, develop, reprocess.*

Appropriation isn't a simple matter.

Take "Gallows Pole," for instance. The song is based on a centuries-old folk ballad called "The Maid Freed from the Gallows." Francis James Child marked down the lyric as "Child Ballad number 95" in the late nineteenth century. The ballad may have originated on continental Europe and certainly traveled with immigrants across the Atlantic. Variants of the song migrated with the people who sang it. Famous African-American folk singer Huddy Ledbetter, called Lead Belly, popularized the song with a 1939 recording. Fred Gerlach, a white musician and luthier, also recorded the song on the famous Folkways label; it was this version that Jimmy Page of Led Zeppelin heard. Page put his own imprint on the song with his instrumentation and arrangement. Creativity—*genius*, if you will—is not born, it is nurtured. Production and creativity stem from inspiration; this inspiration inevitably arises from a foundation of what has come before.

Rapper's Delight

The issue of appropriation arose to the forefront of American popular culture as the genres of rap and hip-hop came into prominence from the late 1970s to the 1990s. Rap and hip-hop use "sampling," that is, musical clips (or samples) of prior recordings. Hip-hop producers reprocess the beats, harmonies, and melodies to produce something new. Jamaican dub or "version" music that started up in the late 1960s influenced American DJs and producers. A "dub" or "version" is an innovative remix of a song track. In Jamaica, and later in the U.S., there were improvisational emcee or DJ versions of a song where the performers rapped their own lyrics (hence "rappers") over top of records blaring in the dance halls or side streets. The term *cultural appropriation* becomes tricky, and probably inaccurate, when you consider the shared traditions and influences of the participants.

Borrowing (some might say stealing) seems to be an essential aspect of the creative act. Famous poet T.S. Eliot, who was accused of plagiarism in composing his modern masterpiece "The Waste Land," put it this way: "Immature poets imitate; mature poets steal." Other creative geniuses (Picasso comes to mind) have been quoted to say essentially the same thing. Confident in their own creativity and their own originality, creative geniuses freely admit that they appropriate what has preceded them. "Bad poets deface what they take, and good poets make it into something better, or at least something different," Eliot writes. Similar quotations have been attributed to Nobel Prize-winning author William Faulkner (1897-1962) and others. Steve Jobs (1955-2011), co-founder of Apple Computer, was fond of quoting Picasso (1881-1973): "Good artists borrow, great artists steal." Picasso is actually reported to have said, "Lesser artists borrow, great artists steal." Were they all borrowing the idea from Eliot (1888-1965)?

Not likely.

It's more likely that as the twentieth century commenced and issues of copyright infringement became a more prominent part of the public discourse (commensurate with the landmark U.S. Copyright Act of 1909), artists and critics focused more intently on the issue of borrowing. Before the twentieth century, society understood borrowing and appropriation as a natural part of creative production. During the twentieth century, legal issues became as important as aesthetic issues. In the twenty-first century, copyright and appropriation remain important public discourses.

Plagiarism

Issues of appropriation and plagiarism overlap.

If a writer borrows without citing or attributing information, he or she risks being accused of plagiarism. The student writer must ask: When am I obligated to attribute or cite source material? When, if ever, is it OK to appropriate without attribution or citation?

In one sense, plagiarism is not complicated. You can't "borrow" someone else's words verbatim. *Copy & paste* plagiarism doesn't happen by accident. Excuses like "I forgot to cite" don't hold water. By denotation, "plagiarism" is fairly straightforward. As discussed further in unit nine, sometimes it is unclear when a citation is required. For example, someone can use *common knowledge* facts without violating the rules of academia. See unit nine for a definition of "common knowledge."

In academia, and specifically in college composition classes, we must attribute and cite sources of information. Crediting the work of others is central to the academic endeavor. If in doubt, cite. Do it as a safeguard. Moreover, as an ethical concern and a matter of respect, we want to credit the words and ideas of others. *And we want to leave no doubt regarding our own intentions.* If your intention is not clear to your reader, then your paper needs revision.

Attributing and citing experts is a primary means of strengthening our own voices and arguments. It is essential to evaluate the validity of the sources we cite. Proper citation lends authority to the author. **Plagiarism is a serious ethical violation within academia, and it is the responsibility of the student to understand what it is and how to avoid it.**

While plagiarism is an academic violation, *copyright infringement* and *trademark infringement* are legal violations.

Outside of academia, is it ever OK to reference someone else's creative work without explicit acknowledgement? It doesn't always seem possible to credit inspiration. If you are working in a professional environment, you would consult your producer or publisher. Journalists have clear ethical and practical guidelines that they must know and follow.

There are some good litmus tests: *Is the purpose of the reference or appropriation to deceive or to create something new? Is the goal to take a short cut or cheat on an assignment or to explore a concept in meaningful ways?*

Questions to Consider

Answer these questions as you read and annotate the text:

- Define "cryptomnesia" and "higher cribbing." Put these terms in context. How are they relevant?
- Why is Bob Dylan a culturally significant figure (especially for Baby Boomers)?
- Who was guilty of "an action I knew my teachers would have called plagiarism"?
- "In nearly one breath, [Muddy] Waters offers five accounts" of the authorship of a song. Explain. Is he confused? Is he a liar?
- "Sine qua non" is Latin for *an essential condition*, literally, "without which it is not." What does the passage mean where this phrase is used?

- What was an important legal question in the early days of photography? How could different judicial decisions have changed the practice and art of photography?
- Lethem is a novelist. He "briefly passed through" a workshop led by a certain "gray eminence." What was the specific nature of the transgenerational discourse that broke down?
- Copyright is enshrined in the U.S. Constitution. How did Jefferson's vision of copyright law differ from the subsequent reality of copyright law, according to Lethem? On a literal level, how has the idea of making a "copy" of something changed since the eighteenth century (when the constitution was ratified)?
- What is the "first life" and the "second life" of a creative property? What illuminating example(s) does Lethem provide?

*All mankind is of one author, and is one volume; when one man dies, one chapter is not torn out of the
book, but translated into a better language; and every chapter must be so translated. …*

—John Donne

Love and Theft

Consider this tale: a cultivated man of middle age looks back on the story of an *amour fou*, one beginning when, traveling abroad, he takes a room as a lodger. The moment he sees the daughter of the house, he is lost. She is a preteen, whose charms instantly enslave him. Heedless of her age, he becomes intimate with her. In the end she dies, and the narrator—marked by her forever—remains alone. The name of the girl supplies the title of the story: *Lolita*.

The author of the story I've described, Heinz von Lichberg, published his tale of Lolita in 1916, forty years before Vladimir Nabokov's novel. Lichberg later became a prominent journalist in the Nazi era, and his youthful works faded from view. Did Nabokov, who remained in Berlin until 1937, adopt Lichberg's tale consciously? Or did the earlier tale exist for Nabokov as a hidden, unacknowledged memory? The history of literature is not without examples of this phenomenon, called cryptomnesia. Another hypothesis is that Nabokov, knowing Lichberg's tale perfectly well, had set himself to that art of quotation that Thomas Mann, himself a master of it, called "higher cribbing." Literature has always been a crucible in which familiar themes are continually recast. Little of what we admire in Nabokov's *Lolita* is to be found in its predecessor; the former is in no way deducible from the latter. Still: did Nabokov consciously borrow and quote?

"When you live outside the law, you have to eliminate dishonesty." The line comes from Don Siegel's 1958 film noir, *The Lineup*, written by Stirling Silliphant. The film still haunts revival houses, likely thanks to Eli Wallach's blazing portrayal of a sociopathic hit man and to Siegel's long, sturdy auteurist career. Yet what were those words worth—to Siegel, or Silliphant, or their audience—in 1958? And again: what was the line worth when Bob Dylan heard it (presumably in some Greenwich Village repertory cinema), cleaned it up a little, and inserted it into "Absolutely Sweet Marie"? What ate they worth now, to the culture at large?

Appropriation has always played a key role in Dylan's music. The songwriter has grabbed not only from a panoply of vintage Hollywood films but from Shakespeare and F. Scott Fitzgerald and Junichi Saga's *Confessions of a Yakuza*. He also nabbed the title of Eric Lott's study of minstrelsy for his 2001 album *Love and Theft*. One imagines Dylan liked the general resonance of the title, in which emotional misdemeanors stalk the sweetness of love, as they do so often in Dylan's songs. Lott's title is, of course, itself a riff on Leslie Fiedler's *Love and Death in the American Novel*, which famously identifies the literary motif of the interdependence of a white man and a dark man, like Huck and Jim or Ishmael and Queequeg—a series of nested references to Dylan's own appropriating, minstrel-boy self. Dylan's art offers a paradox: while it famously urges us not to look back, it also encodes a knowledge of past sources that might otherwise have little home in contemporary culture, like the Civil War poetry of the Confederate bard Henry Timrod, resuscitated in lyrics on Dylan's newest record, *Modern Times*. Dylan's originality and his appropriations are as one.

The same might be said of *all* art. I realized this forcefully when one day I went looking for the John Donne passage quoted above. I know the lines, I confess, not from a college course but from the movie version of 84, *Charing Cross Road* with Anthony Hopkins and Anne Bancroft. I checked out 84, *Charing Cross Road* from the library in the hope of finding the Donne passage, but it wasn't in the book. It's alluded to in the play that was adapted from the book, but it isn't reprinted. So I rented the movie again, and there was the passage, read in voice-over by Anthony Hopkins but without attribution. Unfortunately, the line was also abridged so that, when I finally turned to the Web, I found myself searching for the line "all mankind is of one volume" instead of "all mankind is of one author, and is one volume."

> Define "open source." What does it mean in the world of computer software? What does it mean in the world of culture, according to Lethem?

My Internet search was initially no more successful than my library search. I had thought that summoning boob from the vasty deep was a matter of a few keystrokes, but when I visited the website of the Yale library, I found that most of its books don't yet exist as computer text. As a last-ditch effort I searched the seemingly more obscure phrase "every chapter must be so translated." The passage I wanted finally came to me, as it turns out, not as part of a scholarly library collection but simply because someone who loves Donne had posted it on his homepage. The lines I sought were from Meditation 17 in *Devotions upon Emergent Occasions*, which happens to be the most famous thing Donne ever wrote, containing as it does the line "never send to know for whom the bell tolls; it tolls for thee." My search had led me from a movie to a book to a play to a website and back to a book. Then again, those words may be as famous as they are only because Hemingway lifted them for his book title.

Literature has been in a plundered, fragmentary state for a long time. When I was thirteen I purchased an anthology of Beat writing. Immediately, and to my very great excitement, I discovered one William S. Burroughs, author of something called *Naked Lunch*, excerpted there in all its coruscating brilliance. Burroughs was then as radical a literary man as the world had to offer. Nothing, in all my experience of literature since, has ever had as strong an effect on my sense of the sheer possibilities of writing. Later, attempting to understand this impact, I discovered that Burroughs had incorporated snippets of other writers' texts into his work, an action I knew my teachers would have called plagiarism. Some of these borrowings had been lifted from American science fiction of the Forties and Fifties, adding a secondary shock of recognition for me. By then I knew that this "cut-up method," as Burroughs called it, was central to whatever he thought he was doing, and that he quite literally believed it to be akin to magic. When he wrote about his process, the hairs on my neck stood up, so palpable was the excitement. Burroughs was interrogating the universe with scissors and a paste pot, and the least imitative of authors was no plagiarist at all.

Contamination Anxiety

In 1941, on his front porch, Muddy Waters recorded a song for the folklorist Alan Lomax. After singing the song, which he told Lomax was entitled "Country Blues," Waters described how he came to write it. "I made it on about the eighth of October '38," Waters said. "I was fixin' a puncture on a car. I had been mistreated by a girl. I just felt blue, and the song fell into my mind and it come to me just like that and I started singing." Then Lomax, who knew of the Robert Johnson recording called "Walkin' Blues," asked Waters if there were any other songs that used the same tune. "There's been some blues played like that," Waters replied. "This song comes from the cotton field and a boy once put a record out—Robert Johnson. He put it out as named 'Walkin' Blues.' I heard the tune before I heard it on the record. I learned it from

> Define "intellectual property,"
> "trademark," and "copyright."
> Is Lethem building a case
> against IP (intellectual prop-
> erty) and copyright protec-
> tion? How so?

Son House." in nearly one breath, Waters offers five accounts: his own active authorship: he "made it" on a specific date. Then the "passive" explanation: "it come to me just like that." After Lomax raises the question of influence, Waters, without shame, misgivings, or trepidation, says that he heard a version by Johnson, but that his mentor, Son House, taught it to him. In the middle of that complex genealogy, Waters declares that "this song comes from the cotton field."

Blues and jazz musicians have long been enabled by a kind of "open source" culture, in which pre-existing melodic fragments and larger musical frameworks are freely reworked. Technology has only multiplied the possibilities; musicians have gained the power to *duplicate* sounds literally rather than simply approximate them through allusion. In Seventies Jamaica, King Tubby and Lee "Scratch" Perry deconstructed recorded music, using astonishingly primitive pre-digital hardware, creating what they called "versions." The recombinant nature of their means of production quickly spread to DJs in New York and London. Today an endless, gloriously impure, and fundamentally social process generates countless hours of music.

Visual, sound, and text collage—which for many centuries were relatively fugitive traditions (a cento here, a folk pastiche there)—became explosively central to a series of movements in the twentieth century: futurism, cubism, Dada, musique concrète, situationism, pop art, and appropriationism. In fact, collage, the common denominator in that list, might be called *the* art form of the twentieth century, never mind the twenty-first. But forget, for the moment, chronologies, schools, or even centuries. As examples accumulate—Igor Stravinsky's music and Daniel Johnston's, Francis Bacon's paintings and Henry Darger's, the novels of the Oulipo group and of Hannah Crafts (the author who pillaged Dickens's *Bleak House* to write *The Bondwoman's Narrative*), as well as cherished texts that become troubling to their admirers after the discovery of their "plagiarized" elements, Like Richard Condon's novels or Martin Luther King Jr.'s sermons—it becomes apparent that appropriation, mimicry, quotation, allusion, and sublimated collaboration consist of a kind of sine qua non of the creative act, cutting across all forms and genres in the realm of cultural production.

In a courtroom scene from *The Simpsons* that has since entered into the television canon, an argument over the ownership of the animated characters Itchy and Scratchy rapidly escalates into an existential debate on the very nature of cartoons. "Animation is built on plagiarism!" declares the show's hot-tempered cartoon-producer-within-a-cartoon, Roger Meyers Jr. "You take away our right to steal ideas, where are they going to come from?" If nostalgic cartoonists had never borrowed from *Fritz the Cat*, there would be no *Ren & Stimpy Show*; without the Rankin/Bass and Charlie Brown Christmas specials, there would be no *South Park*; and without *The Flint-stones*—more or less *The Honeymooners* in cartoon loincloths—*The Simpsons* would cease to exist. If those don't strike you as essential losses, then consider the remarkable series of "plagiarisms" that links Ovid's "Pyramus and Thisbe" with Shakespeare's *Romeo and Juliet* and Leonard Bernstein's *West Side Story*, or Shakespeare's description of Cleopatra, copied nearly verbatim from Plutarch's life of Mark Antony and also later nicked by T. S. Eliot for *The Waste Land*. If these are examples of plagiarism, then we want more plagiarism.

Most artists are brought to their vocation when their own nascent gifts are awakened by the work of a master. That is to say, most artists are converted to art by art itself. Finding one's voice isn't just an emptying and purifying oneself of the words of others but an adopting and embracing of filiations, communities, and discourses. Inspiration could be called inhaling the memory of an act never experienced. Invention, it must be humbly admitted, does not consist in creating out of void but out of chaos. Any artist knows these truths, no matter how deeply he or she submerges that knowing.

What happens when an allusion goes unrecognized? A closer look at *The Waste Land* may help make this point. The body of Eliot's poem is a vertiginous mélange of quotation, allusion, and "original" writing. When Eliot alludes to Edmund Spenser's "Prothalamion" with the line "Sweet Thames, run softly, till I end my song," what of readers to whom the poem, never one of Spenser's most popular, is unfamiliar? (Indeed, the Spenser is now known largely because of Eliot's use of it.) Two responses are possible: grant the line to Eliot, or later discover the source and understand the line as plagiarism. Eliot evidenced no small anxiety about these matters; the notes he so carefully added to *The Waste Land* can be read as a symptom of modernism's contamination anxiety. Taken from this angle, what exactly is postmodernism, except modernism without the anxiety?

> How would calling a "copyright" a monopoly on use change the discourse?

Surrounded by Signs

The surrealists believed that objects in the world possess a certain but unspecifiable intensity that had been dulled by everyday use and utility. They meant to reanimate this dormant intensity, to bring their minds once again into close contact with the matter that made up their world. André Breton's maxim "Beautiful as the chance encounter of a sewing machine and an umbrella on an operating table" is an expression of the belief that simply placing objects in an unexpected context re invigorates their mysterious qualities.

This "crisis" the surrealists identified was being simultaneously diagnosed by others. Martin Heidegger held that the essence of modernity was found in a certain technological orientation he called "enframing." This tendency encourages us to see the objects in our world only in terms of how they can serve us or be used by us. The task he identified was to find ways to resituate ourselves vis-à-vis these "objects," so that we may see them as "things" pulled into relief against the ground of their functionality. Heidegger believed that art had the great potential to reveal the "thingness" of objects.

The surrealists understood that photography and cinema could carry out this reanimating process automatically; the process of framing objects in a lens was often enough to create the charge they sought. Describing the effect, Walter Benjamin drew a comparison between the photographic apparatus and Freud's psychoanalytic methods. Just as Freud's theories "isolated and made analyzable things which had heretofore floated along unnoticed in the broad stream of perception," the photographic apparatus focuses on "hidden details of familiar objects," revealing "entirely new structural formations of the subject."

It's worth noting, then, that early in the history of photography a series of judicial decisions could well have changed the course of that art: courts were asked whether the photographer, amateur or professional, required permission before he could capture and print an image. Was the photographer *stealing* from the person or building whose photograph he shot, pirating something of private and certifiable value? Those early decisions went in favor of the pirates. Just as Walt Disney could take inspiration from Buster Keaton's *Steamboat Bill, Jr.*, the Brothers Grimm, or the existence of real mice, the photographer should be free to capture an image without compensating the source. The world that meets our eye through the lens of a camera was judged to be, with minor exceptions, a sort of public commons, where a cat may look at a king.

Novelists may glance at the stuff of the world too, but we sometimes get called to task for it. For those whose ganglia were formed pre-TV, the mimetic deployment of pop-culture icons seems at best an annoying tic and at worst a dangerous vapidity that compromises fiction's seriousness by dating it out of the Platonic Always, where it ought to reside. In a graduate workshop I briefly passed through, a certain gray eminence tried to convince us that a literary story should always eschew "any feature which serves

> What is the idea of a "commons" in the world of music, and why can't Red Robin servers sing "Happy Birthday to you" to their customers?

to date it" because "serious fiction must be Timeless." When we protested that, in his own well-known work, characters moved about electrically lit rooms, drove cars, and spoke not Anglo-Saxon but postwar English—and further, that fiction he'd himself ratified as great, such as Dickens, was liberally strewn with innately topical, commercial, and timebound references—he impatiently amended his proscription to those explicit references that would date a story in the "frivolous Now." When pressed, he said of course he meant the "trendy mass-popular-media" reference. Here, trans-generational discourse broke down.

I was born in 1964; I grew up watching Captain Kangaroo, moon landings, zillions of TV ads, the Banana Splits, *M*A*S*H*, and *The Mary Tyler Moore Show*. I was born with words in my mouth—"Band-Aid," "Q-tip," "Xerox"—object-names as fixed and eternal in my logosphere as "taxicab" and "toothbrush." The world is a home littered with pop-culture products and their emblems. I also came of age swamped by parodies that stood for originals yet mysterious to me—I knew Monkees before Beatles, Belmondo before Bogart, and "remember" the movie *Summer of '42* from a *Mad* magazine satire, though I've still never seen the film itself. I'm not alone in having been born backward into an incoherent realm of texts, products, and images, the commercial and cultural environment with which we've both supplemented and blotted out our natural world. I can no more claim it as "mine" than the sidewalks and forests of the world, yet I do dwell in it, and for me to stand a chance as either artist or citizen, I'd probably better be permitted to name it.

Consider Walker Percy's *The Moviegoer*:

> Other people, so I have read, treasure memorable moments in their lives: the time one climbed the Parthenon at sunrise, the summer night one met a lonely girl in Central Park and achieved with her a sweet and natural relationship, as they say in books. I too once met a girl in Central Park, but it is not much to remember. What I remember is the time John Wayne killed three men with a carbine as he was falling to the dusty street in *Stage-coach*, and the time the kitten found Orson Welles in the doorway in *The Third Man*.

Today, when we can eat Tex-Mex with chopsticks while listening to reggae and watching a YouTube re-broadcast of the Berlin Wall's fall—i.e., when damn neat *everything* presents itself as familiar—it's not a surprise that some of today's most ambitious art is going about trying to *make the familiar strange*. In so doing, in reimagining what human life might truly be like over there across the chasms of illusion, mediation, demographics, marketing, imago, and appearance, artists are paradoxically trying to restore what's taken for "real" to three whole dimensions, to reconstruct a univocally round world out of disparate streams of flat sights.

Whatever charge of tastelessness or trademark violation may be attached to the artistic appropriation of the media environment in which we swim, the alternative—to flinch, or tiptoe away into some ivory tower of irrelevance—is far worse. We're surrounded by signs; our imperative is to ignore none of them.

Use Monopoly

The idea that culture can be property—*intellectual* property—is used to justify everything from attempts to force the Girl Scouts to pay royalties for singing songs around campfires to the infringement suit brought by the estate of Margaret Mitchell against the publishers of Alice Randall's *The Wind Done Gone*. Corporations like Celera Genomics have filed for patents for human genes, while the Recording

Industry Association of America has sued music downloaders for copyright infringement, reaching out-of-court settlements for thousands of dollars with defendants as young as twelve. ASCAP bleeds fees from shop owners who play background music in their stores; students and scholars are shamed from placing texts facedown on photocopy machines. At the same time, copyright is revered by most established writers and art-

> What do you think Lethem means when he writes, "The case for perpetual copyright is a denial of the essential gift-aspect of the creative act"?

ists as a birthright and bulwark, the source of nurture for their infinitely fragile practices in a rapacious world. Plagiarism and piracy, after all, are the monsters we working artists are taught to dread, as they roam the woods surrounding our tiny preserves of regard and remuneration.

A time is marked not so much by ideas that are argued about as by ideas that are taken for granted. The character of an era hangs upon what needs no defense. In this regard, few of us question the contemporary construction of copyright. It is taken as a law, both in the sense of a universally recognizable moral absolute, like the law against murder, and as naturally inherent in our world, like the law of gravity. In fact, it is neither. Rather, copyright is an ongoing social negotiation, tenuously forged, endlessly revised, and imperfect in its every incarnation.

Thomas Jefferson, for one, considered copyright a necessary evil: he favored providing just enough incentive to create, nothing more, and thereafter allowing ideas to flow freely, as nature intended. His conception of copyright was enshrined in the Constitution, which gives Congress the authority to "promote the Progress of Science and useful Arts, by securing for limited Times to Authors and Inventors the exclusive Right to their respective Writings and Discoveries." This was a balancing act between creators and society as a whole; second comers might do a much better job than the originator with the original idea.

But Jefferson's vision has not fared well, has in fact been steadily eroded by those who view the culture as a market in which everything of value should be owned by someone or other. The distinctive feature of modern American copyright law is its almost limitless bloating—its expansion in both scope and duration. With no registration requirement, every creative act in a tangible medium is now subject to copyright protection: your email to your child or your child's finger painting, both are automatically protected. The first Congress to grant copyright gave authors an initial term of fourteen years, which could be renewed for another fourteen if the author still lived. The current term is the life of the author plus seventy years. It's only a slight exaggeration to say that each time Mickey Mouse is about to fall into the public domain, the mouse's copyright term is extended.

Even as the law becomes more restrictive, technology is exposing those restrictions as bizarre and arbitrary. When old laws fixed on reproduction as the compensable (or actionable) unit, it wasn't because there was anything fundamentally invasive of an author's tights in the making of a copy. Rather it was because copies were once easy to find and count, so they made a useful benchmark for deciding when an owner's rights had been invaded. In the contemporary world, though, the act of "copying" is in no meaningful sense equivalent to an infringement—we make a copy every time we accept an emailed text, or send or forward one—and is impossible anymore to regulate or even describe.

At the movies, my entertainment is sometimes lately preceded by a dire trailer, produced by the lobbying group called the Motion Picture Association of America, in which the purchasing of a bootleg copy of a Hollywood film is compared to the theft of a car or a handbag—and, as the bullying super-titles remind us, "You wouldn't steal a handbag!" This conflation forms an incitement to quit thinking. If I were to tell you that pirating DVDs or downloading music is in no way different from loaning a friend a book, my own arguments would be as ethically bankrupt as the MPAA's. The truth lies somewhere in the vast gray area between these two overstated positions. For a car or a handbag, once stolen, no longer

> Can you explain Disney's business model, as characterized by Lethem?

is available to its owner, while the appropriation of an article of "intellectual property" leaves the original untouched. As Jefferson wrote, "He who receives an idea from me, receives instruction himself without lessening mine; as he who lights his taper at mine, receives light without darkening me."

Yet industries of cultural capital, who profit not from creating but from distributing, see the sale of culture as a zero-sum game. The piano-roll publishers fear the record companies, who fear the cassette-tape manufacturers, who fear the online vendors, who fear whoever else is next in line to profit most quickly from the intangible and infinitely reproducible fruits of an artist's labor. It has been the same in every industry and with every technological innovation. Jack Valenti, speaking for the MPAA: "I say to you that the VCR is to the American film producer and the American public as the Boston Strangler is to the woman home atone."

Thinking clearly sometimes requires unbraiding our language. The word "copyright" may eventually seem as dubious in its embedded purposes as "family values," "globalization," and, sure, "intellectual property." Copyright is a "right" in no absolute sense; it is a government-granted monopoly on the use of creative results. So let's try calling it that—not a right but a *monopoly on use*, a "usemonopoly"—and then consider how the rapacious expansion of monopoly rights has always been counter to the public interest, no matter if it is Andrew Carnegie controlling the price of steel or Walt Disney managing the fate of his mouse. Whether the monopolizing beneficiary is a living artist or some artist's heirs or some corporation's shareholders, the loser is the community, including living artists who might make splendid use of a healthy public domain.

The Beauty of Second Use

A few years ago someone brought me a strange gift, purchased at MoMA's downtown design store: a copy of my own first novel, *Gun, With Occasional Music*, expertly cut into the contours of a pistol. The object was the work of Robert The, an artist whose specialty is the reincarnation of everyday materials. I regard my first book as an old friend, one who never fails to remind me of the spirit with which I entered into this game of art and commerce—that to be allowed to insert the materials of my imagination onto the shelves of bookstores and into the minds of readers (if only a handful) was a wild privilege. I was paid $6,000 for three years of writing, but at the time I'd have happily published the results for nothing. Now my old friend had come home in a new form, one I was unlikely to have imagined for it myself. The gun-book wasn't readable, exactly, but I couldn't take offense at that. The fertile spirit of stray connection this appropriated object conveyed back to me—the strange beauty of its second use—was a reward for being a published writer I could never have fathomed in advance. And the world makes room for both my novel and Robert The's gun-book. There's no need to choose between the two.

In the first life of creative property, if the creator is lucky, the content is sold. After the commercial life has ended, our tradition supports a second life as well. A newspaper is delivered to a doorstep, and the next day wraps fish or builds an archive. Most books fall out of print after one year, yet even within that period they can be sold in used bookstores and stored in libraries, quoted in reviews, parodied in magazines, described in conversations, and plundered for costumes for kids to wear on Halloween. The demarcation between various possible uses is beautifully graded and hard to define, the more so as artifacts distill into and repercuss through the realm of culture into which they've been entered, the more so as they engage the receptive minds for whom they were presumably intended.

Active reading is an impertinent raid on the literary preserve. Readers are like nomads, poaching their way across fields they do not own—artists are no more able to control the imaginations of their audiences than the culture industry is able to control second uses of its artifacts. In the children's classic *The Velveteen Rabbit*, the old Skin Horse offers the Rabbit a lecture on the practice of textual poaching. The value of a new toy lies not it its material qualities (not "having things that buzz inside you and a stick-out

> Explain *imperial plagiarism*, which might also be called "cultural appropriation."

handle"), the Skin Horse explains, but rather in how the toy is used. "Real isn't how you are made. ... It's a thing that happens to you. When a child loves you for a long, long time, not just to play with, but REALLY loves you, then you become Real." The Rabbit is fearful, recognizing that consumer goods don't become "real" without being actively reworked: "Does it hurt?" Reassuring him, the Skin Horse says: "It doesn't happen all at once. ... You become. It takes a long time. ... Generally, by the time you are Real, most of your hair has been loved off, and your eyes drop out and you get loose in the joints and very shabby." Seen from the perspective of the toymaker, the Velveteen Rabbit's loose joints and missing eyes represent vandalism, signs of misuse and rough treatment; for others, these are marks of its loving use.

Artists and their surrogates who fall into the trap of seeking recompense for every possible second use end up attacking their own best audience members for the crime of exalting and enshrining their work. The Recording Industry Association of America prosecuting their own record-buying public makes as little sense as the novelists who bristle at autographing used copies of their books for collectors. And artists, or their heirs, who fall into the trap of attacking the collagists and satirists and digital samplers of their work are attacking the next generation of creators for the crime of being influenced, for the crime of responding with the same mixture of intoxication, resentment, lust, and glee that characterizes all artistic successors. By doing so they make the world smaller, betraying what seems to me the primary motivation for participating in the world of culture in the first place: to make the world larger.

Source Hypocrisy, or, Disnial

The Walt Disney Company has drawn an astonishing catalogue from the work of others: *Snow White and the Seven Dwarfs, Fantasia, Pinocchio, Dumbo, Bambi, Song of the South, Cinderella, Alice in Wonderland, Robin Hood, Peter Pan, Lady and the Tramp, Mulan, Sleeping Beauty, The Sword in the Stone, The Jungle Book*, and, alas, *Treasure Planet*, a legacy of cultural sampling that Shakespeare, or De La Soul, could get behind. Yet Disney's protectorate of lobbyists has policed the resulting cache of cultural materials as vigilantly as if it were Fort Knox—threatening legal action, for instance, against the artist Dennis Oppenheim for the use of Disney characters in a sculpture, and prohibiting the scholar Holly Crawford from using any Disney-related images—including artwork by Lichtenstein, Warhol, Oldenburg, and others—in her monograph *Attached to the Mouse: Disney and Contemporary Art*.

This peculiar and specific act—the enclosure of commonwealth culture for the benefit of a sole or corporate owner—is close kin to what could be called *imperial plagiarism*, the free use of Third World or "primitive" artworks and styles by more privileged (and better-paid) artists. Think of Picasso's *Les Demoiselles d'Avignon*, or some of the albums of Paul Simon or David Byrne: even without violating copyright, those creators have sometimes come in for a certain skepticism when the extent of their outsourcing became evident. And, as when Led Zeppelin found themselves sued for back royalties by the bluesman Willie Dixon, the act can occasionally be an expensive one. *To live outside the law, you must be honest*: perhaps it was this, in part, that spurred David Byrne and Brian Eno to recently launch a "remix" website, where anyone can download easily disassembled versions of two songs from *My Life in the Bush of Ghosts*, an album reliant on vernacular speech sampled from a host of sources. Perhaps it also explains why Bob Dylan has never refused a request for a sample.

> What is "source hypocrisy" or "Disnial"?

Kenneth Koch once said, "I'm a writer who likes to be influenced." It was a charming confession, and a rare one. For so many artists, the act of creativity is intended as a Napoleonic imposition of one's uniqueness upon the universe—*après moi le déluge* of copycats! And for every James Joyce or Woody Guthrie or Martin Luther King Jr., or Walt Disney, who gathered a constellation of voices in his work, there may seem to be some corporation or literary estate eager to stopper the bottle: cultural debts flow in, but they don't flow out. We might call this tendency "source hypocrisy." Or we could name it after the most pernicious source hypocrites of all time: Disnial.

You Can't Steal a Gift

My reader may, understandably, be on the verge of crying, "Communist!" A large, diverse society cannot survive without property; a large, diverse, and modem society cannot flourish without some form of intellectual property. But it takes little reflection to grasp that there is ample value that the term "property" doesn't capture. And works of art exist simultaneously in two economies, a market economy and a *gift economy*.

The cardinal difference between gift and commodity exchange is that a gift establishes a feeling-bond between two people, whereas the sale of a commodity leaves no necessary connection. I go into a hardware store, pay the man for a hacksaw blade, and walk out. I may never see him again. The disconnectedness is, in fact, a virtue of the commodity mode. We don't want to be bothered, and if the clerk always wants to chat about the family, I'll shop elsewhere. I just want a hacksaw blade. But a gift makes a connection. There are many examples, the candy or cigarette offered to a stranger who shares a seat on the plane,

© agsandrew/Shutterstock.com

the few words that indicate goodwill between passengers on the late-night bus. These tokens establish the simplest bonds of social life, but the model they offer may be extended to the most complicated of unions—marriage, parenthood, mentorship. If a value is placed on these (often essentially unequal) exchanges, they degenerate into something else.

> Can you clarify the difference between market economy (commodity exchange) and gift economy?

Yet one of the more difficult things to comprehend is that the gift economies—like those that sustain open-source software—coexist so naturally with the market. It is precisely this doubleness in art practices that we must identify, ratify, and enshrine in our lives as participants in culture, either as "producers" or "consumers." Art that matters to us—which moves the heart, or revives the soul, or delights the senses, or offers courage for living, however we choose to describe the experience—is received as a gift is received. Even if we've paid a fee at the door of the museum or concert hall, when we are touched by a work of art something comes to us that has nothing to do with the price. The daily commerce of our lives proceeds at its own constant level, but a gift conveys an uncommodifiable surplus of inspiration.

The way we treat a thing can change its nature, though. Religions often prohibit the sale of sacred objects, the implication being that their sanctity is lost if they are bought and sold. We consider it unacceptable to sell sex, babies, body organs, legal rights, and votes. The idea that something should never be commodified is generally known as *inalienability* or *unalienability*—a concept most famously expressed by Thomas Jefferson in the phrase "endowed by their Creator with certain unalienable Rights ..." A work of art seems to be a hardier breed; it can be sold in the market and still emerge a work of art. But if it is true that in the essential commerce of art a gift is carried by the work from the artist to his audience, if I am right to say that where there is no gift there is no art, then it may be possible to destroy a work of art by converting it into a pure commodity. I don't maintain that art can't be bought and sold, but that the gift portion of the work places a constraint upon our merchandising. This is the reason why even a really beautiful, ingenious, powerful ad (of which there are a lot) can never be any kind of real art: an ad has no status as gift; i.e., it's never really *for* the person it's directed at.

The power of a gift economy remains difficult for the empiricists of our market culture to understand. In our times, the rhetoric of the market presumes that everything should be and can be appropriately bought, sold, and owned—a tide of alienation lapping daily at the dwindling redoubt of the unalienable. In free-market theory, an intervention to halt propertization is considered "paternalistic," because it inhibits the free action of the citizen, now reposited as a "potential entrepreneur." Of course, in the real world, we know that child-rearing, family life, education, socialization, sexuality, political life, and many other basic human activities require insulation from market forces. In fact, paying for many of these things can ruin them. We may be willing to peek at *Who Wants to Marry a Multi-millionaire* or an eBay auction of the ova of fashion models, but only to reassure ourselves that some things are still beneath our standards of dignity.

What's remarkable about gift economies is that they can flourish in the most unlikely places—in run-down neighborhoods, on the Internet, in scientific communities, and among members of Alcoholics Anonymous. A classic example is commercial blood systems, which generally produce blood supplies of lower safety, purity, and potency than volunteer systems. A gift economy may be superior when it comes to maintaining a group's commitment to certain extra-market values.

The Commons

Another way of understanding the presence of gift economies—which dwell like ghosts in the commercial machine—is in the sense of a *public commons*. A commons, of course, is anything like the streets over which we drive, the skies through which we pilot airplanes, or the public parks or beaches on which we

> Explain "undiscovered public knowledge," as named by library scientist Don Swanson.

dally. A commons belongs to everyone and no one, and its use is controlled only by common consent. A commons describes resources like the body of ancient music drawn on by composers and folk musicians alike, rather than the commodities, like "Happy Birthday to You," for which ASCAP, 114 years after it was written, continues to collect a fee. Einstein's theory of relativity is a commons. Writings in the public domain are a commons. Gossip about celebrities is a commons. The silence in a movie theater is a transitory commons, impossibly fragile, treasured by those who crave it, and constructed as a mutual gift by those who compose it.

The world of art and culture is a vast commons, one that is salted through with zones of utter commerce yet remains gloriously immune to any overall commodification. The closest resemblance is to the commons of a *language*: altered by every contributor, expanded by even the most passive user. That a language is a commons doesn't mean that the community owns it; rather it belongs *between* people, possessed by no one, not even by society as a whole.

Nearly any commons, though, can be encroached upon, partitioned, enclosed. The American commons include tangible assets such as public forests and minerals, intangible wealth such as copyrights and patents, critical infrastructures such as the Internet and government research, and cultural resources such as the broadcast airwaves and public spaces. They include resources we've paid for as taxpayers and inherited from previous generations. They're not just an inventory of marketable assets; they're social institutions and cultural traditions that define us as Americans and enliven us as human beings. Some invasions of the commons are sanctioned because we can no longer muster a spirited commitment to the public sector. The abuse goes unnoticed because the theft of the commons is seen in glimpses, not in panorama. We may occasionally see a former wetland paved; we may hear about the breakthrough cancer drug that tax dollars helped develop, the rights to which pharmaceutical companies acquired for a song. The larger movement goes too much unremarked. The notion of a *commons of cultural materials* goes more or less unnamed.

Honoring the commons is not a matter of moral exhortation. It is a practical necessity. We in Western society are going through a period of intensifying belief in private ownership, to the detriment of the public good. We have to remain constantly vigilant to prevent raids by those who would selfishly exploit out common heritage for their private gain. Such raids on our natural resources are not examples of enterprise and initiative. They ate attempts to take from all the people just for the benefit of a few.

Undiscovered Public Knowledge

Artists and intellectuals despondent over the prospects for originality can take heart from a phenomenon identified about twenty years ago by Don Swanson, a library scientist at the University of Chicago. He called it "undiscovered public knowledge." Swanson showed that standing problems in medical research may be significantly addressed, perhaps even solved, simply by systematically surveying the scientific literature. Left to its own devices, research tends to become more specialized and abstracted from the real-world problems that motivated it and to which it remains relevant. This suggests that such a problem may be tackled effectively not by commissioning mote research but by assuming that most or all of the solution can already be found in various scientific journals, waiting to be assembled by someone willing to read across specialties. Swanson himself did this in the case of Raynaud's syndrome, a disease that causes the fingers of young women to become numb. His finding is especially striking—perhaps even scandalous—because it happened in the ever-expanding biomedical sciences.

Undiscovered public knowledge emboldens us to question the extreme claims to originality made in press releases and publishers' notices: Is an intellectual or creative offering truly novel, or have we just forgotten a worthy precursor? Does solving certain scientific problems realty require massive additional funding, or could a computerized search engine, creatively deployed, do the same job more quickly and cheaply? Lastly, does our appetite for creative vitality require the violence and exasperation of another avant-garde, with its wearisome killing-the-father imperatives, or might we be better off ratifying *the ecstasy of influence*—and deepening our willingness to understand the commonality and timelessness of the methods and motifs available to artists?

> What should be "the price of a rare success" when it comes to cultural production, according to Lethem?

Give All

A few years ago, the Film Society of Lincoln Center announced a retrospective of the works of Dariush Mehrjui, then a fresh enthusiasm of mine. Mehrjui is one of Iran's finest filmmakers, and the only one whose subject was personal relationships among the upper-middle-class intelligentsia. Needless to say, opportunities to view his films were—and remain—rare indeed. I headed up-town for one, an adaptation of J. D. Salinger's *Franny and Zooey*, titled *Pari*, only to discover at the door of the Walter Reade Theater that the screening had been canceled: its announcement had brought threat of a lawsuit down on the Film Society. True, these were Salinger's rights under the law. Yet why would he care that some obscure Iranian film-maker had paid him homage with a meditation on his heroine? Would it have damaged his book or robbed him of some crucial remuneration had the screening been permitted? The fertile spirit of stray connection—one stretching across what is presently seen as the direst of international breaches—had in this case been snuffed out. The cold, undead hand of one of my childhood literary heroes had reached out from its New Hampshire redoubt to arrest my present-day curiosity.

A few assertions, then:

Any text that has infiltrated the common mind to the extent of *Gone With the Wind* or *Lolita* or *Ulysses* inexorably joins the language of culture. A map-turned-to-landscape, it has moved to a place beyond enclosure or control. The authors and their heirs should consider the subsequent parodies, refractions, quotations, and revisions an honor, or at least the price of a rare success.

A corporation that has imposed an inescapable notion—Mickey Mouse, Band-Aid—on the cultural language should pay a similar price.

The primary objective of copyright is not to reward the labor of authors but "to promote the Progress of Science and useful Arts." To this end, copyright assures authors the right to their original expression, but encourages others to build freely upon the ideas and information conveyed by a work. This result is neither unfair nor unfortunate.

Contemporary copyright, trademark, and patent law is presently corrupted. The case for perpetual copyright is a denial of the essential gift-aspect of the creative act. Arguments in its favor are as un-American as those for the repeal of the estate tax.

Art is sourced. Apprentices graze in the field of culture.

Digital sampling is an art method like any other, neutral in itself.

Despite hand-wringing at each technological turn—radio, the Internet—the future will be much Like the past. Artists will sell some things but also give some things away. Change may be troubling for those who crave less ambiguity, but the life of an artist has never been filled with certainty.

> What is the "key" to this article (not metaphorically but literally)? How does this "key" lend a wry glint of humor to the concept of Lethem's authorship?

The dream of a perfect systematic remuneration is nonsense. I pay rent with the price my words bring when published in glossy magazines and at the same moment offer them for almost nothing to impoverished literary quarterlies, or speak them for free into the air in a radio interview. So what are they worth? What would they be worth if some future Dylan worked them into a song? Should I care to make such a thing impossible?

Any text is woven entirely with citations, references, echoes, cultural languages, which cut across it through and through in a vast stereophony. The citations that go to make up a text are anonymous, untraceable, and yet *already read*; they are quotations without inverted commas. The kernel, the soul—let us go further and say the substance, the bulk, the actual and valuable material of all human utterances—is plagiarism. For substantially all ideas are secondhand, consciously and unconsciously drawn from a million outside sources, and daily used by the garnerer with a pride and satisfaction born of the superstition that he originated them; whereas there is not a rag of originality about them anywhere except the little discoloration they get from his mental and moral caliber and his temperament, and which is revealed in characteristics of phrasing. Old and new make the warp and woof of every moment. There is no thread that is not a twist of these two strands. By necessity, by proclivity, and by delight, we all quote. Neurological study has lately shown that memory, imagination, and consciousness itself is stitched, quilted, pastiched. If we cut-and-paste our selves, might we not forgive it of our artworks?

Artists and writers—and our advocates, our guilds and agents—too often subscribe to implicit claims of originality that do injury to these truths. And we too often, as hucksters and bean counters in the tiny enterprises of our selves, act to spite the gift portion of our privileged roles. People live differently who treat a portion of their wealth as a gift. If we devalue and obscure the gift-economy function of our art practices, we turn our works into nothing more than advertisements for themselves. We may console ourselves that our lust for subsidiary rights in virtual perpetuity is some heroic counter to rapacious corporate interests. But the truth is that with artists pulling on one side and corporations pulling on the other, the loser is the collective public imagination from which we were nourished in the first place, and whose existence as the ultimate repository of our offerings makes the work worth doing in the first place.

As a novelist, I'm a cork on the ocean of story, a leaf on a windy day. Pretty soon I'll be blown away. For the moment I'm grateful to be making a living, and so must ask that for a limited time (in the Thomas Jefferson sense) you please respect my small, treasured usemonopolies. Don't pirate my editions; do plunder my visions. The name of the game is Give All. You, reader, are welcome to my stories. They were never mine in the first place, but I gave them to you. If you have the inclination to pick them up, take them with my blessing.

Key: I is Another

This key to the preceding essay names the source of every line I stole, warped, and cobbled together as I "wrote" (except, alas, those sources I forgot along the way). First uses of a given author or speaker are highlighted in red. Nearly every sentence I culled I also revised, at least slightly—for necessities of space, in order to produce a more consistent tone, or simply because I felt like it.

Title

The phrase "the ecstasy of influence," which embeds a rebuking play on Harold Bloom's "anxiety of influence," is lifted from spoken remarks by Professor Richard Dienst of Rutgers.

Love and Theft

"… a cultivated man of middle age …" to "… hidden, unacknowledged memory?" These lines, with some adjustments for tone, belong to the anonymous editor or assistant who wrote the dust-flap copy of Michael Maar's *The Two Lolitas*. Of course, in my own experience, dust-flap copy is often a collaboration between author and editor. Perhaps this was also true for Maar.

"The history of literature …" to "… borrow and quote?" comes from Maar's book itself.

"Appropriation has always …" to "… Ishmael and Queequeg …" This paragraph makes a hash of remarks from an interview with Eric Lott conducted by David McNair and Jayson Whitehead, and incorporates both interviewers' and interviewee's observations. (The text-interview form can be seen as a commonly accepted form of multivocal writing. Most interviewers prime their subjects with remarks of their own—Leading the witness, so to speak—and gently refine their subjects' statements in the final printed transcript.)

"I realized this …" to "… for a long time." The anecdote is cribbed, with an elision to avoid appropriating a dead grandmother, from Jonathan Rosen's *The Talmud and the Internet*. I've never seen *84, Charing Cross Road*, nor searched the Web for a Donne quote. For me it was through Rosen to Donne, Hemingway, website, et al.

"When I was thirteen …" to "… no plagiarist at all." This is from William Gibson's "God's Little Toys," in *Wired* magazine. My own first encounter with William Burroughs, also at age thirteen, was less epiphanic. Having grown up with a painter father who, during family visits to galleries or museums, approvingly noted collage and appropriation techniques in the visual arts (Picasso, Claes Oldenburg, Stuart Davis), I was gratified, but not surprised, to learn that literature could encompass the same methods.

Contamination Anxiety

"In 1941, on his front porch …" to "… 'this song comes from the cotton field.'" Siva Vaidhyanathan, *Copyrights and Copywrongs*.

"… enabled by a kind … freely reworked." Kembrew McLeod, *Freedom of Expression*. In *Owning Culture*, McLeod notes that, as he was writing, he

happened to be listening to a lot of old country music, and in my casual listening I noticed that *six* country songs shared *exactly* the same vocal melody, including Hank Thompson's "Wild Side of Life," the Carter Family's "I'm Thinking Tonight of My Blue Eyes," Roy Acuff's "Great Speckled Bird," Kitty Wells's "It Wasn't God Who Made Honky Tonk Angels," Reno & Smiley's "I'm Using My Bible for a Roadmap," and Townes Van Zandt's "Heavenly Houseboat Blues." … In his extensively researched book, *Country: The Twisted Roots of Rock 'n' Roll*, Nick Tosches documents that the melody these songs share is both "ancient and British." There were no recorded lawsuits stemming from these appropriations.…

"… musicians have gained … through allusion." Joanna Demers, *Steal This Music*.

"In Seventies Jamaica …" to "… hours of music." Gibson.

"Visual, sound, and text collage…" to "… realm of cultural production." This plunders, rewrites, and amplifies paragraphs from McLeod's *Owning Culture*, except for the line about collage being the art form of the twentieth and twenty-first centuries, which I heard filmmaker Craig Baldwin say, in defense of sampling, in the trailer for a forthcoming documentary, *Copyright Criminals*.

"In a courtroom scene …" to "… would cease to exist." Dave Itzkoff, *New York Times*.

"… the remarkable series of 'plagiarisms' …" to "… we want more plagiarism." Richard Posner, combined from The Becker-Posner Blog and *The Atlantic Monthly*.

"Most artists are brought…" to "… by art itself." These words, and many more to follow, come from Lewis Hyde's *The Gift*. Above any other book I've here plagiarized, I commend *The Gift* to your attention.

"Finding one's voice … filiations, communities, and discourses." Semanticist George L. Dillon, quoted in Rebecca Moore Howard's "The New Abolitionism Comes to Plagiarism."

"Inspiration could be … act never experienced." Ned Rorem, found on several "great quotations" sites on the Internet.

"Invention, it must be humbly admitted … out of chaos." Mary Shelley, from her introduction to *Frankenstein*.

"What happens …" to "… contamination anxiety." Kevin J.H. Dettmar, from "The Illusion of Modernist Allusion and the Politics of Postmodern Plagiarism."

Surrounded By Signs

"The surrealists believed …" to the Walter Benjamin quote. Christian Keathley's *Cinephilia and History, or the Wind in the Trees*, a book that treats fannish fetishism as the secret at the heart of film scholarship. Keathley notes, for instance, Joseph Cornell's surrealist-influenced 1936 film *Rose Hobart*, which simply records "the way in which Cornell himself watched the 1931 Hollywood potboiler *East of Borneo*, fascinated and distracted as he was by its B-grade star"—the star, of course, being Rose Hobart herself. This, I suppose, makes Cornell a sort of father to computer-enabled fan-creator re-workings of Hollywood product, like the version of George Lucas's *The Phantom Menace* from which the noxious Jar Jar Binks character was purged; both incorporate a viewer's subjective preferences into a revision of a filmmaker's work.

"… early in the history of photography" to "… without compensating the source." From *Free Culture*, by Lawrence Lessig, the greatest of public advocates for copyright reform, and the best source if you want to get radicalized in a hurry.

"For those whose ganglia …" to "… discourse broke down." From David Foster Wallace's essay "E Unibus Pluram," reprinted in *A Supposedly Fun Thing I'll Never Do Again*. I have no idea who Wallace's "gray eminence" is or was. I inserted the example of Dickens into the paragraph; he strikes me as overlooked in the lineage of authors of "brand-name" fiction.

"I was born … *Mary Tyler Moore Show*." These are the reminiscences of Mark Hosler from Negativland, a collaging musical collective that was sued by U2's record label for their appropriation of "I Still Haven't Found What I'm Looking For." Although I had to adjust the birth date, Hosler's cultural menu fits me like a glove.

"The world is a home … pop-culture products …" McLeod.

"Today, when we can eat …" to "… flat sights." Wallace.

"We're surrounded by signs, ignore none of them." This phrase, which I unfortunately tendered somewhat leaden with the word "imperative," comes from Steve Erickson's novel *Our Ecstatic Days*.

Usemonopoly

"… everything from attempts …" to "defendants as young as twelve." Robert Boynton, *The New York Times Magazine*, "The Tyranny of Copyright?"

"A time is marked …" to "… what needs no defense." Lessig, this time from *The Future of Ideas*.

"Thomas Jefferson, for one …" to "'… respective Writings and Discoveries.'" Boynton.

"… second comers might do a much better job than the originator …" I found this phrase in Lessig, who is quoting Vaidhyanathan, who himself is characterizing a judgment written by Learned Hand.

"But Jefferson's vision … owned by someone or other." Boynton.

"The distinctive feature …" to "… term is extended." Lessig, again from *The Future of Ideas*.

"When old laws …" to "… had been invaded." Jessica Litman, *Digital Copyright*.

"'I say to you … woman home alone.'" I found the Valenti quote in McLeod. Now fill in the blank: Jack Valenti is to the public domain as _____ is to _____.

The Beauty of Second Use

"In the first …" to "… builds an archive." Lessig.

"Most books … one year …" Lessig.

"Active reading is …" to "… do not own …" This is a mashup of Henry Jenkins, from his *Textual Poachers: Television Fans and Participatory Culture*, and Michel de Certeau, whom Jenkins quotes.

"In the children's classic …" to "… its loving use." Jenkins. (Incidentally, have the holders of the copyright to *The Velveteen Rabbit* had a close look at *Toy Story*? There could be a lawsuit there.)

Source Hypocrisy, or, Disnial

"The Walt Disney Company … alas, *Treasure Planet* …" Lessig.

"Imperial Plagiarism" is the title of an essay by Marilyn Randall.

"…spurred David Byrne …*My Life in the Bush of Ghosts* …" Chris Dahlen, *Pitchfork*—though in truth by the time I'd finished, his words were so utterly dissolved within my own that had I been an ordinary cutting-and-pasting journalist it never would have occurred to me to give Dahlen a citation. The effort of preserving another's distinctive phrases as I worked on this essay was sometimes beyond my capacities; this form of plagiarism was oddly hard work.

"Kenneth Koch …" to "…*déluge* of copycats!" Emily Nussbaum, *The New York Times Book Review*.

You Can't Steal a Gift

"You can't steal a gift." Dizzy Gillespie, defending another player who'd been accused of poaching Charlie Parker's style: "You can't steal a gift. Bird gave the world his music, and if you can hear it you can have it."

"A large, diverse society … intellectual property." Lessig.

"And works of art …" to "… marriage, parenthood, mentorship." Hyde.

"Yet one … so naturally with the market." David Bollier, *Silent Theft*.

"Art that matters …" to "… bought and sold." Hyde.

"We consider it unacceptable…" to "'… certain unalienable Rights …'" Bollier, paraphrasing Margaret Jane Radin's *Contested Commodities*.

"A work of art …" to "… constraint upon our merchandising." Hyde.

"This is the reason…person it's directed at." Wallace.

"The power of a gift …" to "… certain extra-market values." Bollier, and also the sociologist Warren O. Hagstrom, whom Bollier is paraphrasing.

The Commons

"Einstein's theory …" to "… public domain are a commons." Lessig.

"That a language is a commons … society as a whole." Michael Newton, in the *London Review of Books*, reviewing a book called *Echolalias: On the Forgetting of Language* by Daniel Heller-Roazen. The paraphrases of book reviewers are another covert form of collaborative culture; as an avid reader of reviews, I know much about books I've never read. To quote Yann Martel on how he came to be accused of imperial plagiarism in his Booker-winning novel *Life of Pi*,

> Ten or so years ago, I read a review by John Updike in the *New York Times Review of Books* [sic]. It was of a novel by a Brazilian writer, Moacyr Scliar. I forget the title, and John Updike did worse: he clearly thought the book as a whole was forgettable. His review—one of chose that makes you suspicious by being mostly descriptive ... oozed indifference. But one thing about it struck me: the premise. ... Oh, the wondrous things I could do with this premise.

Unfortunately, no one was ever able to locate the Updike review in question.

"The American commons ..." to "... for a song." Bollier.

"Honoring the commons ..." to "... practical necessity." Bollier.

"We in Western ... public good." John Sulston, Nobel Prize–winner and co-mapper of the human genome.

"We have to remain ..." to "... benefit of a few." Harry S Truman, at the opening of the Everglades National Park. Although it may seem the height of presumption to rip off a president—I found claiming Truman's stolid advocacy as my own embarrassing in the extreme—I didn't rewrite him at all. As the poet Marianne Moore said, "If a thing had been said in the *best* way, how can you say it better?" Moore confessed her penchant for incorporating lines from others' work, explaining, "I have not yet been able to outgrow this hybrid method of composition."

Undiscovered Public Knowledge

"... intellectuals despondent ..." to "... quickly and cheaply?" Steve Fuller, *The Intellectual*. There's something of Borges in Fuller's insight here; the notion of a storehouse of knowledge waiting passively to be assembled by future users is suggestive of both "The Library of Babel" and "Kafka and his Precursors."

Give All

"... one of Iran's finest ..." to "... meditation on his heroine?" Amy Taubin, *Village Voice*, although it was me who was disappointed at the door of the Walter Reade Theater.

"The primary objective ..." to "... unfair nor unfortunate." Sandra Day O'Connor, 1991.

"... the future will be much like the past" to "... give some things away." Open-source film archivist Rick Prelinger, quoted in McLeod.

"Change may be troubling ... with certainty." McLeod.

"... woven entirely ..." to "... without inverted commas." Roland Barthes.

"The kernel, the soul ..." to "... characteristics of phrasing." Mark Twain, from a consoling letter to Helen Keller, who had suffered distressing accusations of plagiarism (!). In fact, her work included unconsciously memorized phrases; under Keller's particular circumstances, her writing could be understood as a kind of allegory of the "constructed" nature of artistic perception. I found the Twain quote in the aforementioned *Copyrights and Copywrongs*, by Siva Vaidhyanathan.

"Old and new ..." to "... we all quote." Ralph Waldo Emerson. These guys all sound alike!

"People live differently ... wealth as a gift." Hyde.

"... I'm a cork ..." to "... blown away." This is adapted from The Beach Boys song "'Til I Die," written by Brian Wilson. My own first adventure with song-lyric permissions came when I tried to have a character in my second novel quote the lyrics "There's a world where I can go and/Tell my secrets to/In my room/In my room." After learning the likely expense, at my editor's suggestion I replaced those with "You take the high road/I'll take the low road/I'll be in Scotland before you," a lyric in the public domain. This capitulation always bugged me, and in the subsequent British publication of the same book I restored the Brian Wilson lyric, without permission. *Ocean of Story* is the title of a collection of Christina Stead's short fiction.

Saul Bellow, writing to a friend who'd taken offense at Bellow's fictional use of certain personal facts, said: "The name of the game is Give All. You are welcome to all my facts. You know them, I give them to you. If you have the strength to pick them up, take them with my blessing." I couldn't bring myself to retain Bellow's "strength," which seemed presumptuous in my new context, though it is surely the more elegant phrase. On the other hand, I was pleased to invite the suggestion that the gifts in question may actually be light and easily lifted.

Key to the Key

The notion of a collage text is, of course, not original to me. Walter Benjamin's incomplete *Arcades Project* seemingly would have featured extensive interlaced quotations. Other precedents include Graham Rawle's novel *Diary of an Amateur Photographer*, its text harvested from photography magazines, and Eduardo Paolozzi's collage-novel *Kex*, cobbled from crime novels and newspaper clippings. Closer to home, my efforts owe a great deal to the recent essays of David Shields, in which diverse quotes are made to closely intertwine and reverberate, and to conversations with editor Sean Howe and archivist Pamela Jackson. Last year David Edelstein, in *New York* magazine, satirized the Kaavya Viswanathan plagiarism case by creating an almost completely plagiarized column denouncing her actions. Edelstein intended to demonstrate, through ironic example, how bricolage such as his own was ipso facto facile and unworthy. Although Viswanathan's version of "creative copying" was a pitiable one, I differ with Edelstein's conclusions.

The phrase *Je est un autre*, with its deliberately awkward syntax, belongs to Arthur Rimbaud. It has been translated both as "I is another" and "I is someone else," as in this excerpt from Rimbaud's letters:

> For *I* is someone else. If brass wakes up a trumpet, it is not its fault. To me this is obvious: I witness the unfolding of my own thought: I watch it, I listen to it: I make a stroke of the bow: the symphony begins to stir in the depths, or springs on to the stage.

> If the old fools had not discovered only the *false* significance of the Ego, we should not now be having to sweep away those millions of skeletons which, since time immemorial, have been piling up the fruits of their one-eyed intellects, and claiming to be, themselves, the authors!

Questions for Comprehension

Answer these questions as a comprehension gauge and/or for further clarification on the text:

1. Lethem observes, "It becomes apparent that appropriation, mimicry, quotation, allusion, and sublimated collaboration consist of a kind of sine qua non of the creative act, cutting across all forms and genres in the realm of cultural production." As briefly as possible, and in your own words, explain Lethem's claim.

2. Lethem mentions Shakespeare and the famous poet T.S. Eliot, then writes, "If these are examples of plagiarism, then we want more plagiarism." Explain what he means.

3. True or False. The Walt Disney corporation amassed most of its twentieth century intellectual property by paying licensing fees to authors and artists.

4. Who owns public lands and public radio waves?

5. Library scientist Don Swanson discovered that significant medical issues could be addressed and maybe even solved by doing what?

6. After reading Lethem's article, what is your take on the concept of "originality"?

Finding Connections: Copyright Era and The Public Domain

Discussions of creativity, appropriation, and plagiarism lead to discussions of copyright, trademark, and the public domain.

So now lawyers get in on the discourse.

The current and seemingly ever-changing state of copyright law in the Internet era is certainly as complicated as issues of appropriation and plagiarism.

To introduce the subject in class, I ask my students why Hollywood and London producers are so in love with Sherlock Holmes, the famous detective.

Well into the twenty-first century, Holmes continues to appear in stage, TV, and film productions. Students might guess that the appeal of Arthur Conan Doyle's mythic detective stems from the character's timeless internal paradoxes or unmatched intellect.

But that's not the answer.

There's a more prosaic explanation for Holmes' popularity. Holmes—who first appeared in 1887—exists in the "public domain," meaning that stage, TV, and film producers don't have to pay the author's estate any licensing fees or royalties.

"What about Philip Marlowe?" I ask my students. No one has heard of him. He is Raymond Chandler's famous detective who first appeared in the 1939 novel *The Big Sleep*. Under the U.S. Copyright Act of 1909, Chandler's detective Marlowe does not exist in the public domain, meaning that anyone who wants to produce a show starring this fictional detective must pay for the right to do so.

It would be interesting to ask Raymond Chandler (1888-1959) which he would prefer—the monies he garnered as a result of copyright protections following his death or the kind of universal renown that Arthur Conan Doyle and Sherlock Holmes have enjoyed.

Questions surrounding copyright protection are complicated. Think about musicians and songwriters of the twenty-first century. Citizens of the Internet era seem to think that all creative production should be available to the public for free. (Examine the history of Napster and music piracy, or BitTorrent and film piracy.) How do we expect artists to continue to produce music if they don't have money to buy groceries? Yet Chance the Rapper tells *Vanity Fair* and other outlets, "I never wanted to sell my music, because I thought putting a price on it put a limit on it and inhibited me from making a connection." Artists like Chance the Rapper, whose 2016 *Coloring Book* was the first streaming-only album to top a Billboard chart, have adopted and expanded the "open source" concept of computer pioneers who advocated an Internet filled with "shareware."

Despite the growth of Open Movements such as OER Commons (*oercommons.org*) and Creative Commons (*creativecommons.org*), creative appropriation largely continues to be treated as violation of law (copyright infringement) under American law.

Examine Lethem's article for its meditation upon issues of copyright and appropriation.

© Fabio Alcini/Shutterstock.com

Open Movements

Many artists continue to value copyright protection, which ensures both payment and the integrity of their work. On the other hand, say critics, copyright can be used as an instrument of creative repression.

The non-profit organization Creative Commons aims to "build a more equitable, accessible, and innovative world" by making it easier for people "to share their creative and academic work, as well as to access and build upon the work of others." Creative Commons wants to fight what it sees as the unfair application of copyright law that infringes on the rights of artists and scholars to produce new work.

The sources listed in each unit bibliography come from free online sources and from Open Educational Resources (OER) databases. As a writer, artist, and teacher, I value aspects of copyright as well as aspects of OER. Copyright law, however, often seems at odds with the realities of creative production. In many cases, only wealthy corporations or artists can afford the necessary licenses and legal protections to allow for creative productions that reference or allude to copyrighted work. This dynamic is especially relevant in film and music, where independent artists cannot access protected film clips and audio samples.

One of my own short stories was quashed by the estate of Johnny Cash because it appeared in an anthology entitled *Just to Watch Him Die*, an allusion to the famous Cash lyric from his song "Folsom Prison Blues." No Cash lyric had been published, only this five-word allusion in the volume's title. I told the small publisher to fight it—I'm certain he would have won under "fair use" in a court of law—but he didn't have the time or money to risk legal action. I had worked hard on the story and stood to make no money from it whatsoever. Then to have the estate of our musical hero condemn it was both bizarre and disheartening. How would Cash's estate have been harmed had my publisher sold 50 or 100 copies of the anthology? Independent artists in the twenty-first century certainly have cause for concern regarding copyright law. Hip-hop artists I know sample, record, and distribute from their home studios, ignoring copyright laws and maybe hoping to get sued: any publicity is good publicity. Yet the dynamic also condemns them to the recesses of the Internet since independent record labels cannot risk liability.

Twenty-first century "Open" movements are bound to challenge outdated legal notions of copyright and IP (intellectual property). Gen Z and college students of the twenty-first century will in all likelihood discover increasingly blurry lines separating issues of appropriation, copyright protection, and the public domain.

Finding Connections Works Cited

Creative Commons, *creativecommons.org.*

Robinson, Lisa. "Why Chance the Rapper Makes Music for Free (and How He Actually Makes Money)." *Vanity Fair,* 9 Feb. 2017, *https://www.vanityfair.com/hollywood/2017/02/why-chance-the-rapper-music-is-free-and-how-he-makes-money.*

Schultz, Colin. "'Sherlock Holmes' Is Now Officially Off Copyright and Open for Business." *Smithsonian.com,* 19 June 2014, *https://www.smithsonianmag.com/smart-news/sherlock-holmes-now-officially-copyright-and-open-business-180951794/.*

The idea that mainstream society needs to "get woke" about cultural appropriation is not entirely new, nor is it a simple result of the 1980s social movement called PC or "political correctness."

Author William Styron published his novel *The Confessions of Nat Turner* (1967) in a time of social upheaval in the United States. The Civil Rights movement was ongoing, the "second wave" of the women's movement was gaining ground in popular consciousness, and the counterculture movement took a stance against social norms of compliance and conformity, questioning, among other things, the legitimacy of the war in Vietnam. San Francisco's so-called Summer of Love (1967) boosted hippie culture, heralding new social norms in dress, behavior, and consciousness.

Styron won the 1968 Pulitzer Prize in Fiction for his novel, but not everyone was a fan of the work.

In order to understand the controversy, we need to understand the history behind the novel. Nat Turner (1800-1831) was an enslaved African-American preacher who led the nation's most successful and bloodiest slave revolt in Southampton County, Virginia. The uprising resulted in the deaths of at least 60 white men, women, and children, as well as the subsequent executions of perhaps 120 Black men, women, and children, many of whom were not involved in the uprising. Nat Turner's Revolt scared Southern slaveholders. Literacy for Black folk had always been discouraged; now it was largely outlawed as a capital crime. The death penalty was codified in many states and counties for the crime of Black folk learning how to read.

Growing up in the same area of Virginia where the rebellion took place, Styron was fascinated with the life and death of Nat Turner. Little was known about the man. Styron aimed to elevate Turner's status in the national consciousness. Famous African-American writer James Baldwin happened to be living with Styron and his wife for a time while Styron was struggling with early drafts of the novel. One night, Baldwin challenged Styron to write his book from Nat Turner's point of view. Something clicked for Styron, and for the next three or four years he banged away at the typewriter, telling the story from the rebel leader's point of view.

An 1831 court document called "The Confessions of Nat Turner" purports to express Turner's thoughts in his own words. It is purportedly a voluntary statement, recorded by a white lawyer named Thomas Gray. The statement was taken after Turner's arrest and prior to his execution. The document answers questions but leaves many other questions unanswered.

This gap between historical fact and imagination is where fiction thrives.

African-American actor and director Nate Parker dismisses Styron's literary efforts at representation as an inappropriate instance of cultural appropriation. Parker produced *The Birth of a Nation* (2016), a film about Nat Turner. Parker represents Turner's life through an African-American consciousness, attempting to right the wrongs he sees in William Styron's literary text.

Parker faults Styron for leaving out the historical fact that Turner had a wife, for instance. Parker faults Styron for representing Turner as lusting after an 18-year-old white girl, whom he subsequently murders. The destructive cultural stereotype of a Black man in sexual pursuit of a white woman is a gross offense to the memory of Nat Turner. Parker, it must be noted, also includes at least one major historical inaccuracy in his narrative. (Nat Turner did not turn himself in.)

In Styron's defense, Turner's feelings toward the white girl as expressed in the novel are decidedly more complicated than simple sexual desire. Nevertheless, Styron chooses this subplot and chooses to vacate the existence of Nat's actual wife. He may have had artistic reasons for doing so; nonetheless, it strikes critics as the wrong choice, a prime example of inappropriate white cultural appropriation of a Black hero's narrative.

Whatever else he did, and however flawed the representation, the novelist did elevate Nat Turner's position in the American story. In a country where the most painful aspects of our history are often buried and forgotten, as well as neglected in our schools, Styron drew attention to Nat Turner. Narrating the story from Turner's point of view demonstrates a sympathetic connection, even if Styron's efforts at representation are flawed.

The debate over cultural appropriation is not a twenty-first century phenomenon.

In 1968, James Baldwin moderated a debate between his friend William Styron and his friend Ossie Davis, the African-American actor who had refused the part of Nat Turner in a proposed film version of Styron's book. Black critics lined up against Styron's narrative, and Black activists ensured that the book would never be made into a movie. Black Americans at that time were well aware of what we call "cultural appropriation." A discourse that was alive in the Civil Rights Era remains so in the Internet era through the Black Lives Matter and related social justice movements.

Finding Connections Works Cited

Cunningham, Vinson. "'The Birth of a Nation' Isn't Worth Defending." *The New Yorker,* 10 Oct. 2016, https://www.newyorker.com/magazine/2016/10/10/the-birth-of-a-nation-isnt-worth-defending.

Klein, Christopher. "10 Things You May Not Know About Nat Turner's Rebellion." *History.com,* 24 May 2016, updated 31 Aug. 2018, https://www.history.com/news/10-things-you-may-not-know-about-nat-turners-rebellion.

Parker, Nate. Director, *The Birth of a Nation.* Fox Searchlight Pictures, 2016.

Styron, William. *The Confessions of Nat Turner.* Random House, 1967.

Tanenhaus, Sam. "The Literary Battle for Nat Turner's Legacy." *Vanity Fair,* 3 Aug. 2016, https://www.vanityfair.com/culture/2016/08/the-literary-battle-for-nat-turners-legacy.

Resources

The Rhetorical Situation

Analyzing the Rhetorical Situation of a Text

First, let's define "text." A **text** can mean any form of human communication, including, but not limited to, a literary text. Various forms of texts may include: a music video, a song, a novel, a film, a photograph, a blog, or a post. And, of course, any article that appears in *Engaging Discourse 2.0* qualifies as a "text." Editorial introductions, too, qualify as texts.

The **rhetorical situation** of a given "text" consists of:

✓ The **text** itself which communicates in words, in images, in sounds, or in a combination of ways,
✓ An **author** or set of authors,
✓ An **audience**, that is, the recipient(s) of the communication,
✓ The **purpose**, that is, the reason(s) for the communication, and
✓ A **context**, the time/setting/place/situation/environment which encompasses the text/instance of communication.

When we compose essays or analyze literary texts (and other forms of texts), it is important to remain aware of the *rhetorical situation*. Understanding the rhetorical situation informs our text analysis.

An abundance of valuable resource materials regarding rhetorical situation are available online.

Text: Author or Audience

As a reader or recipient of any sort of "text," you are probably also part of its **audience**. At times, as you study a text, you may discover that you feel yourself to be either inside or outside of the text's intended audience. Analyzing the rhetorical situation of a text helps you to discover where you stand, so to speak, in this dynamic.

As the **author** of a text, you must assess the situation and needs of your audience so that your own authored text communicates effectively.

A simple example: You are on your way to the grocery store, and you write yourself out a list. This list is a text. *Who is your audience?* Yourself. *What is your purpose?* To get food to feed yourself. The *context* in this case is pretty nondescript. The list exists within the here-and-now of the daily grind. *Is it OK to use emoticons and indecipherable symbols that only you can understand?* Sure. It's your list. You yourself are the only audience. You achieve your goal, and I hope it involves some fresh fruits and vegetables too.

Another example: You wish to contribute to a *Star Trek* fan blog. *Who is your audience?* Fans of the long-running TV and movie series who obsess over every detail of the various productions. There might even be sub-groups who specialize in "new" Trekkie lore or "old" Trekkie lore. These folks get bored pretty quickly if posts aren't hyper-focused on details, and they don't mind specialized terminology. In fact, they like insider lingo. **An awareness of the audiences who might appreciate your blog post determines how you will compose.** The rhetorical situation is pretty clear, especially if you find a particular sub-group that shares your special interest in Vulcan culture.

If you were to write an article in an **academic journal**, the situation would be much the same, minus the interest in Vulcan culture. Sociologists and psychologists have their own specialized terminology, as do other academicians and scholars. **An understanding of audience and rhetorical situation must guide your writing efforts.**

If you write for a **general interest audience**—let's say an essay that requires interviews and research for a popular magazine—your editor will be pleased when you write in clear prose with standard usage that is widely accepted by a broad, educated audience. I encourage my students to write in this general mode—using clear, simple prose to explain complicated ideas in straightforward, comprehensible language. Cultivating a capacity to communicate to a wide audience provides the practice and habit of linguistic flexibility that will serve you well in a variety of career and academic situations.

Not all writing instructors share this philosophy of practicing to write for a general audience. In fact, there is merit in developing your ability to communicate with a specialized audience as well. **Initiate a discussion with your instructor regarding rhetorical situation and the audience whom he or she expects you to address.**

Understanding the Rhetorical Situation

Typically, as we read or analyze an article or piece of literature, we approach the text first as an audience member. Sometimes, as mentioned above, we discover an intimate connection to the text. Students in the twenty-first century say it's "relatable," which is not a word I like too much, but which seems to be here to stay. (As long as you don't vague out and you can tell me *why* it's relatable, I might be able to handle it.) At other times, we feel completely outside of the text. Either of these situations—inside or outside—is worth examining. Your own relationship to the text may in some instances become a key component of literary analysis.

We must (metaphorically) step back from the text to consider the author's *purpose* and the author's *context*, which may involve the author's historical situation. Usually, if we understand an author's historical context or the original publication context of the text, for example, we are in a much better position to develop a meaningful literary analysis.

Take control of your curriculum: *Write a 300–500 word post to an imaginary online fanzine that specializes in the study of (or obsession with) your favorite book series, Netflix show, film, video game, or whatever. Now "translate" that post for a general interest audience. Write a separate 300–500 word article that expresses your same subject matter in language that would appeal to a broad general readership. Present these compositions side by side to your instructor in order to demonstrate your comprehension of* audience *and* rhetorical situation.

See Unit Nine Research in the Twenty-First Century for detailed information on the research paper composition process.

Essay Prompts

Level I: Analysis-Response

1. Offer a detailed analysis-response to the concept of "borrowing" as it is addressed in Lethem's article.
2. Analyze and respond to Lethem's article with a focus on the concept of "authenticity." Reflect on "authenticity," particularly as it is relevant to the music industry or art world. Why is "authenticity" important, and what does it mean?
3. How does Lethem's article address the issue of "cultural appropriation"? Analyze and respond to Lethem's article with a focus on the concept of "cultural appropriation."
4. What is the so-called "Fair Use" doctrine? How does Fair Use relate to Lethem's article?

Level II: Making Connections

1. What is the connection between brain plasticity and creativity? Investigate the concept of creativity and/or genius from a scientific standpoint.
2. How do digital and Internet technologies affect the issue of artistic influence and borrowing in the twenty-first century? Explore art forms that depend on digital technologies or borrowing. How have digital technologies expanded, sped up, or made possible these forms of borrowing (such as "sampling," for example).
3. Do Gen Z attitudes regarding artistic copyright and IP (intellectual property) differ from prior generations? How and why do Gen Z attitudes regarding copyright and IP (intellectual property) differ from prior generations, i.e. Baby Boomers?

Level III: Research

1. Has it become culturally acceptable for people to "appropriate" artistic productions as in *steal* or *obtain for personal use*? Why or why not? What are the issues that have arisen in regard to illegal taking in the Internet era? Examine the history of Napster and music piracy, or BitTorrent and film piracy. What issues remain relevant in the age of digital streaming?
2. Research the current state of copyright law, including the status of the so-called "fair use" doctrine. What contemporary controversies surround copyright protection?
3. What exactly is *plagiarism*? You have likely heard a great deal about plagiarism in your English and composition classes. Study the history of this concept. Has the definition of plagiarism changed over time? Do all world cultures share the same ideas regarding plagiarism? Is plagiarism ever a legal matter? What is the difference between "plagiarism" and "copyright infringement"? Why is plagiarism such a big deal in academia, the publishing industry, and/or other areas of commerce?
4. Examine Internet era "open" movements, especially as they pertain to copyright. Check out the non-profit CreativeCommons.org. What is the organization's mission and main activities? What is the "public domain"? What is "fair use"? Examine the history of copyright law and how it developed in the twentieth century. Take a position on the roles of copyright and the public domain in the twenty-first century.
5. Research the controversy surrounding William Styron's 1967 novel, *The Confessions of Nat Turner*. Explore allegations of cultural appropriation in this instance and explore other instances where critics have leveled a charge of cultural appropriation against an artist or institution.

Further Inquiry

Bergland, Christopher. "The Neurochemicals of Happiness." *Psychology Today*, 29 Nov. 2012. https://www.psychologytoday.com/us/blog/the-athletes-way/201211/the-neurochemicals-happiness.

Brenner, Grant Hilary. "Your Brain on Creativity." *Psychology Today*, 22 Feb. 2018, www.psychologytoday.com/us/blog/experimentations/201802/your-brain-creativity.

Carson, Shelley. "Creative Thinking and the Brain." *Harvard Health*, Dec. 2010, www.health.harvard.edu/newsletter_article/creative-thinking-and-the-brain.

Cherry, Kendra. "Understanding the Psychology of Creativity." *VeryWellMind*, 15 June 2019, https://www.verywellmind.com/what-is-creativity-p2-3986725.

Deamer, Kacey. "Genius: Can Anybody Be One?" *LiveScience.com*, 9 June 2016, https://www.livescience.com/55028-what-makes-a-genius.html.

DiSalvo, David. "Study Reveals How The Creative Brain Is Wired." *Forbes*, 19 Jan. 2018, www.forbes.com/sites/daviddisalvo/2018/01/19/study-shows-how-the-creative-brain-is-wired-differently.

Eliot, T.S. "Philip Massinger." *The Sacred Wood* (1921), https://www.bartleby.com/200/sw11.html.

Haridy, Rich. "The Neuroscience of Creativity: How the Brains of Innovators Are Wired Differently." *New Atlas*, 18 Jan. 2018, newatlas.com/creative-throught-brain-activity-networks/53025/.

Kaufman, Scott Barry. "The Neuroscience of Creativity: A Q&A with Anna Abraham." *Scientific American Blog Network*, 4 Jan. 2019, blogs.scientificamerican.com/beautiful-minds/the-neuroscience-of-creativity-a-q-a-with-anna-abraham/.

Kotler, Steven. "8 Steps to a World-Class Understanding of Creativity (and How to Hack It)." *StevenKotler.com*, https://www.stevenkotler.com/rabbithole/reiciendis-aut-perspiciatis-et-copy.

Kotler, Steven. "Flow States and Creativity." *Psychology Today*, 25 Feb. 2014. https://www.psychologytoday.com/us/blog/the-playing-field/201402/flow-states-and-creativity.

Laurinavicius, Tomas. "Adaptability: The True Mark of Genius." *HuffPost.com*, 17 Aug. 2016, updated 6 Dec. 2017, https://www.huffpost.com/entry/adaptability-the-true-mar_b_11543680.

Lebowitz, Shana. "8 Personality Traits of Highly Intelligent People (Backed by Science)." *Business Insider*, 21 July 2016, https://www.inc.com/business-insider/8-personality-traits-highly-intelligent-genius-people-share-according-to-science.html.

Newman, Tim. "The Neuroscience of Creativity." *Medical News Today*, 17 Feb. 2016, www.medicalnewstoday.com/articles/306611.

Ridley, Louise. "What's Inside the Brain of a Genius?" *BBC Science Focus Magazine*, 23 Sept.2010, https://www.sciencefocus.com/the-human-body/whats-inside-the-brain-of-a-genius/.

Robinson, Andrew. "Can We Define Genius?" *Psychology Today*, 30 Nov. 2010, https://www.psychologytoday.com/us/blog/sudden-genius/201011/can-we-define-genius.

Weiner, Eric. "Five Myths About Genius." *WashingtonPost.com*, 21 Oct. 2016, https://www.washingtonpost.com/opinions/five-myths-about-genius/2016/10/21/ffecc73c-96e0-11e6-9b7c-57290af48a49_story.html.

"What is Creativity?" Synopsis of Three Source Texts. California State University, Northridge, http://www.csun.edu/~vcpsy00h/creativity/define.htm.

Wickelgren, Ingrid. "How Do You Spot a Genius?" *Scientific American*, Blogs, 18 Oct. 2012, https://blogs.scientificamerican.com/streams-of-consciousness/how-do-you-spot-a-genius/.

Wilson, Tracy V. "How Geniuses Work." *HowStuffWorks.com*, 2005, https://people.howstuffworks.com/genius.htm.

Zaidel, Dahlia W. "Creativity, Brain and Art: Biological and Neurological Considerations." *Frontiers in Human Neuroscience*, 2 June 2014. U.S. National Library of Medicine, National Institutes of Health, https://www.ncbi.nlm.nih.gov/pmc/articles/PMC4041074/. doi: 10.3389/fnhum.2014.00389.

UNIT SIX

The Future of AI

In his book, *Emergence: The Connected Lives of Ants, Brains, Cities, and Software*, writer Steven Johnson draws an analogy between patterns in the natural world and the software methodology that computer scientists use to enable AI, or artificial intelligence. Although futurists, cultural critics, and scientists cannot agree whether AI will prove more productive or catastrophic for humankind, no one argues that changes in the twenty-first century will be anything less than profound. Some thinkers, including MIT physicist Max Tegmark, have gone so far as to question whether we are entering a new phase of human existence.

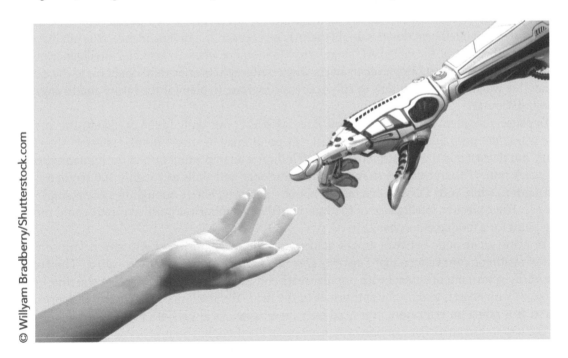

© Willyam Bradberry/Shutterstock.com

In *Life 3.0*, Tegmark imagines humanity moving toward a new evolutionary stage in which AI may live independently, designing its own hardware and software. The repercussions for humanity, needless to say, would be extensive. Such forms of artificial life do not yet exist. Increasingly, scientists and philosophers entertain the possibilities that AI can exist not only as a subservient form of intelligence (that is, in the service of humanity) but as an independent entity that may or may not, depending upon conditions, always act to serve our best interests.

The sci-fi scenarios that play out in popular culture from this basic premise are multi-various: the *Terminator* series (1984-2019), *Ex Machina* (2015) and *Her* (2013) are prime examples of Hollywood's dramatic take on the future of AI.

Are the real questions surrounding the future of AI so frightening as these popular narratives?

It is easy to dismiss such apocalyptic fears as fanciful, childish nightmares, and it is even easier to collapse into an attitude of, "Whatever will happen, will happen. I can't make a difference anyway." As one of my rock-n-roll heroes Joe Strummer noted, however, "The future is unwritten."

Tegmark believes it is important for philosophers and other humanists to become engaged in this important discourse. The future of AI is, in fact, unwritten. In the absence of a script, a national plan, or scientific guidelines, this future could turn out badly, according to Tegmark and others.

Large systems, or "self-organizing systems," as both Johnson and Tegmark point out, do not feature a blueprint of instructions which centrally direct collective behavior and machine learning. Each tiny part of a vast system may operate on a simple binary basis. The simple yes/no functionality of each bit can give rise to vast complexity. In an ant colony, the queen does not control or direct the behaviors of the colony. Only as a large system does the colony exhibit what we might term "intelligence." The queen herself has no intelligence whatsoever. None of the individual ants has intelligence. Only as a colony do they display complex behavioral patterns. This analogy illuminates one of the keys to AI and self-organizing systems.

The emergence of some form of non-biological intelligence seems inevitable at this point in the early twenty-first century. (Some experts argue that it has already occurred.) It is important to note that many highly educated and intelligent skeptics doubt that AI can ever achieve independence, true intelligence, or "free will." In other words, the fabled AI "singularity" (a moment when an artificial intelligence becomes self-aware) will never happen. However, in an era when philosophers offer valid doubts as to the existence of human free will, it is not a pointless or silly academic exercise to plan for the future and to engage this important discourse.

Let's pause a moment to take stock: How does AI affect your daily life? Very likely, the answer is: *in more ways than you realize.* Siri and Alexa, at this point, may be more "dumb assistant" than "smart assistant," but the fact that these assistants exist at all indicates an important turn in the human experience.

Tegmark notes, "Your synapses store all your knowledge and skills as roughly 100 terabytes' worth of information, while your DNA stores merely about a gigabyte, barely enough to store a single movie download." The collective intelligence of the Internet (the metaphorical beehive mind) could provide a starting point for a fundamental change in AI.

In drawing an analogy between an ant colony and the mechanisms of AI, Steven Johnson draws the sort of synthetic connections that *Engaging Discourse 2.0* encourages. A topic called "The Future of AI" can easily sprawl out of control with popular fears and groundless speculation. As you dive into this discourse, rely on experts and on the authorities in the field. You don't need to reinvent or fabricate this discourse. It is going on right now. You need only investigate. As always, it's best to find a "sub-focus" within the larger discourse. For example, you have probably thought about your own prospective career and the impact that AI and robotics will have on the job market. Unit six provides a great opportunity to explore the impact of AI on your own career field.

Seek out timely major research questions. For example: *How is AI employed to fight the spread of Covid-19 and other infectious epidemics? How is AI being employed in hospitals and in the medical field?* You can start with broad topics. Then you must narrow and focus.

AGI: Fact or Fiction?

In the following excerpt, Tegmark focuses on three stages of evolutionary development. The first stage involves "survive and replicate." The second involves "culture" wherein humans adapt to their surroundings and design their own "software," allowing us to learn language and preserve memory even beyond death. He proposes a third evolutionary stage, which he terms "Life 3.0." A life form, in this vision of the future, can "control its own destiny" by designing its own software and hardware, thus obtaining the godlike power to control its own evolutionary development. *Techno-skeptics* view AGI (artificial general intelligence) as extremely unlikely or only possible in the remote future. *Digital utopians* propose that AGI is likely happen within this century and believe that it will be beneficial to our evolution. Others propose that the rise of AGI will not have a good outcome for humanity.

"Life 3.0," writes Tegmark, "is the master of its own destiny, finally fully free from its evolutionary shackles."

What is AGI or "general AI"? What are the chances that AGI will arise in the twenty-first century? In what specific iterations is AGI most likely to develop? As always, instead of relying on Hollywood or popular culture for answers, we must seek credible authorities. What do the experts say?

Questions to Consider

Answer these questions as you read and annotate the text:

- What do physicists like Tegmark mean by the term "complexity"? What do computer scientists mean by the term "complexity"? What do composition instructors mean by "complexity"? (Is it ironic that the word "complexity" has so many shades of meaning?)
- What are "intelligent agents"?
- When it comes to what Tegmark calls Life 2.0, what does he mean by the metaphorical use of "software"? What are the best examples of human "software" under this metaphor?
- Does the concept of Life 3.0 strike you as science or science fiction? Why?
- "Fearing a rise of killer robots is like worrying about overpopulation on Mars." Who said this? The quotation is an articulation of what position on the AI debate?
- Note that the techno-skeptics are not opposed to AI, so what is their disagreement with the digital utopians (especially when it comes to AGI or *artificial general intelligence*)?
- In this first chapter from his book, Tegmark points to various other chapters to come. What are the topics he mentions for these upcoming chapters which do not appear in *Engaging Discourse 2.0*?

Max Tegmark, "Welcome to the Most Important Conversation of Our Time" (2017)

> Technology is giving life the potential to flourish like never before—or to self-destruct.
>
> —Future of Life Institute

Thirteen point eight billion years after its birth, our Universe has awoken and become aware of itself. From a small blue planet, tiny conscious parts of our Universe have begun gazing out into the cosmos with telescopes, repeatedly discovering that everything they thought existed is merely a small part of something grander: a solar system, a galaxy and a universe with over a hundred billion other galaxies arranged into an elaborate pattern of groups, clusters and superclusters. Although these self-aware stargazers disagree on many things, they tend to agree that these galaxies are beautiful and awe-inspiring.

But beauty is in the eye of the beholder, not in the laws of physics, so before our Universe awoke, there was no beauty. This makes our cosmic awakening all the more wonderful and worthy of celebrating: it transformed our Universe from a mindless zombie with no self-awareness into a living ecosystem harboring self-reflection, beauty and hope—and the pursuit of goals, meaning and purpose. Had our Universe never awoken, then, as far as I'm concerned, it would have been completely pointless—merely a gigantic waste of space. Should our Universe permanently go back to sleep due to some cosmic calamity or self-inflicted mishap, it will, alas, become meaningless.

On the other hand, things could get even better. We don't yet know whether we humans are the only stargazers in our cosmos, or even the first, but we've already learned enough about our Universe to know that it has the potential to wake up much more fully than it has thus far. Perhaps we're like that first faint glimmer of self-awareness you experienced when you began emerging from sleep this morning: a premonition of the much greater consciousness that would arrive once you opened your eyes and fully woke up. Perhaps life will spread throughout our cosmos and flourish for billions or trillions of years—and perhaps this will be because of decisions that we make here on our little planet during our lifetime.

A Brief History of Complexity

So how did this amazing awakening come about? It wasn't an isolated event, but merely one step in a relentless 13.8-billion-year process that's making our Universe ever more complex and interesting—and is continuing at an accelerating pace.

As a physicist, I feel fortunate to have gotten to spend much of the past quarter century helping to pin down our cosmic history, and it's been an amazing journey of discovery. Since the days when I was a graduate student, we've gone from arguing about whether our Universe is 10 or 20 billion years old to arguing about whether it's 13.7 or 13.8 billion years old, thanks to a combination of better telescopes, better computers and better understanding. We physicists still don't know for sure what caused our Big Bang or whether this was truly the beginning of everything or merely the sequel to an earlier stage. However, we've acquired a rather detailed understanding of what's happened since our Big Bang, thanks to an avalanche of high-quality measurements, so please let me take a few minutes to summarize 13.8 billion years of cosmic history.

In the beginning, there was light. In the first split second after our Big Bang, the entire part of space that our telescopes can in principle observe ("our observable Universe," or simply "our Universe" for short) was much hotter and brighter than the core of our Sun and it expanded rapidly. Although this may sound spectacular, it was also dull in the sense that our Universe contained nothing but a lifeless, dense, hot and boringly uniform soup of elementary particles. Things looked pretty much the same everywhere, and the only interesting structure consisted of faint random-looking sound waves that made the soup about 0.001% denser in some places. These faint waves are widely believed to have originated as so-called quantum fluctuations, because Heisenberg's uncertainty principle of quantum mechanics forbids anything from being completely boring and uniform.

As our Universe expanded and cooled, it grew more interesting as its particles combined into ever more complex objects. During the first split second, the strong nuclear force grouped quarks into protons (hydrogen nuclei) and neutrons, some of which in turn fused into helium nuclei within a few minutes. About 400,000 years later, the electromagnetic force grouped these nuclei with electrons to make the first atoms. As our Universe kept expanding, these atoms gradually cooled into a cold dark gas, and the darkness of this first night lasted for about 100 million years. This long night gave rise to our cosmic dawn when the gravitational force succeeded in amplifying those fluctuations in the gas, pulling atoms together to form the first stars and galaxies. These first stars generated heat and light by fusing hydrogen into heavier atoms such as carbon, oxygen and silicon. When these stars died, many of the atoms they'd created were recycled into the cosmos and formed planets around second-generation stars.

At some point, a group of atoms became arranged into a complex pattern that could both maintain and replicate itself. So soon there were two copies, and the number kept doubling. It takes only forty doublings to make a trillion, so this first self-replicator soon became a force to be reckoned with. Life had arrived.

The Three Stages of Life

The question of how to define life is notoriously controversial. Competing definitions abound, some of which include highly specific requirements such as being composed of cells, which might disqualify both future intelligent machines and extraterrestrial civilizations. Since we don't want to limit our thinking about the future of life to the species we've encountered so far, let's instead define life very broadly, simply as a process that can retain its complexity and replicate. What's replicated isn't matter (made of atoms) but information (made of bits) specifying how the atoms are arranged. When a bacterium makes a copy of its DNA, no new atoms are created, but a new set of atoms are arranged in the same pattern as the original, thereby copying the information. In other words, we can think of life as a self-replicating information-processing system whose information (software) determines both its behavior and the blueprints for its hardware.

Like our Universe itself, life gradually grew more complex and interesting,[1] and as I'll now explain, I find it helpful to classify life forms into three levels of sophistication: Life 1.0, 2.0 and 3.0. I've summarized these three levels in figure 1.1.

It's still an open question how, when and where life first appeared in our Universe, but there is strong evidence that here on Earth life first appeared about 4 billion years ago. Before long, our planet was teeming with a diverse panoply of life forms. The most successful ones, which soon outcompeted the rest, were able to react to their environment in some way. Specifically, they were what computer scientists call "intelligent agents": entities that collect information about their environment from sensors and then process this information to decide how to act back on their environment. This can include highly complex

---

1 Why did life grow more complex? Evolution rewards life that's complex enough to predict and exploit regularities in its environment, so in a more complex environment, more complex and intelligent life will evolve. Now this smarter life creates a more complex environment for competing life forms, which in turn evolve to be more complex, eventually creating an ecosystem of extremely complex life.

> Why, according to Tegmark, is the question of how to define "life" controversial? How does Tegmark himself define "life"?

information processing, such as when you use information from your eyes and ears to decide what to say in a conversation. But it can also involve hardware and software that's quite simple.

For example, many bacteria have a sensor measuring the sugar concentration in the liquid around them and can swim using propeller-shaped structures called flagella. The hardware linking the sensor to the flagella might implement the following simple but useful algorithm: "If my sugar concentration sensor reports a lower value than a couple of seconds ago, then reverse the rotation of my flagella so that I change direction."

You've learned how to speak and countless other skills. Bacteria, on the other hand, aren't great learners. Their DNA specifies not only the design of their hardware, such as sugar sensors and flagella, but also the design of their software. They never learn to swim toward sugar; instead, that algorithm was hard-coded into their DNA from the start. There was of course a learning process of sorts, but it didn't take place during the lifetime of that particular bacterium. Rather, it occurred during the preceding evolution of that species of bacteria, through a slow trial-and-error process spanning many generations,

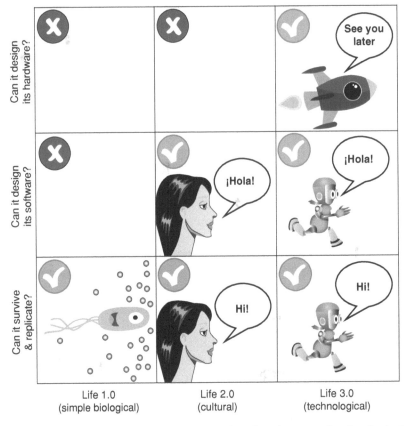

Figure 1.1: The three stages of life: biological evolution, cultural evolution and technological evolution. Life 1.0 is unable to redesign either its hardware or its software during its lifetime: both are determined by its DNA, and change only through evolution over many generations. In contrast, Life 2.0 can redesign much of its software: humans can learn complex new skills—for example, languages, sports and professions—and can fundamentally update their worldview and goals. Life 3.0, which doesn't yet exist on Earth, can dramatically redesign not only its software, but its hardware as well, rather than having to wait for it to gradually evolve over generations.

where natural selection favored those random DNA mutations that improved sugar consumption. Some of these mutations helped by improving the design of flagella and other hardware, while other mutations improved the bacterial information-processing system that implements the sugar-finding algorithm and other software.

Such bacteria are an example of what I'll call "Life 1.0": *life where both the hardware and software are evolved rather than designed.* You and I, on the other hand, are examples of "Life 2.0": *life whose hardware is evolved, but whose software is largely designed.* By your software, I mean all the algorithms and knowledge that you use to process the information from your senses and decide what to do—everything from the ability to recognize your friends when you see them to your ability to walk, read, write, calculate, sing and tell jokes.

You weren't able to perform any of those tasks when you were born, so all this software got programmed into your brain later through the process we call learning. Whereas your childhood curriculum is largely designed by your family and teachers, who decide what you should learn, you gradually gain more power to design your own software. Perhaps your school allows you to select a foreign language: Do you want to install a software module into your brain that enables you to speak French, or one that enables you to speak Spanish? Do you want to learn to play tennis or chess? Do you want to study to become a chef, a lawyer or a pharmacist? Do you want to learn more about artificial intelligence (AI) and the future of life by reading a book about it?

This ability of Life 2.0 to design its software enables it to be much smarter than Life 1.0. High intelligence requires both lots of hardware (made of atoms) and lots of software (made of bits). The fact that most of our human hardware is added after birth (through growth) is useful, since our ultimate size isn't limited by the width of our mom's birth canal. In the same way, the fact that most of our human software is added after birth (through learning) is useful, since our ultimate intelligence isn't limited by how much information can be transmitted to us at conception via our DNA, 1.0-style. I weigh about twenty-five times more than when I was born, and the synaptic connections that link the neurons in my brain can store about a hundred thousand times more information than the DNA that I was born with. Your synapses store all your knowledge and skills as roughly 100 terabytes' worth of information, while your DNA stores merely about a gigabyte, barely enough to store a single movie download. So it's physically impossible for an infant to be born speaking perfect English and ready to ace her college entrance exams: there's no way the information could have been preloaded into her brain, since the main information module she got from her parents (her DNA) lacks sufficient information-storage capacity.

The ability to design its software enables Life 2.0 to be not only smarter than Life 1.0, but also more flexible. If the environment changes, 1.0 can only adapt by slowly evolving over many generations. Life 2.0, on the other hand, can adapt almost instantly, via a software update. For example, bacteria frequently encountering antibiotics may evolve drug resistance over many generations, but an individual bacterium won't change its behavior at all; in contrast, a girl learning that she has a peanut allergy will immediately change her behavior to start avoiding peanuts. This flexibility gives Life 2.0 an even greater edge at the population level: even though the information in our human DNA hasn't evolved dramatically over the past fifty thousand years, the information collectively stored in our brains, books and computers has exploded. By installing a software module enabling us to communicate through sophisticated spoken language, we ensured that the most useful information stored in one person's brain could get copied to other brains, potentially surviving even after the original brain died. By installing a software module enabling us to read and write, we became able to store and share vastly more information than people could memorize. By developing brain software capable of producing technology (i.e., by studying science and engineering), we enabled much of the world's information to be accessed by many of the world's humans with just a few clicks.

This flexibility has enabled Life 2.0 to dominate Earth. Freed from its genetic shackles, humanity's combined knowledge has kept growing at an accelerating pace as each breakthrough enabled the next: language, writing, the printing press, modern science, computers, the internet, etc. This ever-faster cultural evolution of our shared software has emerged as the dominant force shaping our human future, rendering our glacially slow biological evolution almost irrelevant.

Yet despite the most powerful technologies we have today, all life forms we know of remain fundamentally limited by their biological hardware. None can live for a million years, memorize all of Wikipedia, understand all known science or enjoy spaceflight without a spacecraft. None can transform our largely lifeless cosmos into a diverse biosphere that will flourish for billions or trillions of years, enabling our Universe to finally fulfill its potential and wake up fully. All this requires life to undergo a final upgrade, to Life 3.0, which can design not only its software but also its hardware. In other words, Life 3.0 is the master of its own destiny, finally fully free from its evolutionary shackles.

The boundaries between the three stages of life are slightly fuzzy. If bacteria are Life 1.0 and humans are Life 2.0, then you might classify mice as 1.1: they can learn many things, but not enough to develop language or invent the internet. Moreover, because they lack language, what they learn gets largely lost when they die, not passed on to the next generation. Similarly, you might argue that today's humans should count as Life 2.1: we can perform minor hardware upgrades such as implanting artificial teeth, knees and pacemakers, but nothing as dramatic as getting ten times taller or acquiring a thousand times bigger brain.

In summary, we can divide the development of life into three stages, distinguished by life's ability to design itself:

- Life 1.0 (biological stage): evolves its hardware and software
- Life 2.0 (cultural stage): evolves its hardware, designs much of its software
- Life 3.0 (technological stage): designs its hardware and software

After 13.8 billion years of cosmic evolution, development has accelerated dramatically here on Earth: Life 1.0 arrived about 4 billion years ago, Life 2.0 (we humans) arrived about a hundred millennia ago, and many AI researchers think that Life 3.0 may arrive during the coming century, perhaps even during our lifetime, spawned by progress in AI. What will happen, and what will this mean for us? That's the topic of this book.

Controversies

This question is wonderfully controversial, with the world's leading AI researchers disagreeing passionately not only in their forecasts, but also in their emotional reactions, which range from confident optimism to serious concern. They don't even have consensus on short-term questions about AI's economic, legal and military impact, and their disagreements grow when we expand the time horizon and ask about *artificial general intelligence* (AGI)—especially about AGI reaching human level and beyond, enabling Life 3.0. *General intelligence* can accomplish virtually any goal, including learning, in contrast to, say, the narrow intelligence of a chess-playing program.

Interestingly, the controversy about Life 3.0 centers around not one but two separate questions: when and what? When (if ever) will it happen, and what will it mean for humanity? The way I see it, there are three distinct schools of thought that all need to be taken seriously, because they each include a number of world-leading experts. As illustrated in figure 1.2, I think of them as *digital utopians, techno-skeptics* and *members of the beneficial-AI movement*, respectively. Please let me introduce you to some of their most eloquent champions.

Digital Utopians

When I was a kid, I imagined that billionaires exuded pomposity and arrogance. When I first met Larry Page at Google in 2008, he totally shattered these stereotypes. Casually dressed in jeans and a remarkably ordinary-looking shirt, he would have blended right in at an MIT picnic. His thoughtful soft-spoken style and his friendly smile made me feel relaxed rather than intimidated talking with him. On July 18, 2015, we ran into each other at a party in Napa Valley thrown by Elon Musk and his then wife, Talulah, and got into a conversation about the scatological interests of our kids. I recommended the profound literary classic *The Day My Butt Went Psycho*, by Andy Griffiths, and Larry ordered it on the spot. I struggled to remind myself that he might go down in history as the most influential human ever to have lived: my guess is that if superintelligent digital life engulfs our Universe in my lifetime, it will be because of Larry's decisions.

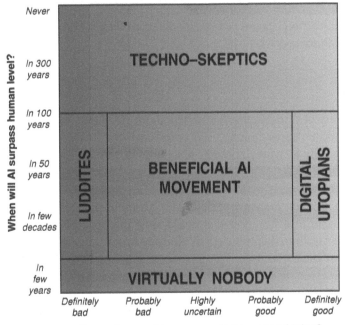

Figure 1.2: Most controversies surrounding strong artificial intelligence (that can match humans on any cognitive task) center around two questions: When (if ever) will it happen, and will it be a good thing for humanity? Techno-skeptics and digital utopians agree that we shouldn't worry, but for very different reasons: the former are convinced that human-level artificial general intelligence (AGI) won't happen in the foreseeable future, while the latter think it will happen but is virtually guaranteed to be a good thing. The beneficial-AI movement feels that concern is warranted and useful, because AI-safety research and discussion now increases the chances of a good outcome. Luddites are convinced of a bad outcome and oppose AI. This figure is partly inspired by Tim Urban. (The AI Revolution: Our Immortality or Extinction?)

With our wives, Lucy and Meia, we ended up having dinner together and discussing whether machines would necessarily be conscious, an issue that he argued was a red herring. Later that night, after cocktails, a long and spirited debate ensued between him and Elon about the future of AI and what should be done. As we entered the wee hours of the morning, the circle of bystanders and kibitzers kept growing. Larry gave a passionate defense of the position I like to think of as *digital utopianism:* that digital life is the natural and desirable next step in the cosmic evolution and that if we let digital minds be free rather than try to stop or enslave them, the outcome is almost certain to be good. I view Larry as the most influential exponent of digital utopianism. He argued that if life is ever going to spread throughout our Galaxy and beyond, which he thought it should, then it would need to do so in digital form. His main concerns were that AI paranoia would delay the digital utopia and/or cause a military takeover of AI that would fall foul of Google's "Don't be evil" slogan. Elon kept pushing back and asking Larry to clarify details of his arguments, such as why he was so confident that digital life wouldn't destroy everything we care about. At times, Larry accused Elon of being "specieist": treating certain life forms as inferior just because they were silicon-based rather than carbon-based. We'll return to explore these interesting issues and arguments in detail, starting in chapter 4.

Although Larry seemed outnumbered that warm summer night by the pool, the digital utopianism that he so eloquently championed has many prominent supporters. Roboticist and futurist Hans Moravec inspired a whole generation of digital utopians with his classic 1988 book *Mind Children*, a tradition continued and refined by inventor Ray Kurzweil. Richard Sutton, one of the pioneers of the AI subfield known as reinforcement learning, gave a passionate defense of digital utopianism at our Puerto Rico conference that I'll tell you about shortly.

Techno-skeptics

Another prominent group of thinkers aren't worried about AI either, but for a completely different reason: they think that building super-human AGI is so hard that it won't happen for hundreds of years, and therefore view it as silly to worry about it now. I think of this as the *techno-skeptic* position, eloquently articulated by Andrew Ng: "Fearing a rise of killer robots is like worrying about overpopulation on Mars." Andrew is the chief scientist at Baidu, China's Google, and he recently repeated this argument when I spoke with him at a conference in Boston. He also told me that he felt that worrying about AI risk was a potentially harmful distraction that could slow the progress of AI. Similar sentiments have been articulated by other techno-skeptics such as Rodney Brooks, the former MIT professor behind the Roomba robotic vacuum cleaner and the Baxter industrial robot. I find it interesting that although the digital utopians and the techno-skeptics agree that we shouldn't worry about AI, they agree on little else. Most of the utopians think human-level AGI might happen within the next twenty to a hundred years, which the techno-skeptics dismiss as uninformed pie-in-the-sky dreaming, often deriding the prophesied singularity as "the rapture of the geeks." When I met Rodney Brooks at a birthday party in December 2014, he told me that he was 100% sure it wouldn't happen in my lifetime. "Are you sure you don't mean 99%?," I asked in a follow-up email, to which he replied, "No wimpy 99%. 100%. Just isn't going to happen."

The Beneficial-AI Movement

When I first met Stuart Russell in a Paris café in June 2014, he struck me as the quintessential British gentleman. Eloquent, thoughtful and soft-spoken, but with an adventurous glint in his eyes, he seemed to me a modern incarnation of Phileas Fogg, my childhood hero from Jules Verne's classic 1873 novel, *Around the World in 80 Days*. Although he was one of the most famous AI researchers alive, having co-authored the standard textbook on the subject, his modesty and warmth soon put me at ease.

> Why has so-called Life 2.0 been able to dominate Earth?

He explained to me how progress in AI had persuaded him that human-level AGI this century was a real possibility and, although he was hopeful, a good outcome wasn't guaranteed. There were crucial questions that we needed to answer first, and they were so hard that we should start researching them now, so that we'd have the answers ready by the time we needed them.

Today, Stuart's views are rather mainstream, and many groups around the world are pursuing the sort of AI-safety research that he advocates. But this wasn't always the case. An article in *The Washington Post* referred to 2015 as the year that AI-safety research went mainstream. Before that, talk of AI risks was often misunderstood by mainstream AI researchers and dismissed as Luddite scaremongering aimed at impeding AI progress. As we'll explore in chapter 5, concerns similar to Stuart's were first articulated over half a century ago by computer pioneer Alan Turing and mathematician Irving J. Good, who worked with Turing to crack German codes during World War II. In the past decade, research on such topics was mainly carried out by a handful of independent thinkers who weren't professional AI researchers, for example Eliezer Yudkowsky, Michael Vassar and Nick Bostrom. Their work had little effect on most mainstream AI researchers, who tended to focus on their day-to-day tasks of making AI systems more intelligent rather than on contemplating the long-term consequences of success. Of the AI researchers I knew who did harbor some concern, many hesitated to voice it out of fear of being perceived as alarmist technophobes.

I felt that this polarized situation needed to change, so that the full AI community could join and influence the conversation about how to build beneficial AI. Fortunately, I wasn't alone. In the spring of 2014, I'd founded a nonprofit organization called the Future of Life Institute (FLI; http://futureoflife.org) together with my wife, Meia, my physicist friend Anthony Aguirre, Harvard grad student Viktoriya Krakovna and Skype founder Jaan Tallinn. Our goal was simple: to help ensure that the future of life existed and would be as awesome as possible. Specifically, we felt that technology was giving life the power either to flourish like never before or to self-destruct, and we preferred the former.

Our first meeting was a brainstorming session at our house on March 15, 2014, with about thirty students, professors and other thinkers from the Boston area. There was broad consensus that although we should pay attention to biotech, nuclear weapons and climate change, our first major goal should be to help make AI-safety research mainstream. My MIT physics colleague Frank Wilczek, who won a Nobel Prize for helping figure out how quarks work, suggested that we start by writing an op-ed to draw attention to the issue and make it harder to ignore. I reached out to Stuart Russell (whom I hadn't yet met) and to my physics colleague Stephen Hawking, both of whom agreed to join me and Frank as co-authors. Many edits later, our op-ed was rejected by *The New York Times* and many other U.S. newspapers, so we posted it on my *Huffington Post* blog account. To my delight, Arianna Huffington herself emailed and said, "thrilled to have it! We'll post at #1!," and this placement at the top of the front page triggered a wave of media coverage of AI safety that lasted for the rest of the year, with Elon Musk, Bill Gates and other tech leaders chiming in. Nick Bostrom's book *Super-intelligence* came out that fall and further fueled the growing public debate.

The next goal of our FLI beneficial-AI campaign was to bring the world's leading AI researchers to a conference where misunderstandings could be cleared up, consensus could be forged, and constructive plans could be made. We knew that it would be difficult to persuade such an illustrious crowd to come to a conference organized by outsiders they didn't know, especially given the controversial topic, so we tried as hard as we could: we banned media from attending, we located it in a beach resort in January (in Puerto Rico), we made it free (thanks to the generosity of Jaan Tallinn), and we gave it the most non-alarmist title we could come up with: "The Future of AI: Opportunities and Challenges." Most importantly, we teamed up with Stuart Russell, thanks to whom we were able to grow the organizing committee to include a group of AI leaders from both academia and industry—including Demis Hassabis from Google's DeepMind, who went on to show that AI can beat humans even at the game of Go. The more I got to know Demis, the more I realized that he had ambition not only to make AI powerful, but also to make it beneficial.

The result was a remarkable meeting of minds. The AI researchers were joined by top economists, legal scholars, tech leaders (including Elon Musk) and other thinkers (including Vernor Vinge, who coined the term "singularity," which is the focus of chapter 4). The outcome surpassed even our most optimistic expectations. Perhaps it was a combination of the sunshine and the wine, or perhaps it was just that the time was right: despite the controversial topic, a remarkable consensus emerged, which we codified in an open letter[2] that ended up getting signed by over eight thousand people, including a veritable who's who in AI. The gist of the letter was that the goal of AI should be redefined: the goal should be to create not undirected intelligence, but beneficial intelligence. The letter also mentioned a detailed list of research topics that the conference participants agreed would further this goal. The beneficial-AI movement had started going mainstream. We'll follow its subsequent progress later in the book. (This open letter, "Research Priorities for Robust and Beneficial Artificial Intelligence," can be found at http://futureoflife.org/ai-open-letter/.)

Another important lesson from the conference was this: the questions raised by the success of AI aren't merely intellectually fascinating; they're also morally crucial, because our choices can potentially affect the entire future of life. The moral significance of humanity's past choices were sometimes great, but always limited: we've recovered even from the greatest plagues, and even the grandest empires eventually crumbled. Past generations knew that as surely as the Sun would rise tomorrow, so would tomorrow's humans, tackling perennial scourges such as poverty, disease and war. But some of the Puerto Rico speakers argued that this time might be different: for the first time, they said, we might build technology powerful enough to permanently end these scourges—or to end humanity itself. We might create societies that flourish like never before, on Earth and perhaps beyond, or a Kafkaesque global surveillance state so powerful that it could never be toppled.

Misconceptions

When I left Puerto Rico, I did so convinced that the conversation we had there about the future of AI needs to continue, because it's the most important conversation of our time.[2] It's the conversation about the collective future of all of us, so it shouldn't be limited to AI researchers. That's why I wrote this book: I wrote it in the hope that you, my dear reader, will join this conversation. What sort of future do you want? Should we develop lethal autonomous weapons? What would you like to happen with job automation? What career advice would you give today's kids? Do you prefer new jobs replacing the old ones, or a jobless society where everyone enjoys a life of leisure and machine-produced wealth? Further down the road, would you like us to create Life 3.0 and spread it through our cosmos? Will we control intelligent machines or will they control us? Will intelligent machines replace us, coexist with us or merge with us? What will it mean to be human in the age of artificial intelligence? What would you like it to mean, and how can we make the future be that way?

---

2 The AI conversation is important in terms of both urgency and impact. In comparison with climate change, which might wreak havoc in fifty to two hundred years, many experts expect AI to have greater impact within decades—and to potentially give us technology for mitigating climate change. In comparison with wars, terrorism, unemployment, poverty, migration and social justice issues, the rise of AI will have greater overall impact—indeed, we'll explore in this book how it can dominate what happens with all these issues, for better or for worse.

The goal of this book is to help you join this conversation. As I mentioned, there are fascinating controversies where the world's leading experts disagree. But I've also seen many examples of boring pseudo-controversies in which people misunderstand and talk past each other. To help ourselves focus on the interesting controversies and open questions, not on the misunderstandings, let's start by clearing up some of the most common misconceptions.

There are many competing definitions in common use for terms such as "life," "intelligence" and "consciousness," and many misconceptions come from people not realizing that they're using a word in two different ways. To make sure that you and I don't fall into this trap, I've put a cheat sheet in table 1.1 showing how I use key terms in this book. Some of these definitions will only be properly introduced and explained in later chapters. Please note that I'm not claiming that my definitions are better than anyone else's—I simply want to avoid confusion by being clear on what I mean. You'll see that I generally go for broad definitions that avoid anthropocentric bias and can be applied to machines as well as humans. Please read the cheat sheet now, and come back and check it later if you find yourself puzzled by how I use one of its words—especially in chapters 4–8.

Terminology Cheat Sheet	
Life	Process that can retain its complexity and replicate
Life 1.0	Life that evolves its hardware and software (biological stage)
Life 2.0	Life that evolves its hardware but designs much of its software (cultural stage)
Life 3.0	Life that designs its hardware and software (technological stage)
Intelligence	Ability to accomplish complex goals
Artificial Intelligence (AI)	Non-biological intelligence
Narrow intelligence	Ability to accomplish a narrow set of goals, e.g., play chess or drive a car
General intelligence	Ability to accomplish virtually any goal, including learning
Universal intelligence	Ability to acquire general intelligence given access to data and resources
[Human-level] Artificial General Intelligence (AGI)	Ability to accomplish any cognitive task at least as well as humans
Human-level AI	AGI
Strong AI	AGI
Superintelligence	General intelligence far beyond human level
Civilization	Interacting group of intelligent life forms
Consciousness	Subjective experience
Qualia	Individual instances of subjective experience
Ethics	Principles that govern how we should behave
Teleology	Explanation of things in terms of their goals or purposes rather than their causes

Goal-oriented behavior	Behavior more easily explained via its effect than via its cause
Having a goal	Exhibiting goal-oriented behavior
Having purpose	Serving goals of one's own or of another entity
Friendly AI	Superintelligence whose goals are aligned with ours
Cyborg	Human-machine hybrid
Intelligence explosion	Recursive self-improvement rapidly leading to superintelligence
Singularity	Intelligence explosion
Universe	The region of space from which light has had time to reach us during the 13.8 billion years since our Big Bang

Table 6.1: Many misunderstanding about AI are caused by people using the words above to mean different things. Here's what I take them to mean in this book. (Some of these definitions will only be properly introduced and explained in later chapters.)

In addition to confusion over terminology, I've also seen many AI conversations get derailed by simple misconceptions. Let's clear up the most common ones.

Timeline Myths

The first one regards the timeline from figure 1.2: how long will it take until machines greatly supersede human-level AGI? Here, a common misconception is that we know the answer with great certainty.

One popular myth is that we know we'll get superhuman AGI this century. In fact, history is full of technological over-hyping. Where are those fusion power plants and flying cars we were promised we'd have by now? AI too has been repeatedly over-hyped in the past, even by some of the founders of the field: for example, John McCarthy (who coined the term "artificial intelligence"), Marvin Minsky, Nathaniel Rochester and Claude Shannon wrote this overly optimistic forecast about what could be accomplished during two months with stone-age computers: "We propose that a 2 month, 10 man study of artificial intelligence be carried out during the summer of 1956 at Dartmouth College ... An attempt will be made to find how to make machines use language, form abstractions and concepts, solve kinds of problems now reserved for humans, and improve themselves. We think that a significant advance can be made in one or more of these problems if a carefully selected group of scientists work on it together for a summer."

On the other hand, a popular counter-myth is that we know we *won't* get superhuman AGI this century. Researchers have made a wide range of estimates for how far we are from superhuman AGI, but we certainly can't say with great confidence that the probability is zero this century, given the dismal track record of such techno-skeptic predictions. For example, Ernest Rutherford, arguably the greatest nuclear physicist of his time, said in 1933—less than twenty-four hours before Leo Szilard's invention of the nuclear chain reaction—that nuclear energy was "moonshine," and in 1956 Astronomer Royal Richard Woolley called talk about space travel "utter bilge." The most extreme form of this myth is that superhuman AGI will never arrive because it's physically impossible. However, physicists know that a brain consists of quarks and electrons arranged to act as a powerful computer, and that there's no law of physics preventing us from building even more intelligent quark blobs.

There have been a number of surveys asking AI research-ers how many years from now they think we'll have human-level AGI with at least 50% probability, and all these surveys have die same conclusion: the world's leading experts disagree, so we simply don't know. For example, in such a poll of the AI researchers at the Puerto Rico AI conference, the average (median) answer was by the year 2055, but some researchers guessed hundreds of years or more.

There's also a related myth that people who worry about AI think it's only a few years away. In fact, most people on record worrying about superhuman AGI guess it's still at least decades away. But they argue that as long as we're not 100% *sure* that it won't happen this century, it's smart to start safety research now to prepare for the eventuality. As we'll see in this book, many of the safety problems are so hard that they may take decades to solve, so it's prudent to start re-searching them now rather than the night before some programmers drinking Red Bull decide to switch on human-level AGI.

> When it comes to AI and AGI, what are the most prevalent myths that exists nowadays, in your view? What are the corresponding facts that Tegmark cites to dispel the myth(s)?

Controversy Myths

Another common misconception is that the only people harboring concerns about AI and advocating AI-safety research are Luddites who don't know much about AI. When Stuart Russell mentioned this during his Puerto Rico talk, the audience laughed loudly. A related misconception is that supporting AI-safety research is hugely controversial. In fact, to support a modest investment in AI-safety research, people don't need to be convinced that risks are high, merely non-negligible, just as a modest investment in home insurance is justified by a non-negligible probability of the home burning down.

My personal analysis is that the media have made the AI-safety debate seem more controversial than it really is. After all, fear sells, and articles using out-of-context quotes to proclaim imminent doom can generate more clicks than nuanced and balanced ones. As a result, two people who only know about each other's positions from media quotes are likely to think they disagree more than they really do. For example, a techno-skeptic whose only knowledge about Bill Gates' position comes from a British tabloid may mistakenly think he believes superintelligence to be imminent. Similarly, someone in the beneficial-AI movement who knows nothing about Andrew Ng's position except his above-mentioned quote about overpopulation on Mars may mistakenly think he doesn't care about AI safety. In fact, I personally know that he does—the crux is simply that because his timeline estimates are longer, he naturally tends to pri-oritize short-term AI challenges over long-term ones.

Myths About What the Risks Are

I rolled my eyes when I saw this headline in the *Daily Mail:* "Stephen Hawking Warns That Rise of Robots May Be Disastrous for Mankind." I've lost count of how many similar articles I've seen. Typically, they're accompanied by an evil-looking robot carrying a weapon, and suggest that we should worry about robots rising up and killing us because they've become conscious and/or evil. On a lighter note, such articles are actually rather impressive, because they succinctly summarize the scenario that my AI colleagues *don't* worry about. That scenario combines as many as three separate misconceptions: concern about *consciousness, evil* and *robots,* respectively.

If you drive down the road, you have a subjective experience of colors, sounds, etc. But does a self-driving car have a subjective experience? Does it feel like anything at all to be a self-driving car, or is it like an unconscious zombie without any subjective experience? Although this mystery of consciousness is interesting in its own right, and we'll devote chapter 8 to it, it's irrelevant to AI risk. If you get struck by a driverless car, it makes no difference to you whether it subjectively feels conscious. In the same way, what will affect us humans is what superintelligent AI *does*, not how it subjectively feels.

The fear of machines turning evil is another red herring. The real worry isn't malevolence, but competence. A superintelligent AI is by definition very good at attaining its goals, whatever they may be, so we need to ensure that its goals are aligned with ours. You're probably not an ant hater who steps on ants out of malice, but if you're in charge of a hydroelectric green energy project and there's an anthill in the region to be flooded, too bad for the ants. The beneficial-AI movement wants to avoid placing humanity in the position of those ants.

The consciousness misconception is related to the myth that machines can't have goals. Machines can obviously have goals in the narrow sense of exhibiting goal-oriented behavior: the behavior of a heat-seeking missile is most economically explained as a goal to hit a target. If you feel threatened by a machine whose goals are misaligned with yours, then it's precisely its goals in this narrow sense that trouble you, not whether the machine is conscious and experiences a sense of purpose. If that heat-seeking missile were chasing you, you probably wouldn't exclaim "I'm not worried, because machines can't have goals!"

I sympathize with Rodney Brooks and other robotics pioneers who feel unfairly demonized by scare-mongering tabloids, because some journalists seem obsessively fixated on robots and adorn many of their articles with evil-looking metal monsters with shiny red eyes. In fact, the main concern of the beneficial-AI movement isn't with robots but with intelligence itself: specifically, intelligence whose goals are misaligned with ours. To cause us trouble, such misaligned intelligence needs no robotic body, merely an internet connection—we'll explore in chapter 4 how this may enable outsmarting financial markets, out-inventing human researchers, out-manipulating human leaders and developing weapons we cannot even understand. Even if building robots were physically impossible, a super-intelligent and super-wealthy AI could easily pay or manipulate myriad humans to unwittingly do its bidding, as in William Gibson's science fiction novel *Neuromancer*.

The robot misconception is related to the myth that machines can't control humans. Intelligence enables control: humans control tigers not because we're stronger, but because we're smarter. This means that if we cede our position as smartest on our planet, it's possible that we might also cede control.

Figure 1.5 summarizes all of these common misconceptions, so that we can dispense with them once and for all and focus our discussions with friends and colleagues on the many legitimate controversies—which, as we'll see, there's no shortage of!

The Road Ahead

In the rest of this book, you and I will explore together the future of life with AI. Let's navigate this rich and multifaceted topic in an organized way by first exploring the full story of life conceptually and chronologically, and then exploring goals, meaning and what actions to take to create the future we want.

In chapter 2, we explore the foundations of intelligence and how seemingly dumb matter can be rearranged to remember, compute and learn. As we proceed into the future, our story branches out into many scenarios defined by the answers to certain key questions. Figure 1.6 summarizes key questions we'll encounter as we march forward in time, to potentially ever more advanced AI.

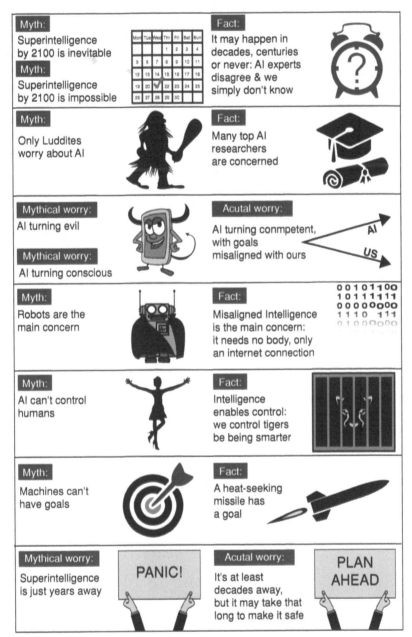

Figure 1.5:   Common myths about superintelligent AI.

Right now, we face the choice of whether to start an AI arms race, and questions about how to make tomorrow's AI systems bug-free and robust. If AI's economic impact keeps growing, we also have to decide how to modernize our laws and what career advice to give kids so that they can avoid soon-to-be-automated jobs. We explore such short-term questions in chapter 3.

If AI progress continues to human levels, then we also need to ask ourselves how to ensure that it's beneficial, and whether we can or should create a leisure society that flourishes without jobs. This also raises the question of whether an intelligence explosion or slow-but-steady growth can propel AGI far beyond human levels. We explore a wide range of such scenarios in chapter 4 and investigate the spectrum of possibilities for the aftermath in chapter 5, ranging from arguably dystopic to arguably utopic. Who's in charge—humans, AI or cyborgs? Are humans treated well or badly? Are we replaced and, if so, do we perceive our replacements as conquerors or worthy descendants? I'm very curious about which of the chapter 5 scenarios you personally prefer! I've set up a website, http://AgeOfAi.org, where you can share your views and join the conversation.

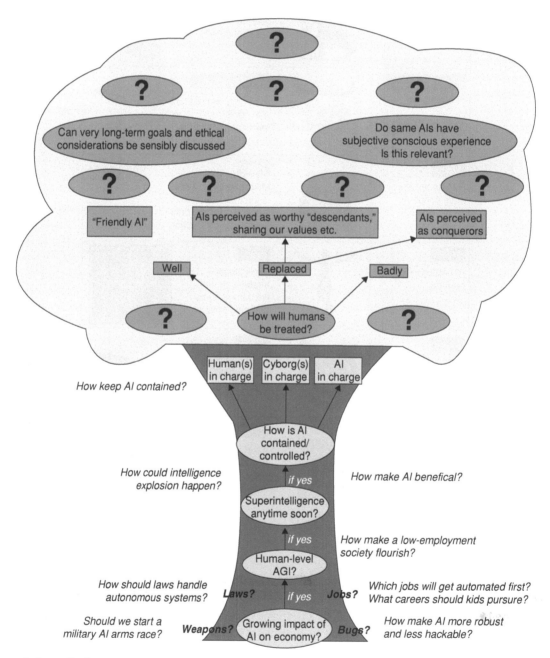

Figure 1.6: Which AI questions are interesting depends on how advanced AI gets and which branch our future takes.

Finally, we forge billions of years into the future in chapter 6 where we can, ironically, draw stronger conclusions than in the previous chapters, as the ultimate limits of life in our cosmos are set not by intelligence but by the laws of physics.

After concluding our exploration of the history of intelligence, we'll devote the remainder of the book to considering what future to aim for and how to get there. To be able to link cold facts to questions of purpose and meaning, we explore the physical basis of goals in chapter 7 and consciousness in chapter 8. Finally, in the epilogue, we explore what can be done right now to help create the future we want.

In case you're a reader who likes skipping around, most chapters are relatively self-contained once you've digested the terminology and definitions from this first chapter and the beginning of the next one. If you're an AI researcher, you can optionally skip all of chapter 2 except for its initial intelligence definitions. If you're new to AI, chapters 2 and 3 will give you the arguments for why chapters 4 through 6 can't be trivially dismissed as impossible science fiction. Figure 1.7 summarizes where the various chapters fall on the spectrum from factual to speculative.

A fascinating journey awaits us. Let's begin!

The Bottom Line:

- Life, defined as a process that can retain its complexity and replicate, can develop through three stages: a biological stage (1.0), where its hardware and software are evolved, a cultural stage (2.0), where it can design its software (through learning) and a technological stage (3.0), where it can design its hardware as well, becoming the master of its own destiny.
- Artificial intelligence may enable us to launch Life 3.0 this century, and a fascinating conversation has sprung up regarding what future we should aim for and how this can be accomplished. There are three main camps in the controversy: techno-skeptics, digital utopians and the beneficial-AI movement.
- Techno-skeptics view building superhuman AGI as so hard that it won't happen for hundreds of years, making it silly to worry about it (and Life 3.0) now.
- Digital utopians view it as likely this century and wholeheartedly welcome Life 3.0, viewing it as the natural and desirable next step in the cosmic evolution.
- The beneficial-AI movement also views it as likely this century, but views a good outcome not as guaranteed, but as something that needs to be ensured by hard work in the form of AI-safety research.
- Beyond such legitimate controversies where world-leading experts disagree, there are also boring pseudo-controversies caused by misunderstandings. For example, never waste time arguing about "life," "intelligence," or "consciousness" before ensuring that you and your protagonist are using these words to mean the same thing! This book uses the definitions in table 1.1.
- Also beware the common misconceptions in figure 1.5: "Superintelligence by 2100 is inevitable/impossible." "Only Luddites worry about AI." "The concern is about AI turning evil and/or conscious, and it's just years away." "Robots are the main concern." "AI can't control humans and can't have goals."
- In chapters 2 through 6, we'll explore the story of intelligence from its humble beginning billions of years ago to possible cosmic futures billions of years from now. We'll first investigate near-term challenges such as jobs, AI weapons and the quest for human-level AGI, then explore possibilities for a fascinating spectrum of possible futures with intelligent machines and/or humans. I wonder which options you'll prefer!
- In chapters 7 through 9, we'll switch from cold factual descriptions to an exploration of goals, consciousness and meaning, and investigate what we can do right now to help create the future we want.
- I view this conversation about the future of life with AI as the most important one of our time—please join it!

Questions for Comprehension

Answer these questions as a comprehension gauge and/or for further clarification on the text:

1. True or False. There is general scientific agreement that AGI, or artificial general intelligence, will most likely exist by the end of the twenty-first century.

2. True or False. Machines can have goals.

3. As briefly as possible, draw meaningful distinctions between "AI" (artificial intelligence) and "AGI" (artificial general intelligence).

The predictions are hard to believe: expert research indicates that one third of the human workforce could be displaced by automation by the year 2030 (Franck). Another study predicts that 8.5 percent of the global workforce could be displaced by robots by 2030 (Lardieri).

Good critical reasoning, however, demands that we do not simply dismiss ideas because they seem unlikely, inconvenient, or frightening. We want to evaluate the credibility of our sources of information; if our sources seem authoritative, then we can proceed by investigating the facts for ourselves and examining the authors' interpretations of the facts.

Anyone who has put much thought into the matter will conclude that AI (artificial intelligence) and robotics are the primary factors shaping the American workforce of the twenty-first century. As our human future intersects with automation and artificial intelligence, two late twentieth century paradigms tend to guide the spectrum of our thinking: on the one hand, we have R2D2 and C3PO from *Star Wars*, friendly robots who are key to human success; on the other hand, we have *The Terminator*, a scary, emotionless soldier of apocalypse bent on human destruction. Of course, the "truth" of our future probably lies somewhere between these science fiction extremes.

Writers such as Max Tegmark (*Life 3.0*, 2017) and Yuval Noah Harari (*21 Lessons for the 21st Century*, 2018) predict radical changes in the workforce stemming from the development of AI and robotics. In 2013, Oxford researchers developed an algorithm to determine the impact of automation on the human workforce. The results were astounding. The researchers concluded that 47 percent of U.S. jobs are at high risk of replacement. These weren't just the sort of traditional blue-collar jobs that many people understand are at risk. For example, everyone realizes that the job of "truck driver" is under threat of replacement due to GPS (global positioning systems) and self-driving vehicles, but not many people realize that insurance underwriters and paralegals might be replaced en masse. The algorithm predicted that by 2033, there is a 99 percent chance that telemarketers and insurance underwriters will be replaced; a 94 percent chance that paralegals will be replaced; a 91 percent chance that tour guides will be replaced;

and an 88 percent chance that construction workers will be replaced. Even lifeguards do not have job security, with a 67 percent chance of replacement according to this algorithm (cited in Harari, *Homo Deus* 330). Is any human activity safe, one wonders? Remember Indiana Jones? He's OK. Archaeologists stand a 0.7 percent chance of replacement. This profession requires highly sophisticated pattern recognition and there's essentially no profit in the field, so corporations and government won't be investing in technologies to displace the profession. Tegmark sums up the human dilemma regarding twenty-first century workforce with a single question: "As mechanical muscles made horses redundant, will mechanical minds do the same to humans?" (126).

Harari speculates:

Since we do not know how the job market would look in 2030 or 2040, already today we have no idea what to teach our kids. Most of what they currently learn at school will probably be irrelevant by the time they are forty. Traditionally, life has been divided into two main parts: a period of learning followed by a period of working. Very soon this traditional model will become utterly obsolete, and the only way for humans to stay in the game will be to keep learning throughout their lives, and to reinvent themselves repeatedly. Many if not most humans may be unable to do so (*Homo Deus* 331).

Other experts concur. Gen Z workers may have three or more distinct careers in a lifetime. Gen Zers are three times more likely to change jobs than Baby Boomers (King). Gen Zers understand that they cannot trust corporate America to provide a career that will result in a lifetime of benefits with a full-funded retirement plan. In the 1970s, the average worker would spend 25 years at a career job; nowadays, that figure stands at 4.2 years (Sasser).

In 1986, political scientist Langdon Winner contemplated people's attitudes about the coming new world order: As is true of all myths, there are scraps of truth in our absent conceptions of a computerized future. "Mythinformation," he writes, is the "almost religious conviction that a widespread adoption of computers and communications systems, along with broad access to electronic information, will automatically produce a better world for humanity" (105). Winner calls instead for reflection and planning. Seven years prior to the official adoption of the term "Internet" by the Federal Networking Council in 1995, Winner cites U.S. Bureau of Labor Statistics studies predicting that the emerging post-industrial economy, or "information society," will provide "plenty of work for janitors, hospital orderlies, and fast-food helpers" (106). In fact, our ever-expanding service sector economy does offer plenty of low wage, part-time jobs for young people and for people of all ages, while "career" jobs have become more difficult to obtain. Wages in the U.S. have been largely static for four decades as automation pervades the workforce.

Is it possible that even Wal-Mart greeters will soon be replaced by robot greeters who do not complain about minimum wage and health benefits? In fact, according to a host of financial experts, Americans will need to keep working later and later into life as the concept of "retirement" becomes an economic fantasy for growing segments of society.

MIT economist Erik Brynjolfsson and MIT researcher Andrew McAfee argue that the main cause of income inequality and wealth disparity is technology (quoted in Tegmark 120):

- Since the mid-1970s, salaries rose 25 percent for those with graduate degrees while the average high school dropout has taken a 30 percent pay cut.
- Since 2000, an ever larger share of capital wealth goes to company owners rather than to those who work for companies.

- In 1990, the "Big Three" automakers (GM, Ford, and Chrysler) earned revenues that were equal to 2014 Google, Apple, and Facebook revenues. However, the tech companies achieved this revenue with *nine times fewer* employees and *thirty times greater* stock market value.
- The digital economy appears to benefit "superstars" over everyone else. This may be one reason behind the growing disparity between the so-called 1 percent and the rest of us.

Getting Ready for the Twenty-First Century

In 2015, the National Association of Colleges and Employers (NACE) defined **career readiness**: *Career readiness is the attainment and demonstration of requisite competencies that broadly prepare college graduates for a successful transition into the workplace.* NACE associates eight core competencies with this definition of career readiness: Critical thinking/problem solving, oral/written communications, teamwork/collaboration, digital technology, leadership, professionalism/work ethic, career management, and global/intercultural fluency.

These competencies address what companies have long reported that they want to see in recent college graduates. Frequently, though, companies report that these competencies are missing in their new hires.

So, what is the role of college in the twenty-first century? It seems clear that the purpose of undergraduate education must remain *to learn how to learn*. Harari and others remind us that the twenty-first century will demand continual reinvention from its most productive workers.

Adaptability, a capacity to fit into a work culture, the willingness to extend past comfort zones, the capacity to think "outside the box"—these are highly sought-after traits that are commonly found in successful people running Fortune 1000 companies. While STEM field education (science, technology, engineering, and math) holds an obvious place of importance in the twenty-first century, the humanistic approach of liberal arts colleges offers opportunities to succeed in a wide variety of fields, and to remain adaptable to ever-changing environments. An impressive number of prominent American CEOs come from the liberal arts and humanities. (Check it out yourself. Do your research.)

In a workforce shaped by robotics and automation, you may want to seek out a profession that cannot be easily displaced by robotics and AI.

Ask Three Questions Regarding a Potential Job:

1. Does the job require social intelligence?
2. Does it require creativity and clever solutions?
3. Does it require working in unpredictable environments?

If you answer "Yes" to each of these questions, then the job will likely continue to belong to humankind for decades to come (Tegmark 121).

Further Inquiry

- *Which jobs and careers are most likely to be replaced by AI in the near future?*
- *What do* employers *in the twenty-first century want from their workforce?*
  - Answer A: They don't know or can't articulate their needs.
  - Answer B: They want workers with specific hard skills to fill niche operations *right now*.

- Answer C: They want independent critical thinkers and problem solvers with strong work ethics and high level social and intellectual skills *for the long term.*

It would be fair in a job interview to ask a potential employer, "Can you tell me what qualities you are seeking from your employees?" Most employers, I imagine, would be impressed with this question.

If you are skeptical regarding the value of a liberal arts degree, it's a good thing. Skepticism is one of the primary characteristics we liberal arts teachers intend to instill in our students. If you can't trust me, trust a shark. In 2017, Dallas Mavericks owner and *Shark Tank* entrepreneur Mark Cuban shared a bold prediction about the future of jobs: within the next decade, as automation becomes the norm, free thinkers who excel in liberal arts will be in high demand. Cuban believes that the amount of change we'll see for jobs in the next five or 10 years will dwarf what we've observed in the past 30 years. As AI and machine learning shape the workforce, there will be a greater need for expertise in subjects such as English, philosophy, and foreign languages (Morad). Some of today's most in-demand skills, such as software coding, will eventually be taken over by AI automation. Skills like communication and critical thinking will become more important.

So if you actually enjoyed your philosophy or art history class, don't despair! Tell your family it will be OK. Self-starters who excel at critical thinking, problem solving, and communication—the very things we attempt to teach in the liberal arts—are likely to remain in demand for a long time to come.

Finding Connections Works Cited

"Career Readiness Define." *National Association of Colleges and Employers*, 2020, https://www.naceweb.org/career-readiness/competencies/career-readiness-defined/.

Franck, Thomas. "McKinsey: One-third of US Workers Could Be Jobless by 2030 Due to Automation." *CNBC.com*, Nov. 29, 2017, updated 29 Nov. 2017, https://www.cnbc.com/2017/11/29/one-third-of-us-workers-could-be-jobless-by-2030-due-to-automation.html.

Harari, Yuval Noah. *Homo Deus*. Harvill Secker, 2015.

Harari, Yuval Noah. *21 Lessons for the 21st Century*. Spiegel & Grau, 2018.

King, Rachel. "Younger Professionals Are More Likely to Switch Jobs at a Rate Faster Than Ever Before." *Fortune*, 11 Oct. 2018, https://fortune.com/2018/10/11/generation-z-baby-boomers-job-turnover/.

Lardieri, Alexa. "Robots Will Replace 20 Million Jobs by 2030, Oxford Report Finds." *U.S. News & World Report*, 26 June 2019, https://www.usnews.com/news/economy/articles/2019-06-26/report-robots-will-replace-20-million-manufacturing-jobs-by-2030.

Morad, Renee. "Why Mark Cuban Believes Liberal Arts Is the Future of Jobs." *Fobres.com*, 28 Feb. 2017, https://www.forbes.com/sites/reneemorad/2017/02/28/why-mark-cuban-believes-liberal-arts-is-the-future-of-jobs/#22e9b12d7a92.

Sasser, Ben. Interview. CBS, *Face the Nation*, 14 Oct. 2018.

Tegmark, Mark. *Life 3.0: Being Human in the Age of Artificial Intelligence*. Alfred A. Knopf, 2017.

Winner, Langdon. *The Whale and the Reactor: A Search for Limits in an Age of High Technology*. University of Chicago Press, 1986.

Resources

Your Major Research Question

The Major Research Question (MRQ) is a key prompt for a good research paper.
This question guides you in the development of an engaging, focused topic.

One of the *Engaging Discourse 2.0* units will inspire you to develop a "major research question."

- Ideally, the "answer" to your MRQ becomes your **thesis** or **major claim**. Remember that your purpose is more than informational. You want to present an argument or a position rather than simply to convey facts and information.

Once you have chosen a general discourse topic, here are some essential concerns when it comes to **drafting** and **developing** an **MRQ, or major research question**:

- An adequate major research question can *never* be answered "Yes" or "No."
- A good major research question is likely to begin with "How" or "Why."
- Your major research question should not already be answered by the article that inspires your topic.
  - The idea is to expand beyond the boundaries of the article that you have read. Synthetic connections with other articles can inspire your research.
- If someone could write an entire book based on the answer to your major research question, then your question needs improvement. We are writing one research paper of modest length. Make sure your MRQ fits the scope of a single research paper.
- In almost every instance, your draft MRQ will need to be narrowed. We all start out with *broad* questions. It's only practical, however, to answer *narrow* questions. The good news is that it is *much easier* to answer narrow questions, so it is *much easier* to write research papers that have a narrow focus.
- **Develop your MRQ in stages: draft and revise.** A clear, narrow MRQ leads to clear, narrow research. Broad research questions become overwhelming and sometimes prove counterproductive.

Considering the pointers above, understand why these are
FAULTY Major Research Questions:

- Is technology good to use in the classroom? (A *Yes/No* question leaves you with nothing left to research.)
- Does AI affect me? (Again, this is binary, i.e. *Yes/No.* "How does AI affect me?" is a much better starting point for your major research question.)
- When did the self-esteem curriculum emerge in U.S. schools? (If one of our experts has already answered this query, then you need to revise. "Why" might produce a better question.)
- When did smartphones become a significant part of American life? (Hasn't one of our experts already answered this question?)
- How does the psychological immune system operate? (To what extent does Gilbert already answer this question in his article? What other questions and concerns, on the other hand, does he leave unanswered? Revise and narrow: *What is the role of the psychological immune system in dealing with grief or heartache resulting from a failed romantic relationship?*)

See Unit Nine Research in the Twenty-First Century for detailed information on the research paper composition process.

Essay Prompts

Level I: Analysis-Response

1. Based on Tegmark's writing, define the concepts of "digital utopians," "techno skeptics," and "beneficial AI advocates." Analyze the positions of each of these groups. Classify yourself within one of these categories. Clarify why you would place yourself in one category and not the others.

2. Examine the treatment of AI in your favorite movie or TV program. Does the show's treatment of AI fit into the worldview of "digital utopian," "techno skeptic," or "beneficial AI advocate"? Justify your response with an analysis of the program's treatment of AI and the positions of the various groups as Tegmark defines them.

3. Consider the role of AI in your daily life. Where and how does AI most affect you? How does Tegmark's article inform your understanding of the current role of AI in your life?

4. Respond to the concept of "life" as it is defined and examined in Tegmark's article. Recount and respond to Tegmark's classifications of the various "levels" of life. You may choose to define and discuss the idea of "consciousness" as well.

5. Using Tegmark's article as a starting point, define the concept of "organized complexity" or "self-organization" (and/or "emergence") as it is relevant to the topic of AI.

Level II: Making Connections

1. Tegmark participates in real life discourse (that is, late night discussions) on the topic of AI with leading experts. Compare Nicholas Carr's concerns with the role of AI and the Internet to the concerns of the experts that Tegmark mentions in his article.

2. In a human brain, the actions of billions of unintelligent neurons result in cognition and consciousness. Explain why scientists such as Tegmark consider the possibility of the development of AGI, or artificial general intelligence, as a real possibility. Draw an analogy between AGI and human neuroplasticity, including neural remapping.

3. What elements of AI are involved in the operation of online dating apps? Explore the sundry algorithms that attempt to match romantic partners.

4. The human experience in the age of AI is in many ways fundamentally different from the human experience of prior ages. For example, having data instantly available to us is a new condition. Considering the many ways that AI affects our daily existence, what specific AI functions might be said to affect our sense of happiness? Specify. How are these experiences fundamentally different from prior ages, and what are the implications when it comes to the topic of human happiness?

Level III: Research

1. Expand one of the Level II topics into a research project. Develop a specific MRQ, or major research question, which your research paper seeks to answer.

2. What are the most significant impacts of artificial intelligence (AI) on the 21st century American job market? Which jobs are most likely to be disrupted or replaced by AI or robotics, and which careers are most likely to remain "human"? Once you have established some broad, expert data, narrow your research focus to a career field and labor market of your choosing, possibly your own field of study. For example, if you are a biology major, what careers await you in the twenty-first century and what types of jobs that biology majors may have taken in the twentieth century may be displaced by AI and/or robotics? Distinguish between short-term and long-term changes in the labor market.

3. Explore and explain the current state of "machine learning," "deep learning," or "deep machine learning." What are the most interesting and significant current applications of deep machine learning? Clarify how deep machine learning is different from AGI, or general artificial intelligence. How is deep network learning or deep machine learning likely to impact our world in the coming century? Be sure to focus your topic. Writing in narrow, specific terms is more engaging than writing in vague, general terms.

4. In the realm of civilian or military applications of AI, where do we face the most significant moral or legal dilemmas? For example, what civil liberty challenges exist when it comes to facial recognition technologies? What moral dilemmas do we face when it comes to the development of robotic weaponry? Do not write on everything you find. Narrow your topic. Remember that you are responding to prompts, not directives. Take control of your own composition.

5. Define the concept of the "singularity," that is, the point at which an artificial intelligence would (in a future scenario) achieve consciousness or self-awareness. (There is no self-aware AI or machine at the moment; some experts believe there never will be.) What does it mean, and why is it significant, if a machine or software program passes the so-called Turing test? Does current scientific thinking indicate that the "singularity" is a matter of science or science fiction? Rely on expert authority rather than popular speculation. How close are we to encountering AGI, or artificial general intelligence, and what are the most significant implications of the development of AGI? Can a machine or a network ever achieve "consciousness"? Why or why not, according to leading experts? What are the most significant implications of the potential development of AGI?

Further Inquiry

Alexander, Calah. "AI Is Growing Rapidly, but it Won't Replace These 2 Human Skills." *Aleteia,* 26 Sept. 2018, https://aleteia.org/2018/09/26/ai-is-growing-rapidly-but-it-wont-replace-these-2-human-skills/.

"Artificial Intelligence: A Special Report." *The New York Times,* 8 Apr. 2002, [Metalinks Page], newyorktimes.com/spotlight/artificial-intelligence.

Cawley, Conor. "Why Artificial Intelligence Will Never Compete With the Human Brain." *Tech.co,* 26 Apr. 2018, https://tech.co/news/artificial-intelligence-human-brain-2018-04.

Columbia School of Engineering and Applied Science. "A Step Closer to Self-Aware Machines—Engineers Create a Robot that Can Imagine Itself." *TechXplore,* 30 Jan. 2019, https://techxplore.com/news/2019-01-closer-self-aware-machinesengineers-robot.html.

Cook, Gareth. "Does Consciousness Pervade the Universe? Philosopher Philip Goff Answers Questions about 'Panpsychism.'" *Scientific American,* 14 Jan. 2020, https://www.scientificamerican.com/article/does-consciousness-pervade-the-universe/.

Franck, Thomas. "McKinsey: One-third of US Workers Could Be Jobless by 2030 Due to Automation." *CNBC.com,* Nov. 29, 2017, updated 29 Nov. 2017, https://www.cnbc.com/2017/11/29/one-third-of-us-workers-could-be-jobless-by-2030-due-to-automation.html.

Franklin, Thomas. "5 Reasons AI Won't Replace Humans… It Will Make Us Superhuman." *Hackernoon.com,* 8 July 2018, https://hackernoon.com/5-reasons-ai-wont-replace-humans-it-will-make-us-superhuman-413c499e1e68.

Hadley, Mark. "How to Build a Computer with Free Will." *Independent,* 22 Mar. 2018, https://www.independent.co.uk/life-style/gadgets-and-tech/build-computer-free-will-artificial-intelligence-a8254101.html.

Harari, Yuval Noah. *Homo Deus.* Harvill Secker, 2015.

Harari, Yuval Noah. *21 Lessons for the 21st Century.* Spiegel & Grau, 2018.

Ismail, Nick. "Why Robots Won't Replace Humans." *Information Age,* 8 Feb. 2017, https://www.information-age.com/robots-wont-replace-humans-123464364/.

Johnson, Steven. *Emergence: The Connected Lives of Ants, Brains, Cities, and Software.* Scribner, 2001.

Kak, Subhash. "Will Robots Take Your Job? Humans Ignore the Coming AI Revolution at Their Peril." NBC News, Opinion, https://www.nbcnews.com/think/opinion/will-robots-take-your-job-humans-ignore-coming-ai-revolution-ncna845366.

King, Rachel. "Younger Professionals Are More Likely to Switch Jobs at a Rate Faster Than Ever Before." *Fortune,* 11 Oct. 2018, https://fortune.com/2018/10/11/generation-z-baby-boomers-job-turnover/.

Krausová, Alžběta and Hananel Hazan. "Creating Free Will in Artificial Intelligence." International Conference Beyond AI (Pilsen, Czech Republic), Nov. 2013, https://www.researchgate.net/publication/278468286_Creating_Free_Will_in_Artificial_Intelligence.

Lardieri, Alexa. "Robots Will Replace 20 Million Jobs by 2030, Oxford Report Finds." *U.S. News & World Report,* 26 June 2019, https://www.usnews.com/news/economy/articles/2019-06-26/report-robots-will-replace-20-million-manufacturing-jobs-by-2030.

MacDonald, Fiona. "A Robot Has Just Passed a Classic Self-Awareness Test For The First Time." *Science Alert,* 17 July 2015, https://www.sciencealert.com/a-robot-has-just-passed-a-classic-self-awareness-test-for-the-first-time.

Manyika, James, et al. "Jobs Lost, Job Gained: What the Future of Work Will Mean for Jobs, Skills, and Wages." McKinsey & Company, Nov. 2017, https://www.mckinsey.com/featured-insights/future-of-work/jobs-lost-jobs-gained-what-the-future-of-work-will-mean-for-jobs-skills-and-wages.

Marcus, Gary. "What Comes After the Turing Test?" *The New Yorker,* 9 June 2014, https://www.newyorker.com/tech/annals-of-technology/what-comes-after-the-turing-test.

Marcus, Gary, et al. "Beyond the Turing Test." *AI Magazine,* vol. 37, no. 1: Spring 2016, https://aaai.org/ojs/index.php/aimagazine/article/view/2650.

McKendrick, Joe. "Artificial Intelligence Will Replace Tasks, Not Jobs." *Forbes,* 14 Aug. 2018, https://www.forbes.com/sites/joemckendrick/2018/08/14/artificial-intelligence-will-replace-tasks-not-jobs/#312a572aa7fa.

Mills, Terence. "How Far Are We From Truly Human-Like AI?" *Forbes,* 28 Aug. 2018, https://www.forbes.com/sites/forbestechcouncil/2018/08/28/how-far-are-we-from-truly-human-like-ai.

Morad, Renee. "Why Mark Cuban Believes Liberal Arts Is the Future of Jobs." *Forbes.com*, 28 Feb. 2017, https://www.forbes.com/sites/reneemorad/2017/02/28/why-mark-cuban-believes-liberal-arts-is-the-future-of-jobs/#22e9b12d7a92.

Morgan, Brent. "Artificial Intelligence: Can it Replace Human Intelligence?" *Medium.com*, 7 Feb. 2017, https://medium.com/@BrentMorgan/artificial-intelligence-can-it-replace-human-intelligence-b250b9aec153.

Rosso, Cami. "The Unbearable Conundrum of AI Consciousness: Will Machines One Day Become Self-Aware?" *Psychology Today*, 4 Jan. 2018, https://www.psychologytoday.com/us/blog/the-future-brain/201801/the-unbearable-conundrum-ai-consciousness.

Rouse, Margaret. "Definition: Turing Test." *Search Enterprise AI*, https://searchenterpriseai.techtarget.com/definition/Turing-test.

Schkolne, Steven. "Machines Demonstrate Self-Awareness." *Becoming Human: Artificial Intelligence Magazine*, 4 Apr. 2018, https://becominghuman.ai/machines-demonstrate-self-awareness-8bd08ceb1694.

Shell, Ellen Ruppel. "AI and Automation Will Replace Most Human Workers Because They Don't Have to Be Perfect—Just Better Than You." *Newsweek*, 20 Nov. 2018, https://www.newsweek.com/2018/11/30/ai-and-automation-will-replace-most-human-workers-because-they-dont-have-be-1225552.html.

Smith, Craig S. "Computers Already Learn From Us. But Can They Teach Themselves?" *The New York Times*, 8 Apr. 2020, https://www.nytimes.com/2020/04/08/technology/ai-computers-learning-supervised-unsupervised.html.

Tegmark, Max. "Benefits & Risks of Artificial Intelligence." Future of Life Institute, https://futureoflife.org/background/benefits-risks-of-artificial-intelligence.

Tegmark, Mark. *Life 3.0: Being Human in the Age of Artificial Intelligence*. Alfred A. Knopf, 2017.

Watson, Simon. "Killer Robots, Free Will and the Illusion of Control." *The Conversation*, 2 Jan. 2018, http://theconversation.com/killer-robots-free-will-and-the-illusion-of-control-87460.

Weisberger, Mindy. "Will AI Ever Become Conscious?" *Live Science*, 24 May 2018, https://www.livescience.com/62656-when-will-ai-be-conscious.html.

Winner, Langdon. *The Whale and the Reactor: A Search for Limits in an Age of High Technology*. University of Chicago Press, 1986.

UNIT SEVEN

Generation Studies

The Narcissism Epidemic (2009) is a book about American culture. Psychologists Jean Twenge and W. Keith Campbell attempt to use scientific data to support their interpretations of culture and their depictions of disturbing sociological trends. "All Play and No Work: *Entitlement*," the article which appears in this unit, is a chapter excerpt from Twenge and Campbell's book.

In the book's concluding chapter, Twenge and Campbell offer dire predictions for the future of a narcissistic America:

> The economic foundations of the United States are already cracking, with the failure of many large companies and financial institutions and the government bailout of others. But the fantasy persists in other areas, with many Americans still bent on self-admiration, getting attention, and looking hot. Many people still buy lots of stuff and put in on their credit cards. If this continues, there will be massive environmental damage as more people feel entitled to whatever they want and global warming skyrockets. Our social fabric will tear under the weight of egotism and incivility. The Chinese will eat our lunch economically as narcissistic American consumers spend themselves into permanent debt and entitled employees demand more money for less work.

The psychological epidemic of narcissism, claim the authors, is a measurable phenomenon that warrants our attention, and our concern.

Arguably, Americans learned important lessons regarding overspending and the culture of want during the Great Recession. (The recession ran from late 2007 to mid-2009, technically speaking, but the economic lag lasted years longer in parts of the country.) Millennials are clearly wary, for example, of the student loan debt that so many have taken on in pursuit of higher education. Young Americans may well have turned away from materialism as they watched their parents and grandparents lose their homes to foreclosure in the first decade of the millennium.

Or did they? Does cultural memory in the twenty-first century last any longer than the latest iOS update?

© garetsworkshop/Shutterstock.com

I, Me, Mine

Can a generation shaped by the realities of the 2008 Recession and the 2020 coronavirus pandemic really be accused of materialism and narcissism?

Jean Twenge is well known for her work on generational studies. Her interpretations of longitudinal data culled from decades of youth surveys inspired *Generation Me* (2006), where she argues that America's youth are overconfident, entitled, and miserable, in large part due to their schooling (which values self-esteem instead of hard work) and the parenting they received (which encourages entitlement and discourages self-reliance). She documents the changing attitudes of America's youth by studying yearly surveys given to college students since the 1960s. Essentially, children have been taught to put themselves first and to believe that they are never wrong (even when they are clearly wrong). Children are encouraged, never criticized. Everyone gets a blue ribbon. Everyone is above average. Rampant grade inflation and a simultaneous decline in real knowledge tell the tale of American education, according to Twenge.

The Economic Factor

How likely is it that Generation Z will experience different social trends from the ones that Twenge and Campbell believe have shaped Gen X and the Millennials? Will selfish *me-first* social trends increase in the twenty-first century? Is there sufficient data to say whether such trends ever existed?

Explore how the economy and the job market shape generational characteristics. Under Further Inquiry, read what Anne Helen Petersen writes about Millennial burnout. Examine Peter Barnes' depictions of a declining middle class. See who Reniqua Allen believes is left out of the picture, and consider the implications of the Kurz et al. report to the federal reserve entitled "Are Millennials Different?"

The economic "context" of Millennials and Gen Z is a significant factor worth considering when assessing the predominant personality traits of whole generations. *The Greatest Generation* (a term coined by journalist Tom Brokaw) was defined and evaluated by its own economic and historical context, that is, its response to the Great Depression and World War II.

The pertinent cultural shifts began with the Baby Boomers (1946-1964). As any historian can attest, the Baby Boomer generation experienced seismic shifts in culture: the civil rights movement, the counter-culture movement, the anti-war movement, the feminist movement—these were unprecedented cultural shifts that defined the generation. Boomers, according to Twenge, were the first generation to dive deep into an exploration of the individual, embracing concepts of individual freedom and individual consciousness. Comparatively speaking, prior generations experienced a collective coherence and unity of purpose—in overcoming the Great Depression and in fighting World War II, for example. Ironically, Baby Boomers enjoyed their journey toward free consciousness and self-actualization as a group, a journey toward individualism experienced as a collective.

The sons and daughters of the Baby Boomers inherited a world where individual freedom was taken for granted. Sensitive Boomer parents raised their children to "believe in themselves," and disturbing social trends took root, Twenge argues, evolving into the brand of American narcissism that we see rampant in today's schools, politics, and media.

"Generation Me," or "Gen Me," is the catchy term Twenge coins to describe Americans born in the 1970s, 80s, and 90s, emphasizing the self-centered nature of Generation X and Millennials. Twenge herself is part of this demographic, as am I.

Social Trends and What the Studies Say

According to Twenge, Generation Me was taught to put *self first*. After all, everyone is a winner (even if you actually lost or did nothing more than show up). In the 1970s and 80s, a well-intentioned "self-esteem curriculum" crept into American education. Kids were now taught to love themselves ... even if they did nothing particularly praiseworthy. The idea was that the "greatest love of all" (love of self) would teach children to be kind to themselves and to others. The effect, according to Twenge, was to teach children that they didn't need to work for anything in order to receive praise. Children came to expect praise for simply being. *I'm special because I am.*

The downsides have become apparent: children who lack a work ethic, who can't stand criticism because they have always been told that they are right and clever too, who value material objects over metaphysical well-being, who think "me" instead of "we."

- *To what extent do you think Twenge's depiction of American education's "self-esteem curriculum" (described above) is accurate?*

The following statistics and observations come in part from the chapters entitled "An Army of One: *Me*" and "You Can Be Anything You Want to Be" in Jean Twenge's book *Generation Me* (2006):

- By the mid-1990s, the average college male had higher self-esteem than 86% of male respondents in 1968.
- From the 1960s to the 1990s, college students were increasingly likely to agree with the statement, "On the whole, I am satisfied with myself."
- A 1997 survey found that 93% answered "Good" when asked, "In general, how do you feel about yourself?" (6% felt "not very good" and 1% chose "bad.")
- A 1998 survey of teens found that 91% described themselves as responsible, 74% as physically attractive and 79% as "very intelligent."
- In 1968, 18% of college freshmen reported an "A" high school average; in 2004, 48% reported an "A" average (despite SAT scores falling over the same period).
- Despite receiving better grades, 33% of college freshmen in 2003 reported studying six or more hours per week in high school, compared to 47% in 1987.
- In 2003, 47% of college freshmen reported that they were bored during their last year in high school; this number went up from 29% in 1985.
- In 2004, 70% of college freshmen reported that their academic ability was "above average" or "highest 10%."
- Alongside trends of grade inflation is an increasing practice of not correcting student mistakes nor requiring students to correct their own mistakes.
- Kids' self-esteem dropped over the course of the 1970s and took a major upswing after 1980.
- A personality trait called "agency" (which involves assertiveness, dominance, independence, and self-promotion) increased 75% in young men and women from the 1970s to the 1990s.
- "Helicopter" parenting is on the rise, along with the belief that "my child is more special than other children."
- Trends toward *perfectionism* are on the rise.
- Parents hand over control to young children and overwhelm them with choices instead of guiding or directing their activities.
- 98% of college freshmen agreed with the statement, "I am sure that one day I will get to where I want to be in life."
- In 1999, teens predicted they would earn on average $75K per year by the time they were 30. That year, the average income of a 30-year-old was $27K.
- In 2000, 65% of high school seniors predicted their lives would be better than their parents; only 4% predicted their lives would be worse. At the same time, 29% of adults surveyed thought the high school seniors would lead better lives, while 32% thought the high school seniors would lead worse lives.
- Young people increasingly hold unrealistic dreams and expectations.
- "You do you" really means "I do me."
- Millennials appear to think that childhood lasts till 30.
- "Adulting" has become a recognized verb (though, at least in my mind, one with only comic connotations).
- Note a connection to Unit Eight Happiness Studies. What are the distinctions between "happiness" of the sort recognized in the list above and other forms or definitions of happiness?

OK, Boomer

"Like McDonald's and Coca-Cola," Twenge writes in *Generation Me*, "American individualism is spreading to all corners of the globe" (7).

Some of the social trends that scholars and critics have identified ought to be understood in the context of a new economy, stagnant wages, wealth inequity, and cost of living. As Twenge herself notes, quoting an Arab proverb, "Men resemble the times more than they resemble their fathers" (3).

Context is crucial. Let's take, for example, the sociological trend that Millennials, compared to prior generations, are not marrying as frequently and are waiting until later in life to marry. Throughout the late twentieth century, it was common to marry in one's early twenties. By the 2000s, people were waiting until their late twenties, if they decided to marry at all. A critic can claim that selfish people don't want to commit to an adult partnership. However, it could be that people don't want to commit to marriage in the face of the economic uncertainty and disruption characteristic of the Internet era.

Cultural commentators remark that Millennials are abandoning the traditional American dream of home ownership. They don't want the responsibility of caring for a property and paying taxes. Yet there's a more simple explanation: they can't afford home ownership as real estate values rise across the country.

Millennials are not good consumers, we are told; they are failing to fuel the economy. *Or:* They have no extra money to spend. (Note the paradox of Millennials being simultaneously criticized for materialism and for not spending enough money.)

Jobs with sustainable wages and benefits are becoming more scarce. Millennials constitute a large portion of the so-called *gig economy*, operating as independent contractors (lower wages, no benefits) rather than career employees (pension or retirement plan with benefits).

Since the inception of the United States, every generation of Americans has had, on the whole, more capital wealth than the prior generation. This upward trend began to flatten in the late twentieth century. It's no wonder that smart young people, reading these generational criticisms, roll their eyes, and say, "OK, Boomer."

Writer Anne Helen Petersen admonishes the critics who cast Millennials as lazy and entitled:

> We're called whiny for talking frankly about just how much we do work, or how exhausted we are by it. But because overworking for less money isn't always *visible*—because job hunting now means trawling LinkedIn, because "overtime" now means replying to emails in bed—the extent of our labor is often ignored, or degraded.

My own wish for students is that they too gain the voice and literary competence to question unfair criticisms. At the same time, as critical thinkers, we can't simply filter out negative commentary because we don't like it. When we do so, we place ourselves in an unhealthy bubble of entitlement and self-obsession. *Skepticism* involves the ability to examine something critically. I encourage you to bring a healthy level of skepticism to these generational studies. Be skeptical of your own generation, and be skeptical of the criticisms of your generation too.

- To what extent are critics justified that American culture encourages narcissism?
  - Where do you see narcissistic or egomaniacal behavior?
- When it comes to self-esteem, work ethic, and regard for others, what values were you taught at school and at home?
  - Have values of entitlement affected you or your classmates?

- Understand that *narcissism* or *narcissistic personality disorder* is a recognized psychological disorder. It does not simply mean "self-centered" or "vain." Symptoms of this disorder include the need for admiration, disregard of others' feelings, an inability to handle criticism, and an unjustified sense of deserving things from life and from other people.
- To what extent are Twenge and Campbell justified in their use of the clinical term "narcissism" to describe what they see happening in society? To what extent could you argue that they are being hyperbolic in their use of this term to describe everyday whininess and vanity?
- Why are the authors' claims significant? What does it matter if there is a "narcissism epidemic"? Who is affected? Why should we care?
- Note that the concept of *self-esteem* is a modern one, stemming from the Enlightenment era and gaining cultural prominence in the late twentieth century.
  - What is the relationship between "self-esteem" and "narcissism"?
  - Is "self-esteem" a necessity? Why or why not?

Questions to Consider

Answer these questions as you read and annotate the text:

- From your perspective, is missing a college exam a big deal? How do you handle the situation when you must miss important schoolwork?
- What is wrong with college students thinking that they deserve extra grade consideration for trying hard?
- Only a "select few" can achieve the fantasy of mid-week snowboarding, according to these authors. What do they mean, and what is the point?
- Why did American companies outsource jobs, according to a U.S. Labor Department survey?
- What is the "Monitoring the Future" survey? What do the authors say it revealed regarding attitudes toward work and school?
- What is "reciprocity" and why is it important in a society?
- What is "one of the best ways to combat entitlement," according to the authors?
- Do you agree that the "old American hero" needs to be our new hero?

Keith recently got a call from a relative eager to relay a scene he was witnessing: an SUV parked in a no-parking zone, facing in the wrong direction, and blocking a stop sign. The SUV had a bumper sticker that said, "I ♥ ME."

Many people in the United States today are simply oblivious to others' needs, or, worse, think that others' needs are just not as important as their own needs. This state of mind is called entitlement, the pervasive belief that one deserves special treatment, success, and more material things. Entitlement is one of the key components of narcissism, and one of the most damaging to others. When narcissists feel entitled to special treatment, someone else invariably gets the shaft. Entitlement may work for some individuals—sometimes demanding students get their grades changed even when they don't deserve it—but it has terrible consequences when everyone in a society feels a sense of entitlement. This is the trap of entitlement: it can be great to think that you are number one, but it is not so great living with or working with others who also think they are number one. Unlike some of the other symptoms of narcissism, such as materialism or vanity, entitlement is like a ghost, difficult to see in solid form, but increasingly wafting its cold, cloudy fingers into everything.

Entitlement is fun while it lasts. You live in a fantasy in which the world owes you more than you contribute. You can feel entitled to a flat-screen TV without earning the money to pay for it. You can park in the handicapped space because you are in a rush. You can graduate from college and expect to get a fulfilling job with a six-figure salary right away.

Or you can literally take candy from children. Keith's lab actually studied this. College students filled out a questionnaire measuring their feelings of entitlement (for example, "If I were on the *Titanic*, I would deserve to be on the *first* lifeboat!" and "I honestly feel I'm just more deserving than others"). Then a confederate passed around a bucket of candy labeled "Child Development Lab" and said casually, "You can take as much candy as you think you deserve." The students who scored the highest on entitlement took the most candy, not really caring that this would leave less for the children.

Historically, entitlement meant having a social position or a claim to ownership granted by some legitimate authority. Having a title (or being entitled) meant having a clear claim to a social rank or piece of property, such as being a lord or duke in British society. As a facet of narcissism, entitlement means acting as if you have a title—or a right—to something even when you don't. There's some overlap with the historical definition: an entitled person acts like he's royalty and isn't like everyone else. A student might demand a high grade as if it is his by right rather than something to be earned. A woman might purchase an expensive car on credit even though she can't afford it because she thinks she deserves to drive a Mercedes.

Entitlement on Campus

College professors often comment that today's students feel they deserve special treatment. In 2007, a Harvard professor noted that, 20 years ago, "When a few students were sick and missed an exam … they used to be apologetic and just grateful that I would even offer a makeup. These days I have kids who think it's no big deal to miss a test if they have any conflict and then they think *they* should decide when I give the makeup." Some students say, "I *need* an A in this course," as if an A were an entitlement rather than something to be earned. Others expect to get good grades just for paying tuition, even telling faculty

> How do the authors define "entitlement"?

members, "You work for me." The most entitled have decided that they get good grades by arguing, saying things like "I'm not leaving your office until you change my grade to an A."

A survey of college students published in 2008 confirmed these perceptions. Two-thirds of students believed their professor should give them special consideration if they explained they were trying hard (apparently missing the point that grades are given for performance, not just for trying). One-third believed they deserved at least a B just for attending class. And—perhaps most incredible—one-third thought they should be able to reschedule their final exam if it interfered with their vacation plans.

One faculty member in North Dakota who responded to our online survey received an e-mail from an angry parent that said, "I am a high school English teacher, and I know that my daughter is an A writer and you have no reason to give her a C." The professor wanted to—but didn't—reply with the truth: "Yes, mom, I do. Your daughter failed to attend class and to turn in all of her work and then enlisted you in the fight for a better grade. PS. She was an average writer." We authors have both received e-mails from students who seemed to think they could get a better grade just for complaining. Others ask to do extra credit—*after* the class is over. Jean's favorite was a student who asked for an extra-credit assignment two weeks after the end of the semester—his e-mail address was "famousstars" and he used the subject line "Please Read ASAP!!"

For the past 15 years, Joan has worked as a financial aid counselor at a satellite campus of the University of North Carolina; she told us her story in our online survey. Students often tell her, "I don't want loans; I want financial aid," and she has to explain that financial aid consists of more than outright gifts of money. One student came into the office and announced, "I was just at the Cashier's Office to pick up my refund check, and they said I didn't have one. I want to know who the slacker is around here." When Joan looked at the file, she found that the student had not even filed a financial aid application. When confronted with the truth that *she* appeared to be the "slacker," the student said, "My parents are so stupid—they were supposed to do that for me."

Of course, professors themselves are not immune from feelings of entitlement. The job itself probably builds narcissism; after all, several times a week, people take notes when we talk.

How Entitlement Corrodes Relationships on and Off the Job

Entitlement causes real problems in relationships. First, entitlement leads to conflict. Everyone at some point does or says something nasty in a relationship, and how you respond to your partner determines whether the nastiness will be a passing squall or turn into a full-blown storm. Ideally, you'll respond in a constructive or positive way when your partner does or says something mean or stupid.

Imagine that your partner comes home and immediately says, "What did you make me for dinner?" You could be accommodating and say something like "Oh, you must have had a tough day at work—would you like to tell me about it?" Or you could just ignore the rude question and say, "Hi, honey, it's great to see you." If you're less accommodating, though, you could say nothing and withdraw for the rest of the evening, giving him the "cold shoulder." Or you could get creative and shoot back, "I made go-to-hell pasta with a side of you're-sleeping-on-the-couch."

Clever, yes, but not the best response—because it invites your partner to verbally hit you back. "Sounds good," he might parry. "Is it better than the usual I-suck-at-cooking-pasta that you usually make?" Incensed, you throw the food against the wall and say, "Actually, we're having my-fat-husband-should-skip-a-meal pasta."

Next thing you know, your husband has said he always hated your cooking, his mom was right about you, and he takes off in a huff. As he drives away, you are yelling at him that maybe a mama's boy like him should move back with his mama. A squall has turned into a hurricane.

Being just a little bit more accommodating can lead to much less conflict in relationships. That's the problem with entitlement: you're special, so how dare anyone not show you respect? Your spouse's nasty comments or behavior are seen as fundamental challenges to your special stature in life, and thus you can't just let them slide. The result is spiraling relationship conflict. The same is true in work relationships. Let's say that Brandon is an entitled employee. If Brandon's boss criticizes his work, he'll think, How dare she criticize me? and might protest "But I worked hard on that!" Entitled people often confuse working hard with actually producing something good. Brandon is also likely to have trouble getting along with his coworkers. If one of them asks him to do something differently, or says something Brandon construes as mean, the conflict is likely to escalate.

Entitled people are also unwilling to see the world through another person's eyes and find it difficult to empathize with another's misfortunes. When you are entitled, all your focus is directed toward your own experience, your own outcomes, and your own needs. This is an obvious recipe for disaster in a romantic relationship, but it doesn't bode well for work relationships, either. Entitlement is also linked to a fundamental lack of respect for other people. The entitled person considers his needs paramount, and others' needs minor.

Entitlement is also expressed in the odd perpetual adolescence of many American adults. Adolescence is the most narcissistic time of life, and adolescence is being extended beyond all previous limits. First there's the well-known phenomenon of twenty-somethings taking longer to settle into careers and marriages, with more and more living in with their parents. But it goes way beyond that. An article in *New York* magazine in 2006 called "Up with Grups" (the term means grown-ups who can't grow up) asked, "When did it become normal for your average 35-year-old New Yorker to … walk around with an iPod plugged into his ears at all times, listening to the latest from Bloc Party, … decide the Sufjan Stevens is the perfect music to play for her 2-year-old, because, let's face it, 2-year-olds have lousy taste in music, and *we will not listen to the Wiggles in this house*; … quit the office job because—you know what?—screw the office and screw jockeying for that promotion to VP, because isn't promotion just another word for 'slavery'? … and besides, now that she's a freelancer, working on her own projects, on her own terms, it's that much easier to kick off in the middle of the week for a quick snowboarding trip to Sugarbush, because she's got to have some balance, right?"

Not that long ago, 40-year-olds wore suits, and 20-year-olds wore T-shirts and jeans. Now both wear T-shirts and jeans. The whole phenomenon is laced with the idea that one should be able to attain individualistic nirvana by keeping the good parts of adolescence (comfortable clothes, self-centeredness, a laissez-faire attitude toward work) while jettisoning the bad parts (not having any money, other people telling you what to do). Only a select few can achieve this fantasy; for the rest, snowboarding in the middle of the week is going to eventually mean no snowboarding at all because they will have run out of the money they need to go snowboarding.

The Employee Problem

In business, entitlement often boils down to an equation: less work for more pay. Plenty of workers today want that, but they also want more flexibility, balance, meaning, and praise for their work. "If you just expect them to stand behind a register and smile, they're not going to do that unless you tell them why that's important and then recognize them for it," says John Spano, a human resources director at a theater chain. Bob runs a business that staffs industrial and clerical jobs in Minneapolis and answered our survey. "It's not uncommon for an employee to call my office before I arrive for the day to inform me, their employer, that they are too tired to go to work and they must get more sleep. They really see nothing wrong with staying home from work to sleep." One employee who did this three times in one week was fired, only to call a few months later wanting another job.

Managers in white-collar businesses have noticed this as well, complaining that workers want to know what the company will do for them (an on-site gym, lots of time off), rather than what they will do for the company. High expectations are also a new norm; stories abound of employees expecting to change established business practices during their first week at work, or believing that they will be running the company within five years. The new employee mantra might be "I want a job that is fulfilling, flexible, and pays six figures." if they don't get it all, and quickly, many workers simply quit, fueling a trend toward job-hopping that has frustrated many managers. In a 2007 survey of 2,500 hiring managers, 87% agreed that younger workers "feel more entitled in terms of compensation, benefits, and career advancement than older generations."

When Jean has surveyed her undergraduate students at San Diego State—admittedly not a nationally representative sample, but still interesting—they have consistently chosen "lazy" when asked to describe the negative characteristics of their generation (materialistic, self-centered, and disrespectful round out the top four). At first Jean was skeptical about this, wondering if her students were simply parroting an accusation they heard from their grumpy elders. No, they said—they'd just noticed many of their peers were lazy.

Unfortunately, many managers and observers are beginning to agree. In a U.S. Labor Department survey of corporate executives, many said that they outsourced jobs to other countries because foreign workers had a better attitude toward work. "American employees … need anger-management and conflict-resolution skills," said U.S. labor secretary Elaine Chao. "Too many young people bristle when a supervisor asks them to do something."

Balance is Bunk

Or take the new business buzzword *work-life balance.* This trend began with the awareness that many people wanted to stop getting home from the office after their kids were already asleep. This is a great goal, and one we're personally glad we both get to achieve most of the time because of the potential flexibility in our professorships. We can cram work into early mornings or late evenings, type at home while a baby bats toys in a bouncy chair, and have cell phone meetings while driving around town. This, however, is far from "work-life balance"—it is more like work-life collision. We still feel lucky to have it, but it's not exactly relaxing.

The real conflict in society that spawned interest in work-life balance—that is, the highly important and often competing goals of caring for children and of working—quickly expanded to include more self-centered goals, such as having plenty of time to travel, pursue your hobbies, and hang out with your friends. The group that talks about work-life balance the most are twenty-somethings, most of whom are childless and want a flexible schedule so they can drop everything to go kayaking with their friend who's in town or take a "mental health day." Even if an employee wants "balance" so she can take time off to volunteer to help others—usually the opposite of entitlement—it's still problematic because the employee feels entitled to do less work for the company while still getting paid the same. If someone who applied for a faculty job on either of our campuses said he wanted to do less teaching and research so he could volunteer in the community, he would not be hired. This may sound harsh until you consider that faculty salaries at public universities are partially funded by tax dollars, and taxpayers expect that money to fund great research and teaching, and not the volunteer organization of the faculty member's choice. Volunteering is a great thing, but when you do it on the back of the tuition payers or taxpayers, it isn't so great.

> What is the essential problem with "entitlement" in personal relationships?

There's hard evidence of the desire to work less in *Monitoring the Future*, an ongoing study that has surveyed a representative sample of American high school seniors every year since the 1970s. Between 1976 and 2006, more and more students agreed that "work is just making a living" and favored jobs with more vacation time. More said that if they got enough money to live comfortably, they wouldn't want to work. Fewer said they were willing to work overtime to do a good job. At the same time, they were more likely to want a job that pays a lot of money and is viewed by other people with respect. Unfortunately, wanting more money for doing less work is a fairly succinct definition of entitlement. As we noted in Chapter 5, young people have been conditioned to expect this: younger generations have gotten better grades in high school even though they do fewer hours of homework.

There is a growing trend to work part-time even in the most prestigious professions. The number of doctors working part-time jumped 46% from 2005 to 2007. Some of the increase comes from women wanting flexible schedules to raise families, but almost a third of male doctors who moved to a part-time schedule said they wanted more time for "unrelated professional or personal pursuits." (Golf?)

As Keith Hammonds notes in a *Fast Company* article titled "Balance is Bunk," work-life balance is now seen as a right rather than a privilege: "In the last generation, balance has won huge cultural resonance. No longer mere cocktail conversation fodder, it has become something like a new inalienable right, creeping into the American ethos if not the Constitution: life, liberty, and the pursuit of balance. Self-actualization and quality time for all!" It's as if people are saying, "I want to be a top performer in my career, but also have a wide-ranging life outside my work." Sure, no problem. You can join the nonexistent ranks of really successful people who give a full 58% to their careers. We have no problem with people who dedicate themselves to their careers and become top performers. We similarly have no problem with people who dedicate themselves to their families but not careers. We even have no problem with people who don't dedicate themselves to their careers or families, but have an active and fun social life. And we empathize with people who want to dedicate themselves to both their careers and families, something we're both struggling to do ourselves. But the narcissism epidemic is clearly spreading into the culture when you have legions of people who don't want to dedicate themselves to their careers and also think they deserve to be top performers.

In a *Wall Street Journal* article in 2007, a partner at a prestigious law firm noted that the young associates demanded praise for their work; some even cried when they got critical feedback. The older partners at the firm were confused: when they were young associates, they remembered, not getting yelled at was considered praise. The partners had to bring in outside assistance to learn how to cope with the new workers. Some companies are hiring "praise consultants" who advise that bosses should not criticize an employee who is late to work; instead they should praise the employee when he or she gets in on time. One praise consultant throws several pounds of confetti a week. In a previous era, the reward one got for coming to work on time was called "not getting fired," and many argue that expecting praise for showing up is the definition of entitlement.

Screw you and the Horse you Rode in on:
Entitlement And Conflict

The willingness to get ahead by harming coworkers is another highly corrosive aspect of entitlement in the workplace. Narcissists often take advantage of their teammates in their attempts to succeed at all costs. These are the "glory hogs," "suck-ups," or "backstabbers"—people who get ahead at the expense of others and jeopardize the success of the organization. When narcissists work with others on a group task, they take credit for the successes of the group and blame their coworkers for their failures, even if they have a close, friendly relationship. This self-serving approach might make the narcissist look good to her boss, but it destroys the narcissist's relationship with her coworkers. In the end, it backfires when no one wants to work with the narcissist again.

Entitlement also has a more far-reaching and corrosive effect on society, destroying practices of reciprocity and obligation. The basic principle of reciprocity is that if someone does something for me, I need to do something for them in return. For example, if you receive a Christmas card from someone, you feel compelled to send them a card as well. If you fail to do this, you feel guilty.

Reciprocity really pays off when the stakes are higher. Let's say a friend helps you when your computer goes down. According to the rules of exchange, you owe her. The next month, your computer-savvy friend calls because she needs to move some furniture into her house and can't do it alone. You are in pretty good shape, so you swing by and help her out. So, both of you helped the other at minimal cost—it wasn't hard for your friend to fix your computer and it wasn't hard for you to move the couch—but both of you gained a great deal. These informal exchanges happen all the time in society and play a huge role in making the world work. The key is that people reciprocate the help at some point.

What happens if you are dealing with someone with a large sense of entitlement? He might ask you for a favor and you comply. You are a helpful person and are happy to do so. You don't get a thank-you, but you let that slide. Then the person asks for a favor again, and again you comply. The next week, however, you ask the person for a little favor in return and he flat out refuses. Maybe he even looks surprised that you would ask him for a favor. You get a little miffed, and the next time he asks for a favor, you decline. You are now a little less helpful in general, and less inclined to trust other people again. This is a major problem with entitlement: entitled people don't see reciprocity as a two-way street, they see favors as a one-way on-ramp that leads to them. The result is that the whole concept of reciprocity gets diminished and life gets a little harder and more isolated for everyone. Reciprocity is the glue that binds society together, and entitlement dissolves that glue.

A Warmer and Depleted Earth,
Courtesy of Entitlement

Entitled people feel it is their right to take more "stuff" from the world, whether it's fish or fuel. If more people feel this way, the resources will run out, leaving nothing for future generations. In one study, Keith and his colleagues asked students to play the role of the CEO of a forestry company, one of four harvesting timber from a forest. Because forests are renewable resources (like fish, cattle, and crops), the forest will grow back and can be harvested in perpetuity if the companies take only a limited amount at a time. However, if they take too much at one time, the forest will be destroyed. Narcissistic participants cut

in the short term, making it appear that being selfish and shortsighted
ne more narcissists were playing the game, the more quickly the forest
ing trees destroyed the forest far more quickly than four less narcissistic
still preserving resources required more cooperative, less narcissistic
the long run when the participants were less entitled. Nonrenewable
a more when entitled people take more. The more Hummers clog the
or the entire planet.

pidemic

ititlement is to be grateful for what you already have. In one fascinating
the things they were grateful for once a week for ten weeks. Compared
do this task, those who thought about everything they were thankful for
being, enjoyed better health, and exercised more. They were also more
. Gratitude is the opposite of entitlement: you think about what you
deserve to have but don't.

de on his or her own, and can also encourage it in families and children.
was the "children are starving in China" argument, which seems to have
cause there's more food in China. When they watch TV, children see all
rely—on TV or in real life—see the lives of less fortunate young people.
nt for children to learn that there are many kids who are worse off. Jean
se to anything bad is the midwestern standby "It could be worse." Most
of the time, that's actually true.

In addition, thoughts of gratitude can be shared with the family at mealtimes and holidays. This is
common practice at Thanksgiving, but not so much the rest of the year. Other small practices can encourage gratitude as well. Thank-you cards, for example, are a great way to express your gratitude to other
people. They do not just have to be for gifts; thanking people for helping you in some way or just being
a good friend, mentor, or parent benefits both people. Of course, one of the best ways to get your kids to
express gratitude is to express it yourself. Ideally, the expressions of gratitude will whittle away at those
feelings of entitlement. Another holiday tradition is also worth adopting—the Jewish practice, at Yom
Kippur, of asking the important people in your life for forgiveness. No matter what your religion, relationships are smoothed by apology and forgiveness. To apologize for anything you've done to wrong someone
is to discard entitlement and move toward a true connection with someone else.

In the workplace, one of the best ways to combat entitlement is to have workers experience a job that
gives them some humility. Summer jobs and career training (so-called paying your dues) teaches people
they were not born on home plate and imparts useful skills. Paying your dues has fallen out of favor lately;
one book by a twenty-something for twenty-somethings is called *Grindhopping: Build a Rewarding Career
Without Paying Your Dues*. Although it's true that it would be great to found your own company and be
the CEO instantly as the book advises, very few people can go this route. And even when you own your
own company, there is plenty of grind involved. Ask anyone who owns a small business—they'll tell you
about the long hours and all the times they had to work the counter.

Here's the unfortunate truth: virtually every job requires some grind, especially at the beginning. We both love our jobs as professors and researchers, but we started out as graduate students like

> Is work-life balance important? Why or why not?

everyone else. We ran seemingly endless studies in windowless labs, entered data for hours from stacks of papers several feet tall, and photocopied article after article on the library copier.

It wasn't working in the salt mines or cleaning hotel rooms, but it wasn't a glamorous intellectual exercise or constant fun, either. Even now, for all the fun times we have, such as writing this book or working with our students on research ideas, we also slog through unreadable student papers, grade exams, go to committee meetings that reliably spark thoughts of self-immolation, and still sometimes enter data. We're not complaining—just the opposite—but we also wouldn't expect to have jobs that were enjoyable all the time. Heck, even recreational pursuits like fishing, golf, or bowling require you to pay your dues.

In general, Americans have lost the idea that there is value in an honest day's work for an honest day's pay, even if the work isn't fulfilling. This issue has come up recently in the heated discussion around illegal immigration. Some on the pro-illegal-immigration side argue that "illegal immigrants do jobs that Americans are unwilling to do." There is something really disturbing about this statement; it implies that certain jobs are beneath Americans, that Americans don't want to get their hands dirty or their backs sore doing the work that keeps the country running, so they have to import people whom they consider beneath them to do it. This is one of the twists of logic of the narcissism epidemic: apparently, being lazy and unwilling to work makes Americans better than the people who are willing to work.

If this is true, it bodes very poorly for our future as a nation. Traditionally, everyone does lousy jobs when he or she is young. This was seen as an opportunity to learn humility and character. One of Keith's great experiences of humility came when he was working the graveyard shift taking inventory in a store in downtown Oakland. The job was very simple: he read numbers on merchandise and wrote them down on a clipboard. Keith was working next to a woman who was likely schizophrenic—while she was working she was having a heated conversation with someone who wasn't there. The manager came by, looked at the schizophrenic woman's work, and said, "good job." He then looked at Keith's sheet and pointed out that Keith was not following directions—he had put hash marks through the middle of his 7s in the European fashion. There were samples to show the employees how to write numbers correctly, which Keith didn't bother to read because he was so smart. Humiliation experienced and humility learned.

Young people, especially from wealthy families, should be encouraged to do some difficult work in order to learn humility, compassion, the link between work and pay, and the value of the dollar. Such work would teach young people a sense of connection to those who make careers of these jobs, rather than a vague sense of superiority over them. We also think it is crucial to treat people who do low-wage work with dignity and respect. It's easier to sit at a desk all day than it is to wait tables at a diner or pound nails into a roof during the Georgia summer; yet somehow many middle- and upper-class Americans feel they are superior to people who do this kind of work. That has to change. Instead of glorifying people who strike it rich with little effort—including many celebrities—the new American hero needs to be the old American hero: the guy or gal who gets up in the morning, works for a living, and doesn't bitch about it all day.

Questions for Comprehension

Answer these questions as a comprehension gauge and/or for further clarification on the text:

1. True or False. In a 2008 survey, one-third of students believed that their professor should give them special consideration if they explained they were trying hard.

2. Fill in the blank. In a 2007 survey of 2,500 hiring managers, 87 percent agreed that younger workers "feel more _____ in terms of compensation, benefits, and career advancement than older workers." A) competent, B) scared, C) optimistic, D) entitled

3. "Unfortunately," write these authors, "wanting more money for doing less work is a fairly succinct definition" of what?

4. Write a short answer to the following question: What is one of the best ways to combat entitlement?

5. One of the common refrains in American discourse on illegal immigration, the authors point out, is that "illegals do the jobs that Americans are unwilling to do." Why do the authors find this attitude to be a disturbing testament to the change that has taken place in the American work ethic, and what do you think?

Is Gen Z more stressed out than any prior generation of Americans?

The data indicate that it could be so.

But why is Gen Z so stressed out?

One answer could be: *the more time a person spends on the Internet or on a mobile device, the more depressed, anxious, and stressed out that person tends to be.*

Psychologist Jean Twenge, who has long studied generational differences, writes in *The Atlantic*:

> Around 2012, I noticed abrupt shifts in teen behaviors and emotional states. The gentle slopes of the line graphs became steep mountains and sheer cliffs, and many of the distinctive characteristics of the millennial generation began to disappear. In all my analyses of generational data—some reaching back to the 1930s—I had never seen anything like it.

Twenge calls them "iGen," the first generation of Americans in the twenty-first century. Essentially, iGen consists of those born between 1995-2012. The main factor distinguishing this generation is that they came of age with mobile Internet devices in hand (as opposed to Millennials who may have obtained their cellular devices in middle or high school).

It is "a generation shaped by the smartphone and by the concomitant rise of social media." Gen Z is less entitled, less optimistic, less narcissistic, less confident and more depressed than the Millennials, according to Twenge. Gen Z is "obsessed with safety and fearful of their economic futures." Depression and teen suicides rates, she writes, have skyrocketed since 2011.

- *To what extent do you agree or disagree with Twenge that Gen Z (iGen, in her parlance) is "on the brink of the worst mental-health crisis in decades"?*
- *To what extent do you agree or disagree that the cause of this deterioration "can be traced to their phones"?*

What Other Factors Are in Play?

In his book *Excellent Sheep*, William Deresiewicz blames the system of "elite" education that we have created in America for Gen Z's stress and anxiety. Students are not taught to appreciate the inherent value of knowledge or the inherent good of learning; they are taught instead to chase material possessions. Deresiewicz proposes a return to the traditional values of a liberal arts education, advocating the enduring legacy of a curious mind. He depicts the benefits of participating in the timeless discourses that are at the core of a humanist education.

Students who experience this kind of education, argues Deresiewicz, will be less stressed out and more fulfilled.

College students who are not part of the "elite" educational system may nevertheless relate to the author's depiction of a stressed-out generation that is being told to achieve at all costs but not being taught how to think for themselves.

Deresiewicz meditates on the meaning of "thinking for yourself":

> The point is not to have a high IQ. The point is to use it. Intelligence is not an aptitude. It's an activity—and an ethical activity, to boot. We don't need students to be radicals; we only need them to be skeptical. "Skeptical" comes from a word that means "to look." A skeptic is someone who bothers to look (144).

Students who know how "to look" develop their intelligence, but critics of America's educational system say that we aren't teaching our students how to look, how to examine, or how to question the world in which they live.

Instead of a *vocation*—a "calling"—Gen Z is told to seek employment. The point of higher education is to make more money, or so the message goes. It's not a bad message, and it's true that college grads make much more money and have better opportunities than high school grads. What employers say they need from college grads, though, are skills of intelligence and passion: the capacity for critical thinking, a solid independent work ethic, problem solving abilities, and a sense of purpose. *(See Finding Connections: The Workforce of the Twenty-First Century in Unit Six The Future of AI.)*

Economic change and a general fearfulness regarding the economic future seem to have a lot to do with the attitude and outlook of Millennials and Gen Z.

Social mobility has stalled, according to Deresiewicz and others. "If you live in a winner-takes-all society," he writes, "you're going to want your child to be among the winners" (41). Parents worrying over their children's future has resulted in a parental overprotection paradox that includes "coddling and pushing, stroking and surveillance" (46).

Parents don't need their kids to grapple with great questions or learn how to appreciate great books. In an uncertain world, they just want their kids to find good employment.

The Overprotection Paradox

When I was young—*yes, I realize how very old I sound when I begin a sentence this way*—when I was young, kids were basically told to go outside and play and be home by dinner. I do not recall a single moment of "supervised play" in my childhood. Now, I see news stories of parents being reported for neglect when they send their kids to play by themselves at the neighborhood park. Google "lawn darts." This hazardous childhood game really says it all: kids like me would throw a dart into the air with no conception that it was a deadly weapon raining death from above. Hey, we were having fun. Seat belts were not required in cars when I was born. There were no such things as child safety seats. Our society has changed much for the better when it comes to safety (thank goodness), but along with that change has arisen so-called "helicopter parenting" and a cultural mania of overprotection. Many psychologists, including Twenge, claim that the psychological effects of parental overprotection are largely negative. Children never learn to thrive on their own, or how to solve their own problems. Instead, from a very young age, children have been taught that an adult will intervene whenever life threatens to become difficult.

In trying to make life easier for kids, adults can unwittingly make their children's lives more difficult. Instead of reading our kids scary folktales, we turn to nice, safe books like *Go, Dog, Go!* (1961). It was one of my own favorites, I admit. I still like dogs.

Author Bruno Bettelheim touts the psychological benefits of old-fashioned folktales, asking mid-century parents to reconsider the dark tales of bygone centuries. For example, a fairytale like "Hansel and Gretel," Bettelheim explains, psychologically prepares small listeners for life's difficulties. "Little Red Riding Hood" and other tales collected by the Grimm Brothers offer coded warnings to young ears. Parents turned away from folktales toward modern stories like *The Little Engine That Could* (1930). In this modern folktale, a choo-choo train chugs up a big mountain with the mantra *I think I can, I think I can.* The little engine achieves its goal. Why? *Because it thinks it can!* The problem, Bettelheim points out, is that children will inevitably face failure in life, and if they are conditioned to believe that they can overcome difficulty simply by thinking that they can overcome it, they will be disenchanted. A parent's desire to protect the child may actually cause the child stress and anxiety later in life.

I encountered and decoded the old folktales only much later in life. In fact, *The Little Engine That Could* constitutes one of my own earliest literary memories. For decades, we Americans have been told that if we want something badly enough, then we can have it. But what kind of message is that? For one thing, it's a horrible lie. You can't always get what you want … just like that sage Mick Jagger sang out to the Baby Boomers long ago: *But if you try sometime you just might find, you get what you need.*

- *Parents naturally want to shelter their children from life's difficulties. While protecting children, how can parents also allow their children to develop necessary psychological defenses and self-motivation? What do the experts say?*
- *Were you "sheltered" at home or in school? How so? On the other hand, were you forced or allowed to struggle in healthy ways at home and at school? Did you ever face a real risk of failure? Was it terrible, or were you able to gain something from having to deal with failure?*
- *A number of critics bemoan the lack of "grit" in young people. Is there any merit to this harsh criticism? Or is it unfair? Why would it be important for a person to develop "grit" or resilience? How can children and young adults cultivate a sense of "grit" or determination in their own lives? ("Grit," by the way, is a personality trait closely aligned with career and personal success.)*
- *Review what psychologist Daniel Gilbert has to say about "resilience" in his work "Paradise Glossed" in unit eight.*
- *Consider the role of mobile devices when analyzing Gen Z from a mental health perspective.*

Finding Connections Works Cited

Deresiewicz, William. "The Disadvantages of an Elite Education." *American Scholar*, 1 June 2008, https://theamericanscholar.org/the-disadvantages-of-an-elite-education/#.W6qK7lJReAw.

Deresiewicz, William. *Excellent Sheep: The Miseducation of the American Elite and the Way to a Meaningful Life.* Free Press, 2014.

Twenge, Jean. "Have Smartphones Destroyed a Generation?" *The Atlantic*, Sept. 2017, https://www.theatlantic.com/magazine/archive/2017/09/has-the-smartphone-destroyed-a-generation/534198/.

Related: See Finding Connections: Generation Stress, version 1.0 in Unit Two.

Resources

How to Start Your Research Paper

The real start of your feature article or research paper is the **research**. Spend 2x or even 3x as long researching as writing. Start by creating a Works Cited bibliography which serves as a de facto guideline for your paper. Your instructor may first ask you to produce an **annotated bibliography**.

Plan ahead:

- **outline**
- **sequence source materials**
- **plan out transitions from source to source**
- **develop a thesis statement or major claim**
- **rely on evidence, data, and expert opinion**
- **draft, revise, edit**

HINT: Remember that you can draft paragraphs and pages "out of order." Start in the middle. Draft a text introduction of important source material. Transition to another important source. Always keep in mind: What is your purpose? What is your focus and your contribution to the discourse? Stake out your own position. Make sure that paragraphs start and end with your own prose. Your voice shapes the discourse.

Drafting Your Introduction

When you are ready to draft your introductory paragraph(s), consider these options:

- Anecdote/Story
  - Relate an anecdote that embodies a main theme you wish to convey.
- Profile
  - Profile an important individual (an expert in the field, for example) in order to introduce your subject matter.
- Brief History
  - Offer your audience a brief summary of necessary background information that the audience needs to know in order to understand your topic, or narrate an intriguing episode that embodies or contextualizes the topic at hand.

- Big Questions/Big Ideas
  - Hook your audience by asking big questions that are relevant to your subject matter, or propose a big idea that will grab the attention of an educated, engaged audience.
- Establish a Public Discourse
  - Outline a current controversy, public debate, or significant public discourse that is relevant to your topic.
- If All Else Fails, Introduce Source Material

Embrace the role of *author*.

By the time your research is completed, you possess some *authority* on your topic. You are not an expert, but you have synthesized the views of leading experts so that you are in a position to present an argument or major claim to your readers. Clarify the discourse for them. They haven't done the research. You have. Share your knowledge.

Find further information in Unit Nine Research in the Twenty-First Century.

Writing Assignments

Making Connections Template Exercise

The verbs cite(s) *and* claim(s) *indicate that you can use a singular or a plural subject to complete the sentence. For examples,* she cites *matches a singular subject, while* they cite *matches a plural subject. Hint: See if you can do better than using a vague pronoun. Identify a specific author by last name.*

Twenge cite(s) research correlating frequent, lengthy use of social media with feelings of anxiety and social isolation. Moreover, *Twenge* claim(s) that *young people* are particularly vulnerable to feelings of *entitlement* resulting from *narcissism.*

Essay Prompts

Level I: Analysis-Response

1. How do psychologists diagnose "narcissism" or "narcissistic personality disorder"? Look up the Narcissistic Personality Inventory (NPI) online. Uncover some of the questions and possible responses. (Maybe even take the test yourself. See Further Inquiry for a link.) In light of the NPI, analyze and respond to "All Play and No Work: *Entitlement*."

2. Analyze and respond to Twenge and Campbell's article by distinguishing between "wants" and "needs." How is this distinction relevant in a discourse on the subject of entitlement? Note that an exploration on *wants versus needs* is also relevant to happiness studies, so this topic can be elevated to a Level II synthesis essay as well.

3. Offer a defense of Gen Z or millennials in the face of Twenge and Campbell's cultural criticisms. How can you begin to develop the case that these psychologists' readings of youthful narcissism are either inaccurate or no longer relevant?

4. Analyze the narcissism that you see around you either in the culture at large or in your generation, possibly even in your acquaintances? Recount the authors' evidence and support their case by offering anecdotal or other evidence of your own.

5. How did narcissists fare in the resources game played out in Campbell's lab? Consider the concept of "entitlement" as a contributing factor to environmental degradation. How do materialism and/or mass consumerism relate to environmental concerns?

Level II: Making Connections

1. As mentioned above, an exploration of the distinctions between "wants" and "needs" is relevant to the topic of happiness studies. Look into the Unit Eight Further Inquiry bibliography for good source material to synthesize with Twenge and Campbell's article.

2. Examine the role of social media in America's "narcissism epidemic."

3. Look into the Unit Three Further Inquiry bibliography on brain plasticity or revisit the unit two feature article. Explain how neuroplasticity may play a role in the development of a personality disorder such as narcissism.

4. Revisit the unit four feature article or examine the Unit Four Further Inquiry bibliography for relevant source material. Why do narcissists never experience "love" as defined by psychologists like Barbara Fredrickson, Jean Twenge, and W. Keith Campbell?

5. A narcissist (as well as someone who is entitled) focuses on "I" instead of "we." Considering the collective nature of the creative process as examined in unit five, how can someone who is narcissistic (or entitled) thrive in a given field of the creative arts? History is rife with artists who possessed "giant egos." Can a narcissist make a good artist? Why or why not? Are there meaningful distinctions to be made between a narcissistic personality and an egocentric or entitled personality? You may want to select one historical example of an egocentric or narcissistic artist as a model for examination.

6. In her book *iGen* (2017), Jean Twenge argues that mobile devices and social media form the major defining characteristic of the generation born between 1985 and 2012. She claims that social media and mobile devices have caused, among other things, a more depressed generation of young people. Explore this claim. Do you see the relationship between mobile devices and youth anxiety as causal or coincidental? Examine the evidence and explain your reasoning.

7. How do the realities of the twenty-first century workforce tend to shape the attitudes and values of Gen Z? How does the contemporary job market, and preparing to enter the job market, affect Gen Z? As AI impacts the workforce, what sorts of jobs and careers will define Gen Z in the twenty-first century?

Level III: Research

1. *Expand one of the Level II topics listed above into a Level III research topic. For example:* How do the realities of the twenty-first century workforce tend to shape the attitudes and values of Gen Z? How does the contemporary job market, and preparing to enter the job market, affect Gen Z? As AI impacts the workforce, what sorts of jobs and careers will define Gen Z in the twenty-first century? *Rather than synthesis, pursue research on this topic.*

2. How could a generation who has experienced the Great Recession of 2008 or the Covid-19 Pandemic be the sort of shallow, entitled, materialistic consumers and narcissists that Twenge and Campbell describe? Examine the data in order to establish the factuality of America's narcissism epidemic. Are millennials part of this trend? How so? Determine whether Gen Z follows the trend. Collect evidence and explain your reasoning.

3. What is the actual definition of "narcissism"? What is "narcissistic personality disorder"? How do clinical psychologists define it and what are the exact features of the condition? (See the Level I prompt on NPI above.) Do Twenge and Campbell, who are trained psychologists, use the term "narcissism" accurately? Explain why so or why not. A clinical diagnosis of narcissism can only be assigned to an individual, not to an entire generation or to a group of people. Examine how Twenge, Campbell, and others negotiate the line between cultural criticism and clinical diagnosis.

4. Research trends in materialism. Have materialistic values changed significantly from the baby boomer generation to the millennials or Gen Z? What sorts of consumer products define or distinguish one generation from another? What do spending habits and trends say about the generations? Is there any kind of "generation gap" when it comes to materialism or the valuing of material goods? You might include an examination of the role of wealth, jobs, and/or charitable contributions.

5. Consider the role of the economy in generational critiques of millennials. To begin your research, under Unit Seven Further Inquiry, examine the 2018 Kurz et al. Federal Reserve System reported entitled "Are Millennials Different?" As you form your topic, you may want to also read Anne Helen Petersen's 2019 *BuzzFeed News* article or Derek Thompson's 2018 *Atlantic* article, also listed in the unit bibliography.

6. Millennials are self-centered and entitled. What are the origins of this criticism? Who is making this critique? To what extent are these criticisms fair or unfair?

7. According to author William Deresiewicz (*Excellent Sheep* 2014), higher education in the United States has become a consumer business model. Students are customers who pay for classes, "Yet a commercial relationship is exactly the opposite of a pedagogical one," he complains. Teachers in the classical mode offer wisdom to students who are willing to learn, not to students who expect to receive a good grade because they have paid for a course. To what extent is Deresiewicz's criticism of the "consumer business model" of higher education accurate or inaccurate, fair or unfair? To what extent, if any, does a consumer business model of higher education in the United States (and consequences such as grade inflation) impact the development of Gen Z and/or the next generation of American youth?

8. What are the most prominent and defining characteristics of college students in twenty-first century America? Consider exterior factors such as the economy and Internet technologies, and consider social trends that might reveal interior factors, such as trends in public and mental health. Rely on data and expert sources rather than anecdotes or intuition.

Further Inquiry

Allen, Reniqua. "The Story We Tell About Millennials—And Who We Leave Out." TED Salon: Doha Debates, Jan. 2019, https://www.ted.com/talks/reniqua_allen_the_story_we_tell_about_millennials_and_who_we_leave_out?language=en.

Barnes, Peter. "How to Save the Middle Class When Jobs Don't Pay." *88 Open Essays: A Reader for Students of Composition and Rhetoric*, edited by Sarah Wangler and Tina Ulrich, 2019,https://www.oercommons.org/courses/88-open-essays-a-reader-for-students-of-composition-rhetoric/view.

Barnes, Peter. *With Liberty and Dividends for All: How to Save Our Middle Class When Jobs Don't Pay Enough.* San Francisco: Berrett-Koehler Publishers, 2014.

Brokaw, Tom. *The Greatest Generation.* Random House, 1998.

Deresiewicz, William. "The Disadvantages of an Elite Education." *American Scholar*, 1 June 2008, https://theamericanscholar.org/the-disadvantages-of-an-elite-education/#.W6qK7lJReAw.

Deresiewicz, William. *Excellent Sheep: The Miseducation of the American Elite and the Way to a Meaningful Life.* Free Press, 2014.

Harris, Malcolm. *Kids These Days: Human Capital and the Making of Millennials.* Little, Brown and Company, 2017.

Kurz, Christopher, Geng Li, and Daniel J. Vine. "Are Millennials Different?" *Finance and Economics Discussion Series 2018-080*, 2018, Washington: Board of Governors of the Federal Reserve System, https://doi.org/10.17016/FEDS.2018.080.

"Narcissistic Personality Inventory: Narcissism Test." *Open-Source Psychometrics Project*, https://openpsychometrics.org/tests/NPI/.

Petersen, Anne Helen. "How Millennials Became The Burnout Generation." *BuzzFeed News*, 5 Jan. 2019, *https://www.buzzfeednews.com/article/annehelenpetersen/millennials-burnout-generation-debt-work.*

Thompson, Derek. "Millennials Didn't Kill the Economy. The Economy Killed Millennials." *The Atlantic*, 6 Dec. 2018, *https://www.theatlantic.com/ideas/archive/2018/12/stop-blaming-millennials-killing-economy/577408/.*

Twenge, Jean M. *Generation Me: Why Today's Young Americans Are More Confident, Assertive, Entitled—and More Miserable Than Ever Before.* Free Press, 2006.

"Have Smartphones Destroyed a Generation?" *The Atlantic*, Sept. 2017, https://www.theatlantic.com/magazine/archive/2017/09/has-the-smartphone-destroyed-a-generation/534198/.

iGen: Why Today's Super-Connected Kids Are Growing Up Less Rebellious, More Tolerant, Less Happy—and Completely Unprepared for Adulthood (and What That Means for the Rest of Us). Simon & Schuster, 2017.

Twenge, Jean and W. Keith Campbell. *The Narcissism Epidemic: Living in the Age of Entitlement.* Free Press, 2009.

UNIT EIGHT

Happiness Studies

Above all else, people seek happiness. Aristotle reached this conclusion more than 2500 years ago. So, what exactly *is* happiness? How can you achieve it, and how do you sustain it? Answers to these questions have varied over the millennia. Even though the pursuit of happiness represents a human concern throughout antiquity, the scientific study of happiness is a relatively new branch of psychology. Prior to the twentieth century, most psychologists, philosophers, and everyday working people took it for granted that life, taken on the whole, is a fairly miserable affair dotted with enough joy to make our endeavors worthwhile. Political philosopher Thomas Hobbes summed up a common view of the natural state of human existence when he famously characterized the life of the human creature in nature as "nasty, brutish, and short." Written during the bloody turmoil of the English Civil War, his book *Leviathan* (1651) takes a political slant: a strong, undivided government, Hobbes argues, provides a stable framework within which citizens can thrive. His work certainly influenced political philosophers in the centuries that followed. In declaring a new, independent nation, America's founders endorsed "the pursuit of Happiness" as an unalienable right—in other words, as something which cannot be taken away from a person.

In his book, *The Second Mountain* (2019), well-known newspaper columnist David Brooks argues that life's first metaphorical mountain typically involves the achievement of personal goals. Like many religious and philosophical commentators before him, Brooks notes that this "first mountain"—built upon a foundation of the self, the ego, and a sense of personal freedom—rarely provides for sustained happiness. In order to achieve true happiness, Brooks claims, one must resist the lies that our culture tells us, mainly, the lie that if you are successful (and if you have money) you will be happy. Life's metaphorical "second mountain" values relationships over the self. When we value service to others over the self, we can achieve real happiness. In his bestseller, *The Purpose Driven Life* (2002), Rick Warren makes a similar argument. The first line of his book reads, "It's not about you."

Critics of the self-help genre may resist this simplified messaging, and with good reason. It's pretty easy, after all, to tell other people how to live life. The famous Russian writer Leo Tolstoy became a spiritual leader in his later years—arguably, one might say, after he had experienced plenty of self-centered fun himself as a young man. Wise elders throughout history have had a tough go convincing energetic youth that "seize the day" fails in the long run. In the face of an uncertain tomorrow, grasping happiness today may seem the wisest path.

It is only in relatively recent times, in wealthy and stable nations like the United States, where humans seem to have decided that happiness is a human birthright extending from cradle to grave. Happiness has become for us something akin to a service dog that travels with us everywhere, constantly at our feet, there to sooth us with its adoring gaze. American culture bombards us with a message that if we are not constantly happy then something must be horribly wrong. And clearly, so the message goes, we are in dire need of the latest tech gadget, the latest beauty product, the latest pharmaceutical product, or at least a new pair of shoes. When did we become so frail, so addicted to the notion that this materialistic brand of "happiness" is a requirement for leading a fulfilling life?

Psychologists Jean Twenge and W. Keith Campbell argue in their book, *The Narcissism Epidemic* (2009) that American culture itself is a contributing factor to a rising "self-worth" epidemic wherein Americans of all ages increasingly prioritize personal feelings and materialism over social values such as duty or purposeful living.

In any case, how do we *objectively* define the *subjective* feeling of happiness? Whether we call it "bliss" or "contentment," being able to sustain the feeling remains an illusive prospect.

I *like* shiny new iPhones, you might say. And if a shiny new iPhone makes me feel happy, then what's the problem?

Aside from what psychologists Twenge and Campbell might have to say in response to this assertion, positive psychologist Daniel Gilbert in his book *Stumbling on Happiness* (2006) points out that humans are terrible at predicting what will actually create future states of happiness. *Affective forecasting* is the prediction of one's own future emotion state, and Gilbert says that we humans are terrible at it. We typically don't know, in fact, what will make us happy.

Gilbert contends that our confusion and misunderstandings over notions of happiness span the realms of philosophy and psychology. He writes, "If philosophers have muddled the moral and emotional meanings of the word *happiness*, then psychologists have muddled the emotional and judgmental meanings equally well and often." He explains that when people express the idea that they are happy *about* something or happy *that* something, they are not expressing the actual emotion of happiness. Instead, they are expressing a judgment: "I am happy that my test is finally over." Or, "I am happy that I have a shiny new iPhone." Or, relevant to this course, "I am happy that I have completed my composition." You may be happy *that* you have completed your essay, but it does not follow that you are now experiencing happiness. The person who utters these phrases, Gilbert points out, may be expressing *relief*, but certainly not *joy*. It's easy to say the word "happiness." It's difficult to sustain it as a stable emotional state of being.

As a positive psychologist, Gilbert specializes in a relatively new branch of psychology that we might term "happiness studies." Oftentimes, in popular culture, the notion of happiness presents itself like a hamster on a metal wheel, the discontented consumer constantly seeking a new product to satisfy some vague yearning. But what in the long run sustains happy bodies and minds? Note that both philosophers and psychologists are able to draw clear distinctions between short-lived happiness and sustainable happiness.

Any scientific study of happiness mandates that we replace subjective notions with objective data. Gilbert and his colleagues, for example, develop experiments to demonstrate psychological principles. Instead of simply theorizing, they want to show these ideas in action. In his publications and in his online TED Talks, Gilbert cites evidence, not just theories. Twenge likewise relies on data culled from ongoing, perennial surveys. The idea is to replace impressions about happiness with data about happiness.

Whenever the subjects being studied are human beings, however, unanswered questions abound. If twenty-first century neuroscientists face difficulties in studying the plastic human *brain*, then psychologists certainly face even greater difficulties in studying the human *mind*. Clearly, there are intimate connections between the physical brain and what we traditionally identify as the metaphysical mind. Philosophers and scientists contend with these distinctions. Some contemporary experimental philosophers posit that the human mind is not metaphysical at all. The mind is only a physical mechanism which lacks the actual ability to make independent decisions. Under this paradigm, the concept of "free will" is an illusion. The human brain takes in sensory data, processes it, and spits out a resulting behavior or "choice." (Note how computer metaphors inform our understandings of cognition in the era of big data.)

What processes within the *mind* (the totality of conscious and unconscious human mental processes) affect our sense of happiness, well-being, and contentment? This may be the main question at the heart of positive psychology.

Leveling Up

What is "happiness" anyway?

Clearly, there is not one type. Philosophers from the ancient world to the present day have identified various types or levels of happiness. Owning a shiny, new iPhone does provide a type of happiness, but it is important to recognize that philosophers categorize this type of happiness as short-lived, the lowest level, so to speak, of all forms of happiness.

Yet even when we intuit that we have achieved a true state or higher level of happiness, why are we humans so bad at sustaining it?

Self-help gurus ask us to look inside. Cultural critics ask us to resist vapid consumerism. Psychologists ask us to look at a long history of family dynamics. Others say to focus mindfully on the present. Existential philosophers and theologians lead us to the counterintuitive notion that true happiness is only achieved through toil and tears.

Twenty-first century science is unlikely to provide clear or simple answers to age-old questions. Yet something new is available to twenty-first century happiness-seekers. Scientifically-informed studies of the "problem" of happiness result in data that may provide new perspectives on this ancient topic.

Questions to Consider

Answer these questions as you read and annotate the text:

- "Rationalization" is a noun defined as "The act of causing something to be or to seem reasonable." How does the following chapter from Gilbert's book, *Stumbling on Happiness* (2006) relate to the noun, *rationalization*?
- The biggest factor in success in life, many experts agree, is the quality we call "grit." How does the idea of psychological "resilience" relate to "grit," in your view? Is "resilience" a rare or a common quality in humans, according to psychologists?
- What is the difference between "objective stimuli" and "subjective stimuli"? How does the human mind process stimuli?
- What three factors are important in order for us to *disambiguate* stimuli?
- How is the "psychological immune system" analogous to our physical immune system? How or where does the analogy fall short? In other words, how are these systems entirely different in terms of operation?
- If the brain and the eye have a contractual relationship, what is the contract?

Daniel Gilbert, "Paradise Glossed" (2006)

For there is nothing either good or bad, but thinking makes it so. Shakespeare,
Hamlet Prince of Denmark

FORGET YOGA. Forget liposuction. And forget those herbal supplements that promise to improve your memory, enhance your mood, reduce your waistline, restore your hairline, prolong your lovemaking, and improve your memory. If you want to be happy and healthy, you should try a new technique that has the power to transform the grumpy, underpaid chump you are now into the deeply fulfilled, enlightened individual you've always hoped to be. If you don't believe me, then just consider the testimony of some folks who've tried it:

- "I am so much better off physically, financially, mentally, and in almost every other way." (*JW from Texas*)
- "It was a glorious experience." (*MB from Louisiana*)
- "I didn't appreciate others nearly as much as I do now." (*CR from California*)

Who are these satisfied customers, and what is the miraculous technique they're all talking about? Jim Wright, former Speaker of the United States House of Representatives, made his remark after committing sixty-nine ethics violations and being forced to resign in disgrace. Moreese Bickham, a former inmate, made his remark upon being released from the Louisiana State Penitentiary where he'd served thirty-seven years for defending himself against the Ku Klux Klansmen who'd shot him. And Christopher Reeve, the dashing star of *Superman*, made his remark after an equestrian accident left him paralyzed from the neck down, unable to breathe without the help of a ventilator. The moral of the story? If you want to be happy, healthy, wealthy, and wise, then skip the vitamin pills and the plastic surgeries and try public humiliation, unjust incarceration, or quadriplegia instead.

Uh-huh. Right. Are we really supposed to believe that people who lose their jobs, their freedom, and their mobility are somehow *improved* by the tragedies that befall them? If that strikes you as a far-fetched possibility, then you are not alone. For at least a century, psychologists have assumed that terrible events—such as having a loved one die or becoming the victim of a violent crime—must have a powerful, devastating, and enduring impact on those who experience them.[1] This assumption has been so deeply embedded in our conventional wisdom that people who *don't* have dire reactions to events such as these are sometimes diagnosed as having a pathological condition known as "absent grief." But recent research suggests that the conventional wisdom is wrong, that the absence of grief is quite normal, and that rather than being the fragile flowers that a century of psychologists have made us out to be, most people are surprisingly resilient in the face of trauma. The loss of a parent or spouse is usually sad and often tragic, and it would be perverse to suggest otherwise. But the fact is that while most bereaved people are quite sad for a while, very few become chronically depressed and most experience relatively low levels of relatively short-lived distress.[2] Although more than half the people in the United States will experience a trauma such as rape, physical assault, or natural disaster in their lifetimes, only a small fraction will ever develop any post-traumatic pathology or require any professional assistance.[3] As one group of researchers noted, "Resilience is often the most commonly observed outcome trajectory following exposure to a potentially traumatic event."[4] Indeed, studies of those who survive major traumas suggest that the vast majority do

> Who are the three people that Gilbert mentions in his opening, and what are we to understand from the quotations attributed to them?

quite well, and that a significant portion claim that their lives were *enhanced* by the experience.[5] I know, I know. It sounds suspiciously like the title of a country song, but the fact is that most folks do pretty darn good when things go pretty darn bad.

If resilience is all around us, then why are statistics such as these so surprising? Why do most of us find it difficult to believe that *we* could ever consider a lifetime behind bars to be "a glorious experience"[6] or come to see paralysis as "a unique opportunity" that gave "a new direction"[7] to our lives? Why do most of us shake our heads in disbelief when an athlete who has been through several grueling years of chemotherapy tells us that "I wouldn't change anything,"[8] or when a musician who has become permanently disabled says, "If I had it to do all over again, I would want it to happen the same way,"[9] or when quadriplegics and paraplegics tell us that they are pretty much as happy as everyone else?[10] The claims made by people who have experienced events such as these seem frankly outlandish to those of us who are merely imagining those events—and yet, who are we to argue with the folks who've actually been there?

The fact is that negative events do affect us, but they generally don't affect us as much or for as long as we expect them to.[11] When people are asked to predict how they'll feel if they lose a job or a romantic partner, if their candidate loses an important election or their team loses an important game, if they flub an interview, flunk an exam, or fail a contest, they consistently overestimate how awful they'll feel and how long they'll feel awful.[12] Able-bodied people are willing to pay far more to avoid becoming disabled than disabled people are willing to pay to become able-bodied again because able-bodied people underestimate how happy disabled people are.[13] As one group of researchers noted, "Chronically ill and disabled patients generally rate the value of their lives in a given health state more highly than do hypothetical patients [who are] imagining themselves to be in such states."[14] Indeed, healthy people imagine that eighty-three states of illness would be "worse than death," and yet, people who are actually in those states rarely take their own lives.[15] If negative events don't hit us as hard as we expect them to, then why do we expect them to? If heartbreaks and calamities can be blessings in disguise, then why are their disguises so convincing? The answer is that the human mind tends to *exploit ambiguity*—and if that phrase seems ambiguous to you, then just keep reading and let me exploit it.

Stop Annoying People

The only thing more difficult than finding a needle in a haystack is finding a needle in a needlestack. When an object is surrounded by similar objects it naturally blends in, and when it is surrounded by dissimilar objects it naturally stands out. Look at figure 16. If you had a stopwatch that counted milliseconds, you'd find that you can locate the letter *O* in the array on the top (where it is surrounded by numbers) a bit more quickly than you can locate it in the array on the bottom (where it is surrounded by other letters). And that makes sense, because it is harder to find a letter among letters than a letter among numbers. And yet, had I asked you to look for "zero" instead of "the letter *O*," you would have been a bit faster to find it in the array at the bottom than in the array at the top.[16] Now, most of us think that a basic sensory ability such as vision is pretty well explained by its wiring, and if you wanted to understand this ability, you would do well to learn about luminance, contrast, rods, cones, optic nerves, retinas, and the like. But once you knew everything there was to know about the physical properties of the arrays shown in figure 16 and everything there was to know about the anatomy of the human eye, you would still not be able to explain why a person can find the circle more quickly in one case than in the other unless you also knew what that person thought the circle *meant*.

Meanings matter for even the most basic psychological processes, and while this may seem perfectly obvious to reasonable folks like you and me, ignorance of this perfectly obvious fact sent psychologists on a wild-goose chase that lasted nearly thirty years and produced relatively few geese. For much of the last half of the twentieth century, experimental psychologists timed rats as they ran mazes and observed pigeons as they pecked keys because they believed that the best way to understand behavior was to map the relation between a stimulus and an organism's response to that stimulus. By carefully measuring what an organism did when it was presented with a physical stimulus, such as a light, a sound, or a piece of food, psychologists hoped to develop a science that linked observable stimuli to observable behavior without using vague and squishy concepts such as *meaning* to connect them. Alas, this simpleminded project was doomed from the start, because while rats and pigeons may respond to stimuli as they are *presented* in the world, people respond to stimuli as they are *represented* in the mind. Objective stimuli in the world create subjective stimuli in the mind, and it is these subjective stimuli to which people react. For instance, the middle letters in the two words in figure 17 are physically identical stimuli (I promise—I cut and pasted them myself), and yet, most English speakers respond to them differently—see them differently, pronounce them differently, remember them differently—because one represents the letter *H* and the other represents the letter *A*. Indeed, it would be more appropriate to say that one *is* the letter *H* and the other *is* the letter *A* because the identity of an inky squiggle has less to do with how it is objectively constructed and more to do with *how we subjectively interpret it*. Two vertical lines with a cross-bar *mean* one thing when flanked by *T* and *E* and they *mean* another thing when flanked by *C* and *T*, and one of the many things that distinguishes us from rats and pigeons is that we respond to the *meanings* of such stimuli and not to the stimuli themselves. That's why my father can get away with calling me "doodlebug" and you can't.

1	5	9	3	1	5	4	4	2	9
6	8	4	2	1	6	2	2	3	3
9	2	7	6	9	7	5	5	1	1
5	3	7	2	7	6	2	7	8	9
3	7	5	9	6	8	8	2	9	8
4	8	3	1	2	1	6	8	1	8
4	3	4	2	3	9	1	7	0	9
6	2	4	1	8	6	7	5	2	3
7	6	4	2	9	6	5	4	4	5
9	5	2	3	6	7	8	4	5	3

L	G	V	C	L	G	E	E	P	V
I	T	E	P	L	I	P	P	C	C
V	Q	R	I	V	R	G	G	L	L
G	C	R	P	R	I	P	R	T	V
C	R	G	V	I	T	T	P	V	T
E	T	C	L	P	L	I	T	L	T
E	C	E	P	C	V	L	R	O	V
I	P	E	L	T	I	R	G	P	C
R	I	E	P	V	I	G	E	E	G
V	G	Q	C	I	R	T	E	G	C

Fig 16.

TAE
CAT

Fig 17. The middle shape has different meanings in different contexts.

Disambiguating Objects

Most stimuli are ambiguous—that is, they can mean more than one thing—and the interesting question is how we *disambiguate* them—that is, how we know which of a stimulus's many meanings to infer on a particular occasion. Research shows that *context, frequency,* and *recency* are especially important in this regard.

- Consider *context*. The word *bank* has two meanings in English: "a place where money is kept" and "the land on either side of a river." Yet we never misunderstand sentences such as "The boat ran into the bank" or "The robber ran into the bank" because the words *boat* and *robber* provide a context that tells us which of the two meanings of *bank* we should infer in each case.
- Consider *frequency*. Our past encounters with a stimulus provide information about which of its meanings we should embrace. For example, a loan officer is likely to interpret the sentence "Don't run into the bank" as a warning about how to ambulate through his place of business and not as sound advice about the steering of boats because in the course of a typical day the loan officer hears the word *bank* used more frequently in its financial than in its maritime sense.
- Consider *recency*. Even a boater is likely to interpret the sentence "Don't run into the bank" as a reference to a financial institution rather than a river's edge if she recently saw an ad for safe-deposit boxes and thus has the financial meaning of *bank* still active in her mind. Indeed, because I've been talking about banks in this paragraph, I am willing to bet that the sentence "He put a check in the box" causes you to generate a mental image of someone placing a piece of paper in a receptacle and not a mental image of someone making a mark on a questionnaire. (I'm also willing to guess that your interpretation of the title of this section depends on whether you annoyed someone more or less recently than someone annoyed you.)

Unlike rats and pigeons, then, we respond to meanings—and context, frequency, and recency are three of the factors that determine which meaning we will infer when we encounter an ambiguous stimulus. But there is another factor of equal importance and greater interest. Like rats and pigeons, each of us has desires, wishes, and needs. We are not merely spectators of the world but investors in it, and we often *prefer*, that an ambiguous stimulus mean one thing rather than another. Consider, for example, the drawing of a box in figure 18. This object (called the Necker cube after the Swiss crystallographer who discovered it in 1832) is inherently ambiguous, and you can prove this to yourself simply by staring at it for a few seconds. At first, the box appears to be sitting on its side and you have the sense that you're looking out at a box that is *across* from you. The dot is inside the box, at the place where the back panel and the bottom panel meet. But if you stare long enough, the drawing suddenly shifts, the box appears to be standing on its end, and you have the sense that you're looking down on a box that is *below* you. The dot is now perched on the upper right corner of the box. Because this drawing has two equally meaningful interpretations, your brain merrily switches back and forth between them, keeping you mildly entertained until you eventually get

> Gilbert asserts that the human mind tends to "exploit ambiguity." Can you explain in your own words what he means?

dizzy and fall down. But what if one of these meanings were better than the other? That is, what if you *preferred* one of the interpretations of this object? Experiments show that when subjects are rewarded for seeing the box across from them or below them, the orientation for which they were rewarded starts "popping out" more often and their brains "hold on" to that interpretation without switching.[17] In other words, when your brain is at liberty to interpret a stimulus in more than one way, it tends to interpret it the way it *wants* to, which is to say that your preferences influence your interpretations of stimuli in just the same way that context, frequency, and recency do.

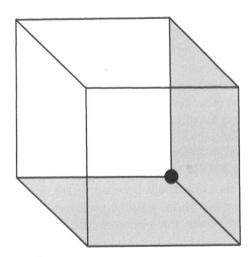

Fig 18. If you stare at a Necker cube, it will appear to shift its orientation.

This phenomenon is not limited to the interpretation of weird drawings. For example, why is it that you think of yourself as a talented person? (C'mon, give it up. You know you do.) To answer this question, researchers asked some volunteers (definers) to write down their definition of *talented* and then to estimate their talent using that definition as a guide.[18] Next, some other volunteers (non-definers) were given the definitions that the first group had written down and were asked to estimate their own talent using those definitions as a guide. Interestingly, the definers rated themselves as more talented than the nondefiners did. Because definers were given the liberty to define the word *talented* any way they wished, they defined it *exactly* the way they wished—namely, in terms of some activity at which they just so happened to excel ("I think *talent* usually refers to *exceptional artistic achievement* like, for example, this painting I just finished," or "*Talent* means *an ability you're born with*, such as being much stronger than other people. Shall I put you down now?"). Definers were able to set the standards for talent, and not coincidentally, they were more likely to meet the standards they set. One of the reasons why most of us think of ourselves as talented, friendly, wise, and fair-minded is that these words are the lexical equivalents of a Necker cube, and the human mind naturally exploits each word's ambiguity for its own gratification.

Disambiguating Experience

Of course, the richest sources of exploitable ambiguity are not words, sentences, or shapes but the intricate, variegated, multi-dimensional *experiences* of which every human life is a collage. If a Necker cube has two possible interpretations and *talent* has fourteen possible interpretations, then *leaving home* or *falling ill* or *getting a job with the U.S. Postal Service* has hundreds or thousands of possible interpretations. The things that *happen* to us—getting married, raising a child, finding a job, resigning from Congress, going to prison, becoming paralyzed—are much more complex than an inky squiggle or a colored cube, and that complexity creates loads of ambiguity that just begs to be exploited. It doesn't have to beg hard. For example, volunteers in one study were told that they would be eating a delicious but unhealthy ice cream sundae (ice cream eaters), and others were told that they would be eating a bitter but healthful plate of fresh kale (kale eaters).[19] Before actually eating these foods, the researchers asked the volunteers to rate the similarity of a number of foods, including ice cream sundaes, kale, and Spam (which everyone considered both unpalatable and unhealthful). The results showed that ice cream eaters thought that Spam was more like kale than it was like ice cream. Why? Because for some odd reason, ice cream eaters were thinking about food in terms of its *taste*—and unlike kale and Spam, ice cream tastes delicious. On the other hand, kale eaters thought that Spam was more like ice cream than it was like kale. Why? Because for some odd reason, kale eaters were thinking about food in terms of its *healthfulness*—and unlike kale, ice cream and Spam are unhealthful. The odd reason isn't really so odd. Just as a Necker cube is both across from you and below you, ice cream is both fattening and tasty, and kale is both healthful and bitter. Your brain and my brain easily jump back and forth between these different ways of thinking about the foods because we are merely reading about them. But if we were preparing to *eat* one of them, our brains would automatically exploit the ambiguity of that food's identity and allow us to think of it in a way that pleased us (delicious dessert or nutritious veggie) rather than a way that did not (fattening dessert or bitter veggie). As soon as our *potential* experience becomes our *actual* experience—as soon as we have a stake in its goodness—our brains get busy looking for ways to think about the experience that will allow us to appreciate it.

Because experiences are inherently ambiguous, finding a "positive view" of an experience is often as simple as finding the "below-you view" of a Necker cube, and research shows that most people do this well and often. Consumers evaluate kitchen appliances more positively after they buy them,[20] job seekers evaluate jobs more positively after they accept them,[21] and high school students evaluate colleges more positively after they get into them.[22] Racetrack gamblers evaluate their horses more positively when they are leaving the betting window than when they are approaching it,[23] and voters evaluate their candidates more positively when they are exiting the voting booth than when they are entering it.[24] A toaster, a firm, a university, a horse, and a senator are all just fine and dandy, but when they become *our* toaster, firm, university, horse, and senator they are instantly finer and dandier. Studies such as these suggest that people are quite adept at finding a positive way to view things once those things become their own.

Cooking with Facts

In Voltaire's classic novel *Candide*, Dr. Pangloss is a teacher of "metaphysico-theologo-cosmolo-nigology" who believes he lives in the best of all possible worlds.

"It is clear," he said, "that things cannot be other than the way they are; for as all things have been created for some end, they must necessarily be created for the best end. For instance, noses were made to support spectacles, hence we wear spectacles. Legs, as anyone can see, were made for breeches, and so we wear breeches. Stones were made to be shaped into castles; thus My Lord has a fine castle because the greatest baron in the province ought to have the finest house. And because pigs were made to be eaten, we eat pork all year round. So those who say that everything is well are speaking foolishly; they should say that everything is best."[25]

The research I've described so far seems to suggest that human beings are hopelessly Panglossian; there are more ways to think about experience than there are experiences to think about, and human beings are unusually inventive when it comes to finding the best of all possible ways. And yet, if this is true, then why aren't we all walking around with wide eyes and loopy grins, thanking God for the wonder of hemorrhoids and the miracle of in-laws? Because the mind may be gullible, but it ain't no patsy. The world is *this* way, we wish the world were *that* way, and our experience of the world—how we see it, remember it, and imagine it—is a mixture of stark reality and comforting illusion. We can't spare either. If we were to experience the world exactly as it is, we'd be too depressed to get out of bed in the morning, but if we were to experience the world exactly as we want it to be, we'd be too deluded to find our slippers. We may see the world through rose-colored glasses, but rose-colored glasses are neither opaque nor clear. They can't be opaque because we need to see the world clearly enough to participate in it—to pilot helicopters, harvest corn, diaper babies, and all the other stuff that smart mammals need to do in order to survive and thrive. But they can't be clear because we need their rosy tint to motivate us to *design* the helicopters ("I'm sure this thing will fly"), *plant* the corn ("This year will be a banner crop"), and *tolerate* the babies ("What a bundle of joy!"). We cannot do without reality and we cannot do without illusion.

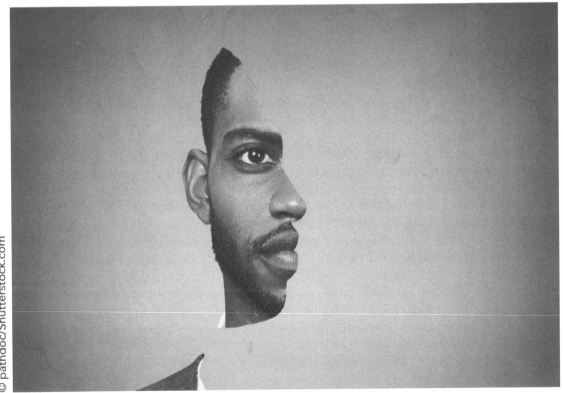

© pathdoc/Shutterstock.com

Each serves a purpose, each imposes a limit on the influence of the other, and our experience of the world is the artful compromise that these tough competitors negotiate.[26]

Rather than thinking of people as hopelessly Panglossian, then, we might think of them as having a *psychological immune system* that defends the mind against unhappiness in much the same way that the *physical immune system* defends the body against illness.[27] This metaphor is unusually appropriate. For example, the physical immune system must strike a balance between two competing needs: the need to recognize and destroy foreign invaders such as viruses and bacteria, and the need to recognize and respect the body's own cells. If the physical immune system is hypoactive, it fails to defend the body against micropredators and we are stricken with infections; but if the physical immune system is hyperactive, it mistakenly defends the body against itself and we are stricken with autoimmune disease. A healthy physical immune system must balance its competing needs and find a way to defend us well—but not *too* well.

Analogously, when we face the pain of rejection, loss, misfortune, and failure, the *psychological* immune system must not defend us too well ("I'm perfect and everyone is against me") and must not fail to defend us well enough ("I'm a loser and I ought to be dead"). A *healthy* psychological immune system strikes a balance that allows us to feel good enough to cope with our situation but bad enough to do something about it ("Yeah, that was a lousy performance and I feel crummy about it, but I've got enough confidence to give it a second shot"). We need to be defended—not defenseless or defensive—and thus our minds naturally look for the best view of things while simultaneously insisting that those views stick reasonably closely to the facts. That's why people seek opportunities to think about themselves in positive ways but routinely reject opportunities to think about themselves in *unrealistically* positive ways.[28] For example, college students request new dorm assignments when their current roommates do not think well of them, but they also request new dorm assignments when their current roommates think *too well* of them.[29] No one likes to feel that they are being duped, even when the duping is a pleasure. In order to maintain the delicate balance between reality and illusion, we seek positive views of our experience, but we only allow ourselves to embrace those views when they seem *credible*. So what makes a view seem credible?

Finding Facts

Most of us put a lot of stock in what scientists tell us because we know that scientists reach their conclusions by gathering and analyzing facts. If someone asked you why you believe that smoking is bad and jogging is good, or that the earth is round and the galaxy is flat, or that cells are small and molecules are smaller, you would point to the facts. You might need to explain that you do not personally *know* the facts to which you are pointing, but that you do know that at some time in the past, a bunch of very earnest people in white lab coats went out and observed the world with stethoscopes, telescopes, and microscopes, wrote down what they observed, analyzed what they wrote down, and then told the rest of us what to believe about nutrition, cosmology, and biology. Scientists are credible because they draw conclusions from observations, and ever since the *empiricists* trumped the *dogmatists* and became the kings of ancient Greek medicine, westerners have had a special reverence for conclusions that are based on things they can see. It isn't surprising, then, that we consider our own views credible when they are based on observable facts but not when they are based on wishes, wants, and fancies. We might *like* to believe that everyone loves us, that we will live forever, and that high-tech stocks are preparing to make a major comeback, and it would be awfully convenient if we could just push a little button at the base of our skulls and instantly believe as we wanted. But that's not how believing works. Over the course of human evolution, the brain and the eye have developed a contractual relationship in which the brain has agreed to believe what the eye sees and not to believe what the eye denies. So if we are to believe something, then it must be supported by—or at least not blatantly contradicted by—the facts.

If views are acceptable only when they are credible, and if they are credible only when they are based on facts, then how do we achieve positive views of ourselves and our experience? How do we manage to think of ourselves as great drivers, talented lovers, and brilliant chefs when the facts of our lives include a pathetic parade of dented cars, disappointed partners, and deflated soufflés? The answer is simple: *We cook the facts*. There are many different techniques for collecting, interpreting, and analyzing facts, and different techniques often lead to different conclusions, which is why scientists disagree about the dangers of global warming, the benefits of supply-side economics, and the wisdom of low-carbohydrate diets. Good scientists deal with this complication by choosing the techniques they consider most appropriate and then accepting the conclusions that these techniques produce, regardless of what those conclusions might be. But *bad* scientists take advantage of this complication by choosing techniques that are especially likely to produce the conclusions they favor, thus allowing them to reach favored conclusions by way of supportive facts. Decades of research suggests that when it comes to collecting and analyzing facts about ourselves and our experiences, most of us have the equivalent of an advanced degree in Really Bad Science.

Consider, for instance, the problem of sampling. Because scientists cannot observe every bacterium, comet, pigeon, or person, they study small samples that are drawn from these populations. A fundamental rule of good science and common sense is that this sample must be drawn from all parts of the population if it is to tell us about that population. There's really no point in conducting an opinion poll if you're only going to call registered Republicans from Orange County or the executive membership of Anarchists Against Organizations Including This One. And yet, that's pretty much what we do when seeking facts that bear on our favored conclusions.[30] For example, when volunteers in one study were told that they'd scored poorly on an intelligence test and were then given an opportunity to peruse newspaper articles about IQ tests, they spent more time reading articles that questioned the validity of such tests than articles that sanctioned them.[31] When volunteers in another study were given a glowing evaluation by a supervisor, they were more interested in reading background information that praised the supervisor's competence and acumen than background information that impeached it.[32] By controlling the sample of information to which they were exposed, these people indirectly controlled the conclusions they would draw.

You've probably done this yourself. For instance, if you've ever purchased a new automobile, you may have noticed that soon after you made the decision to buy the Honda instead of the Toyota, you began lingering over the Honda advertisements in the weekly news-magazine and skimming quickly past ads for the competition.[33] If a friend had noticed this and asked you about it, you would probably have explained that you were simply more interested in learning about the car you'd chosen than about the car you didn't. But *learning* is an odd choice of words here because that word usually refers to the balanced acquisition of knowledge, and the kind of learning one does by reading only Honda ads is more than a little lopsided. Ads contain facts about the advantages of the products they describe and not about the disadvantages, and thus your quest for new knowledge would have the interesting side benefit of ensuring that you would be marinated in those facts—and *only* those facts—that confirmed the wisdom of your decision.

Not only do we select favorable facts from magazines, we also select them from memory. For example, in one study, some volunteers were shown evidence indicating that extraverts receive higher salaries and more promotions than introverts do (successful-extravert group) and other volunteers were shown evidence indicating the opposite (successful-introvert group).[34] When the volunteers were asked to recall specific behaviors from their pasts that would help determine whether they were extraverted or introverted, volunteers in the successful-extravert group tended to recall the time when they'd brazenly walked up to a complete stranger and introduced themselves, whereas volunteers in the successful-introvert group tended to recall the time when they saw someone they liked but had been too shy to say hello.

> Gilbert writes, "We cannot do without reality and we cannot do without illusion." What does he mean?

Of course, other people—and not memories or magazine ads—are the richest sources of information about the wisdom of our decisions, the extent of our abilities, and the irresistible effervescence of our bubbly personalities. Our tendency to expose ourselves to information that supports our favored conclusions is especially powerful when it comes to choosing the company we keep. You've probably noticed that with the exception of Wilt Chamberlain, nobody picks friends and lovers by random sampling. On the contrary, we spend countless hours and countless dollars carefully arranging our lives to ensure that we are surrounded by people who *like* us, and people who *are* like us. It isn't surprising, then, that when we turn to the folks we know for advice and opinions, they tend to confirm our favored conclusions—either because they share them or because they don't want to hurt our feelings by telling us otherwise.[35] Should the people in our lives occasionally fail to tell us what we want to hear, we have some clever ways of helping them.

For example, studies reveal that people have a penchant for asking questions that are subtly engineered to manipulate the answers they receive.[36] A question such as "Am I the best lover you've ever had?" is dangerous because it has only one answer that can make us truly happy, but a question such as "What do you like best about my lovemaking?" is brilliant because it has only one answer that can make us truly miserable (or two if you count "It reminds me of Wilt Chamberlain"). Studies show that people intuitively lean toward asking the questions that are most likely to elicit the answers they want to hear. And when they hear those answers, they tend to believe what they've nudged others to say, which is why "Tell me you love me" remains such a popular request.[37] In short, we derive support for our preferred conclusions by listening to the words that we put in the mouths of people who have already been preselected for their willingness to say what we want to hear.

And it gets worse—because most of us have ways of making other people confirm our favored conclusions without ever engaging them in conversation. Consider this: To be a great driver, lover, or chef, we don't need to be able to parallel park while blindfolded, make ten thousand maidens swoon with a single pucker, or create a *pâte feuilletée* so intoxicating that the entire population of France instantly abandons its national cuisine and swears allegiance to our kitchen. Rather, we simply need to park, kiss, and bake better than most other folks do. How do we know how well most other folks do? Why, we look around, of course—but in order to make sure that we see what we want to see, we look around *selectively*.[38] For example, volunteers in one study took a test that ostensibly measured their social sensitivity and were then told that they had flubbed the majority of the questions.[39] When these volunteers were then given an opportunity to look over the test results of other people who had performed better or worse than they had, they ignored the tests of the people who had done better and instead spent their time looking over the tests of the people who had done worse. Getting a C– isn't so bad if one compares oneself exclusively to those who got a D.

This tendency to seek information about those who have done more poorly than we have is especially pronounced when the stakes are high. People with life-threatening illnesses such as cancer are particularly likely to compare themselves with those who are in worse shape,[40] which explains why 96 percent of the cancer patients in one study claimed to be in better health than the average cancer patient.[41] And if we can't *find* people who are doing more poorly than we are, we may go out and *create* them. Volunteers in one study took a test and were then given the opportunity to provide hints that would either help or hinder a friend's performance on the same test.[42] Although volunteers helped their friends when the test was described as a game, they actively hindered their friends when the test was described as an important measure of intellectual ability. Apparently, when our friends do not have the good taste to come in last so that we can enjoy the good taste of coming in first, we give them a friendly push in the appropriate direction. Once we've successfully sabotaged their performances and ensured their failure, they become the perfect standard for comparison. The bottom line is this: The brain and the eye may have a contractual relationship in which the brain has agreed to believe what the eye sees, but in return the eye has agreed to look for what the brain wants.

Challenging Facts

Whether by choosing information or informants, our ability to cook the facts that we encounter helps us establish views that are both positive and credible. Of course, if you've ever discussed a football game, a political debate, or the six o'clock newscast with someone from the other side of the aisle, you've already discovered that even when people *do* encounter facts that disconfirm their favored conclusions, they have a knack for ignoring them, forgetting them, or seeing them differently than the rest of us do. When Dartmouth and Princeton students see the same football game, both sets of students claim that the facts clearly show that the other school's team was responsible for the unsportsmanlike conduct.[43] When Democrats and Republicans see the same presidential debate on television, both sets of viewers claim that the facts clearly show that their candidate was the winner.[44] When pro-Israeli and pro-Arab viewers see identical samples of Middle East news coverage, both proponents claim that the facts clearly show that the press was biased against their side.[45] Alas, the only thing these facts *clearly* show is that people tend to see what they want to see.

Inevitably, however, there will be times when the unkind facts are just too obvious to set aside. When our team's defensive tackle is caught wearing brass knuckles, or when our candidate confesses to embezzlement on national television, we find it difficult to overlook or forget such facts. How do we manage to maintain a favored conclusion when the brute facts just won't cooperate? Although the word *fact* seems to suggest a sort of unquestionable irrefutability, facts are actually nothing more than conjectures that have met a certain standard of proof. If we set that standard high enough, then nothing can ever be proved, including the "fact" of our own existence. If we set the standard low enough, then all things are true and equally so. Because nihilism and postmodernism are both such unsatisfying philosophies, we tend to set our standard of proof somewhere in the middle. No one can say precisely where that standard should be set, but one thing we do know is that wherever we set it, we must keep it in the same place when we evaluate the facts we favor and the facts we don't. It would be unfair for teachers to give the students they like easier exams than those they dislike, for federal regulators to require that foreign products pass stricter safety tests than domestic products, or for judges to insist that the defense attorney make better arguments than the prosecutor.

And yet, this is just the sort of uneven treatment most of us give to facts that confirm and disconfirm our favored conclusions. In one study, volunteers were asked to evaluate two pieces of scientific research on the effectiveness of capital punishment as a deterrent.[46] They were shown one research study that used the "between-states technique" (which involved comparing the crime rates of states that had capital punishment with the crime rates of states that did not) and one research study that used the "within-states technique" (which involved comparing the crime rates of a single state before and after it instituted or outlawed capital punishment). For half the volunteers, the between-states study concluded that capital punishment was effective and the within-states study concluded it was not. For the other half of the volunteers, these conclusions were reversed. The results showed that volunteers favored whichever technique produced the conclusion that verified their own personal political ideologies. When the within-states technique produced an unfavorable conclusion, volunteers immediately recognized that within-states comparisons are worthless because factors such as employment and income vary over time, and thus crime rates in one decade (the 1980s) can't be compared with crime rates in another decade

> Look up the terms "impact bias" and "confirmation bias." How are these concepts related to the processes that Gilbert describes in this article?

(the 1990s). But when the between-states technique produced an unfavorable conclusion, volunteers immediately recognized that between-states comparisons are worthless because factors such as employment and income vary with geography, and thus crime rates in one place (Alabama) can't be compared with crime rates in another place (Massachusetts).[47] Clearly, volunteers set the methodological bar higher for studies that disconfirmed their favored conclusions. This same technique allows us to achieve and maintain a positive and credible view of ourselves and our experiences. For example, volunteers in one study were told that they had performed very well or very poorly on a social-sensitivity test and were then asked to assess two scientific reports—one that suggested the test was valid and one that suggested it was not.[48] Volunteers who had performed well on the test believed that the studies in the validating report used sounder scientific methods than did the studies in the invalidating report, but volunteers who performed poorly on the test believed precisely the opposite.

When facts challenge our favored conclusion, we scrutinize them more carefully and subject them to more rigorous analysis. We also require a lot more of them. For example, how much information would you require before you were willing to conclude that someone was intelligent? Would their high school transcripts be enough? Would an IQ test suffice? Would you need to know what their teachers and employers thought of them? Volunteers in one study were asked to evaluate the intelligence of another person, and they required considerable evidence before they were willing to conclude that the person was truly smart. But interestingly, they required much *more* evidence when the person was an unbearable pain in the ass than when the person was funny, kind, and friendly.[49] When we *want* to believe that someone is smart, then a single letter of recommendation may suffice; but when we *don't want* to believe that person is smart, we may demand a thick manila folder full of transcripts, tests, and testimony.

Precisely the same thing happens when we want or don't want to believe something about ourselves. For instance, volunteers in one study were invited to take a medical test that would supposedly tell them whether they did or did not have a dangerous enzyme deficiency that would predispose them to pancreatic disorders.[50] The volunteers placed a drop of their saliva on a strip of ordinary paper that the researchers falsely claimed was a medical test strip. Some volunteers (positive-testers) were told that if the strip turned green in ten to sixty seconds, then they had the enzyme deficiency. Other volunteers (negative-testers) were told that if the strip turned green in ten to sixty seconds, then they *didn't* have the enzyme deficiency. Although the strip was an ordinary piece of paper and hence never turned green, the negative-testers waited much longer than the positive-testers before deciding that the test was complete. In other words, the volunteers gave the test strip plenty of time to prove that they were well but much less time to prove that they were ill. Apparently it doesn't take much to convince us that we are smart and healthy, but it takes a whole lotta facts to convince us of the opposite. We ask whether facts *allow* us to believe our favored conclusions and whether they *compel* us to believe our disfavored conclusions.[51] Not surprisingly, disfavored conclusions have a much tougher time meeting this more rigorous standard of proof.[52]

Onward

In July 2004, the City Council of Monza, Italy, took the unusual step of banning goldfish bowls. They reasoned that goldfish should be kept in rectangular aquariums and not in round bowls because "a fish kept in a bowl has a distorted view of reality and suffers because of this."[53] No mention was made of the bland diet, the noisy pump, or the silly plastic castles. No, the problem was that round bowls deform the visual experience of their inhabitants, and goldfish have the fundamental right to see the world as it really is. The good counselors of Monza did not suggest that human beings should enjoy the same right, perhaps because they knew that our distorted views of reality are not so easily dispelled, or perhaps because they understood that we suffer less with them than we would without them. Distorted views of reality are made possible by the fact that experiences are ambiguous—that is, they can be credibly viewed in many ways, some of which are more positive than others. To ensure that our views are credible, our brain accepts what our eye sees. To ensure that our views are positive, our eye looks for what our brain wants. The conspiracy between these two servants allows us to live at the fulcrum of stark reality and comforting illusion. So what does all of this have to do with forecasting our emotional futures? As we are about to see, we may live at the fulcrum of reality and illusion, but most of us don't know our own address.

Questions for Comprehension

Answer these questions as a comprehension gauge and/or for further clarification on the text:

1. True or False. The psychological immune system works to rationalize unpleasant events, allowing a person to conceive of a more pleasant future.

2. In one study, participants were asked to evaluate scientific research on the effectiveness of capital punishment as a deterrent. Participants were asked to judge whether the "between-states" study or the "within-states" study was more accurate. What was the point of this psychological study?

3. Explain the following quotation: "Apparently it doesn't take much to convince us that we are smart and healthy, but it takes a whole lotta facts to convince us of the opposite."

Finding Connections: Can We Choose Happiness? Or Can We Even Choose?

There are some practical, grounded concerns at the heart of this unit. For example, *How do I shape a life in which I'll be happy? What actions will bring me contentment, and what actions would result in misery?* If you're like me as a college student, you've only considered these questions vaguely and tangentially, if at all.

They are not new questions, of course. The ancient Greek philosopher Epicurus (341-270 BCE) is considered by many to be the father of Hedonism, a life philosophy which seeks to maximize happiness and minimize misery. Epicurus' actual advice is often misunderstood as a rabid *carpe diem* (seize the day) mentality of pleasure-seeking. In fact, Epicurus focused on sustained happiness, emphasizing repose, serenity, friendship, simple pleasures, and the avoidance of public and political life.

It seems clear that Epicurus believed that happiness stems from personal choices. American psychologist Daniel Gilbert also believes that "Most of us make at least three important decisions in our lives: where to live, what to do, and with whom to do it. We choose our towns and our neighborhoods, we choose our jobs and our hobbies, we choose our spouses and our friends" (235).

This seems like common sense. Yet, increasingly, twenty-first century social scientists and philosophers emphasize the importance of a person's "context" (one's situation or environment) more than his or her free will when it comes to the apparent decisions that we make in life. Is it possible that, in fact, we do not choose our jobs, our residences, our romantic partners, our political alignments, or even our friends? To use an old-fashioned philosophical term, are these things fated to us rather than the result of conscious choices that we make?

In our unit on "The Future of AI," the question of *free will* also arises. Some experimental scientists, such as Benjamin Libet, and some psychologists, such as Daniel Wegner, have gone so far as to conclude that the concept of free will (i.e. making choices) is nothing more than an illusion. Our brains trick us into thinking that we are making choices when, in fact, the choices are made for us by a plethora of environmental factors and sensory inputs of which we are not conscious.

To what extent, then, can we choose happiness? Happiness itself, it seems, would be a matter of predetermination if we cannot make choices to influence our states of being.

At the same time, as you recall from our unit on "Brain Plasticity," experts believe that our neural networks are capable of positive training at any age. The facts of neuroplasticity and positive brain training seem to present evidence of the human capacity for conscious decision-making.

The "psychological immune system" is yet another factor in discourse on human happiness. In his book, *Stumbling on Happiness*, Daniel Gilbert cites multiple studies that reveal a typical human resilience in the face of traumatic life events. Our brains are not only resilient, he argues, they are able to *synthesize* happiness when tragic circumstances befall us. In a 2004 TED Talk, Gilbert explains that the "psychological immune system" is a survival mechanism. Were we to allow tragedy to devastate us forever, we could not have survived as a species. The prospect of happiness—the ability to conceive of a bright future—may be one of the evolutionary mechanisms keeping humankind on the pathways of procreation.

Just as "synthetic happiness" does not mean "fake happiness" (see Gilbert's TED Talk), a "synthetic connection" between AI and Happiness Studies or between Happiness Studies and Romance in the Twenty-First Century does not mean a "fake connection." *To synthesize* means to combine things into a coherent whole. Your brain can synthesize happiness out of a wide array of life events. And you—as you struggle to combine words, sentences, and ideas—can discover new concepts as you seek information from various fields of study.

Nothing New Under the Sun

The pursuit of happiness is as ancient as love poetry, as ancient as discourse concerning free will and fate. Contemporary experts may use terms like *choice and context* instead of *free will and fate*, but these explorations remain as important in the twenty-first century as they were in the ancient world.

- *When it comes to the study of happiness, where do you stand on the power of context and the power of free will?*
- *What conscious choices is a person able to make in regard to achieving happiness? What environmental factors tend to be deterministic?*
- *What is the role of the human mind in determining one's happiness? What is the role of the heart? Can we separate mind and heart?*

Focus on data and expertise. It is crucial to note the supporting evidence behind a concept, not just the concept itself. For example, you can easily define the "psychological immune system" and even give an example of it in action based on Gilbert's writing. But what supporting evidence does he offer to validate his claims? Convey the thesis or main idea at the heart of any given text, but detail supporting evidence as well. How can you or your reader be confident in an idea if there is no supporting evidence to bolster it? Offering details regarding the supporting evidence persuades an audience. Like the experts and scientists who author these texts, the essay writer or researcher must also rely on evidence. Writers who include convincing details in their work become *authors*, that is, authoritative voices on a given topic. It is well within your purview and capacities to *synthesize* connections between source articles and to *author* a meaningful research paper on topics of interest.

Finding Connections Works Cited

"Aristotle." History of Happiness, *The Pursuit of Happiness,* 2018, https://www.pursuit-of-happiness.org/history-of-happiness/aristotle/.

Gilbert, Daniel. *Stumbling on Happiness.* Alfred A. Knopf, 2006.

Gilbert, Daniel. "The Surprising Science of Happiness." TED Talk, Feb. 2004, https://www.ted.com/talks/dan_gilbert_the_surprising_science_of_happiness.

Resources

Sample Student Paper

J. Doe
Feature Article Essay
Word Count: 3,000

Wealth and Happiness

Happiness is loosely defined as existing in a state of contentment. Everyone strives to achieve this condition of existence through numerous methods and approaches. One focus that seems to have a difference of opinion is the role of wealth and materialism in happiness. There are various scholars that have mixed ideas on this matter, including psychologists in "happiness studies," economists, authors, and many others. Can happiness be achieved if one's net worth doubled overnight or is the pursuit of wealth meaningless when it comes to this issue? Because happiness is hard to define, this argument seems to have no black and white answers and there are also varying degrees of complexity in achieving this state of being.

In the book, *Measuring Happiness: The Economics of Well-Being*, written by Joachim Weimann, Andreas Knabe, and Ronnie Schöb, the authors mention that after World War II, the Western society had visions of wealth and prosperity to forget the horrors of the long and brutal war. Happiness at the time would mean to have a future that they could believe in, which entailed financial success and security for every individual and their families. The authors state that, "Inhabitants of industrialized countries have been enjoying a constantly rising standard of living for a very long time. In most countries, this has manifested itself not only as an increase in average income but also in better provision of cultural and social goods" (Weimann et al. 22). Having that rise in the standard of living meant that there was financial stability in postwar Western society, signifying the happiness and satisfaction from reaching their intended goal of economic success.

It is generally known that income and work directly affect a person's lifestyle and way of living. Work is also seen as a determinant of one's identity and self-perception, which can have a major impact on a person's mental state. Because of these factors, loss of income can contribute to a dramatic decline in an individual's happiness. Covering the years, 1984–2019, happiness researchers collected data based on how unemployment reduces life satisfaction at a worldwide level:

Unemployment reduces average life satisfaction of men by more than 22 percent (1.6 points) and that of women by about 17 percent (1.18 points). Women suffer somewhat less when unemployed than men do, but the loss of quality of life caused by unemployment is also substantial in their case. Both of the preceding observations are valid worldwide. In a study in which Stavrova et al. (2011) compared data from 28 countries, all the data point to a huge difference in life satisfaction between the employed and the unemployed… losing your job means losing your income. You are then reliant on other support, and that is generally considerably less than your old salary. It is the loss of income accompanying unemployment that sees to it that life satisfaction declines (Weimann et al. 58).

These findings attribute to the fact that money directly has a role in happiness and when a person is faced with unemployment, it can take a major hit to that person's life satisfaction. These happiness researchers also discovered that the longer an individual is unemployed, the lower the life satisfaction becomes. This can lead to debilitating depression and anxiety solely based on the feelings of inadequacy.

Anxiety can have a major role when it comes to financial instability and possessing a lower income, which can negatively influence happiness levels. In a business article in *Fast Company*, Charlie Sorrel states that wealth is heavily related to a person's well-being and happiness. Research was done resulting in most participants agreeing that living in a household that is financially sound attributes to overall happiness and contentment. Reports from this research mention, "Life satisfaction, sense of worth and happiness are higher, and anxiety less, as the level of household wealth increases, meaning that on the whole individuals living in households with higher wealth report lower anxiety levels, holding other factors equal" (qtd. in Sorrel). This implies that possessing enough money to live a comfortable life can alleviate anxiety levels to a point where a person can actually enjoy his or her life without the worry and stress of not knowing if you can keep up with bills and payments for the basic necessities of life. Sorrel also states that individual wealth also gives a person a perception of self-worth. This leads to people valuing themselves based off their income and salary. According to this article, the wealthier an individual is, the higher level of life satisfaction that person will obtain.

In a TED Talk speech by Michael Norton, he states that the reason why some people don't think that money can buy happiness is because they are spending it wrong. People that have this view typically spend it on themselves in this materialistic world, which leads to an anti-social type of behavior where it influences behaviors of selfishness. He mentions, "We wondered what would happen if we made people spend more of their money on others. So instead of being antisocial with your money, what if you were more pro-social with it?" (Norton 2:06). Norton conducted a research experiment where half of the participants were given envelopes of money to spend on themselves and the other half had to spend it on others. At the end of the experiment, each participant was asked how happy it made them feel in terms of the method in which they spent the money. The individuals that spent money on others acquired more happiness than what they were feeling before the experiment. However, the people that spent money on themselves felt no different from what they were feeling before. Norton also received data from the Gallup Organization where they asked people from around the world if they donated to charity and how happy they were with life in general. Results showed that people that gave to charity were in fact happier with their lives than the people that didn't give to charity. This shows that it isn't just a cultural or national phenomenon but includes every nation in this world. In terms of receiving happiness, Norton concludes that spending money on others will result in a bigger return of happiness than the act of spending it on yourself.

Wealth directly correlates with materialism because the more money you have, the more things you can buy. In Tim Kasser's book, *The High Price of Materialism*, he brings up the topic of how people seek happiness through wealth because it allows that individual to live a lifestyle that only the rich can obtain. Yet people that have reached this level of status, with a materialistic mindset, seem to experience higher levels of anxiety and depression which directly impedes happiness. This can lead to issues like drunk driving, drug abuse, domestic violence, and many other problems. Kasser states there is a couple of reasons why unhappiness can be led by materialism:

The first concerns the burdens that materialism places on the human soul. Desires to have more and more material goods drive us into an ever more frantic pace of life. Not only must we work harder, but, once possessing the goods, we have to maintain, upgrade, replace, insure, and constantly manage them. Thus, in the journey of life, materialists end up carrying an ever-heavier load, one that expends the energy necessary for living, loving, and learning—the really satisfying aspects of that journey. Thus materialism, although promising happiness, actually creates strain and stress.

Yet if materialism causes unhappiness, it is also the case that unhappiness "causes" materialism. Kasser shows how enhanced desires or "needs" to have more or consume more are deeply and dynamically connected with feelings of personal insecurity. Materialism, it appears, tends to ripen best among people who feel uncertain about matters of love, self-esteem, competence, or control. (Ryan, xiii-xiv)

This creates a delusional dependency on materialistic goods which will keep encouraging an individual to make more money to buy more things, resulting in a vicious cycle of unhappiness. Kasser also mentions that materialism is taught to children due to growing up in homes where possessions and products seem to be one of the most important parts of a household lifestyle. The parents that crave material possessions drive them to work more hours to acquire the means to buy the products that they feel like they need for their children and family. This way of life is then passed down to their children resulting in the possession of this mindset when they grow up and have a family of their own. In these materialistic households, socializing with the family, intimacy with the spouse, interaction between the children and parents seemed to be pushed to the side in terms of prioritization. Richard M. Ryan mentions in the Forward to Kasser's book, "Not much time for living remains after the working, spending, and consuming are completed" (xiv). The remainder of the time is often busy with the consumption of media outlets usually bombarded with advertisements of even more material goods resulting in a never-ending loop of unhappiness and the lack of life satisfaction.

However, in an article called "4 Levels of Happiness" by the website, *The World Counts*, it talks about how happiness can in fact be gained from material objects in the 1st level of happiness. It is also conveyed that people shouldn't focus solely on the first level because it can lead to situations of unhappiness. The article states, "People focusing exclusively on level 1 risk to hit a crisis where life seems shallow and without meaning. In other words, there is a limit to the pleasure you get from a new car, a holiday, a nice meal, etc. if this is the only source of happiness." It also mentions that it is fine to enjoy material goods as long as you don't ignore the other three levels of happiness. The second level of happiness is called ego gratification and the happiness from comparison. This includes being better than others in specific aspects and traits. An example would be winning in a competitive sport or receiving a promotion. The third level is happiness from living for the sake of others and making this world a better place to live in. This deeper level of happiness has to do with one's social connection to other people, by stepping away from our selfish tendencies and focusing more on the happiness of others around you. The fourth level of happiness is considered the deepest and includes the fulfillment in life through means like philosophy, religion, spirituality, scientific ventures, and many other examples. All four levels of happiness can have an accumulating, contributing factor to an individual's overall degree of life satisfaction.

In Daniel Gilbert's, "Immune to Reality," he discusses the difficulty in the prediction of an individual's emotional future. This can tie in with a person that has goals and aspirations of being wealthy and successful and will receive long term happiness when he or she finally gets there. According to Gilbert, that person will have overestimated the length of happiness that the individual will receive from this specific occurrence. This can result in disappointment when people obtain that wealth and success, not to mention all the unhappiness it could cause in the journey to get to that point from hiccups or bad events occurring along the way. He writes, "In short, we do not realize that our views will change because we are normally unaware of the process that change them" (132). This is implying that one day a person's view might include the correlation of wealth and happiness, but certain processes, events, and ways of thinking might change his or her perspective on this issue and the person might not see wealth as a source of joy anymore.

But what if you can create a life you can enjoy without being tied down to a job and where your life is just one big vacation? In order for this to happen, you would need a source of income that can actually assist this type of lifestyle. In her book, *Be a Free Range Human: Escape the 9-5, Create a Life You Love and Still pay the Bills*, Marianne Cantwell writes about how happiness can come from being free from this "career cage" that society revolves around in the typical 9-5 job, while not worrying about financial instability. This kind of lifestyle can bring life to an individual by avoiding the mundane and monotonous life of having a scheduled job/career. However, to accomplish this, money is of the utmost importance when it comes to fueling this way of living. She talks about how it is important to set your income level and to actually make money based off of your "money motivator":

> That means going back to what's important. For me, at the end of the day, it's not really about having nice shoes, or supporting my foodie restaurant habit (though they are important extras in my life). Ultimately, money is about the ability to take care of myself and the people I love, now and in the future. For another free ranger, who is also a mum, her motivator is taking care of her son and daughter. She says, 'My kids were my main motivator for making the move to a free range life and they are the main motivator making sure I charge what I'm worth. When agreeing a fee, every £100 I compromise on is £100 that could have been spent on my kids. Show me a mum that will let a stranger take money from their children!' (Cantwell 226).

Everyone has different motivations for accumulating wealth, and it all depends on what personal values that an individual is aware of including time away, a nice house, future security, or many other things. With the freedom that comes with this lifestyle, provided by money, it can yield copious amounts of life satisfaction and happiness. This shows that you don't have to be extremely wealthy, but you do need a certain amount of money to live a free-range lifestyle while providing essential necessities for individuals and family members.

Christopher Peterson agrees that income can have a positive connection to happiness and that you don't need to be filthy rich. In his *Psychology Today* article, he states, "As income increases, its added contribution to life satisfaction becomes smaller. The impact of additional income is greatest among those who have little money, but it does not stop mattering, even after someone is able to meet basic needs." He is conveying that there is a diminishing return from gaining more wealth with its direct effect on happiness. Thomas Hurka agrees with this viewpoint in his book The Best Things in Life: *A Guide to What Really Matters*. Hurka writes about how money does make a difference in happiness levels going from poverty to moderate wealth. It can alleviate anxieties about the individual's financial instability in the future while providing physical and material comfort. But going past that point of income, the less effect it has on life satisfaction. He also mentions that there is an income baseline and when you surpass that baseline, you receive a short burst of happiness. But that happiness and initial excitement eventually dissipates because your new income becomes the new baseline that you want to surpass. Hurka gives an example of an individual winning the lottery who receives that short term, spike of happiness. But by the sixth month, that person is back to the level of happiness he or she had before the lottery win took place.

With all these different perspectives on the relationship between wealth and happiness, it is hard to find a concrete answer whether they are directly correlated or not. Instead of looking for a black and white answer, I decided to find a conclusion in the grey areas of this issue. It seems to me that there is a role that wealth has on happiness, but it isn't as extreme as some people paint this topic to be. There is a limit that wealth plays in happiness but being financially successful doesn't mean that it makes a person unhappy. There are also numerous factors when it comes to the correlation of wealth and happiness due to different perspectives, circumstances, events, how one spends their money, how much freedom it gives an individual, motivation, mental health, and many other issues.

This apparent division between scholars regarding this topic leads me to ponder what happiness actually is. By looking at all the different approaches and perspectives on happiness I can conclude that everyone has their own specific definition of happiness that fits each person's environment, mindset, lifestyle, and many other factors regarding this subject. Passion in the things we do and the meaningful connections we create can also have a major impact on life satisfaction and contentment. One might lose certain passions and connections, but the beauty of being human means that we can rebuild what we once lost. There is a lot of research being conducted in the field of happiness psychology with varying results. But one thing for certain is that happiness can even be found in the most simple and mundane things. Money can certainly help find an individual's definition of happiness by providing certain necessities of life so one doesn't have to spend time thinking about surviving in this world of consumerism. Instead, a person can use that time for the pursuit of happiness, whether it is watching T.V. with friends, comfort food at a new restaurant, or finding that significant other. My own definition of happiness requires me to at least make a comfortable living by reaching the middle-class salary so I can live my life without the anxieties of living from paycheck to paycheck. This way ensures that I can use that extra energy from all the worries and stress for the pursuit of my own happiness.

Works Cited

"4 Levels of Happiness." *Life Potentials*: Four Levels of Happiness. The World Counts, www.theworldcounts.com.

Cantwell, Marianne. *Be a Free Range Human: Escape the 9-5, Create a Life You Love and Still Pay the Bills*. London: Krogan Page, 2013.

Gilbert, Daniel. "Immune to Reality." *Stumbling on Happiness*, Knopf, 2006.

Hurka, Thomas. *The Best Things in Life: A Guide to What Really Matters*. Oxford University Press, 2011.

Norton, Michael. "Money Can Buy Happiness." TED Talk, 28 Jan. 2012, *YouTube*, https://youtu.be/ZwGEQcFo9RE.

Peterson, Christopher. "Money and Happiness." *Psychology Today*, June 6, 2008, www.psychologytoday.com.

Ryan, Richard M. Forward to Kasser, Tim. *The High Price of Materialism*. Cambridge, Mass: A Bradford Book, 2002.

Sorrel, Charlie. "Money Will Make You Happy Because Life Without Money Is Really Hard." *Fast Company*, 20 Jan. 2016, www.fastcompany.com.

Weimann, Joachim, et al. *Measuring Happiness: The Economics of Well-Being*. Cambridge, Mass: The MIT Press, 2015.

*Accessed on dates (recommended under MLA 8th edition) are missing from these citations. Other minor errors may appear in this uncorrected sample paper.

Writing Assignments

Paragraph "Translation" Exercise

Rewrite the article abstract below in everyday language. Do not expand; do not condense. To the best of your ability, rewrite this article abstract in standard written English language usage for the benefit of a general readership, as the information might appear in a popular interest magazine or on a popular interest web site. This is not a "creative writing" assignment. You do not need to add your own voice into the mix so much as to act as a "translator" between a specialized audience and a general audience. You may want to look up unfamiliar terms. Be clear on all terms and definitions before you begin your rewrite.

The following article abstract comes from the *Journal of Happiness Studies.* (See the Further Inquiry unit bibliography for a citation.)

Article Abstract, "The Effects of Income Levels and Income Inequalities on Happiness"

The standard of living reflected by one's income and consumption is the primary explanation for the utility or satisfaction of the private consumer. However, empirical evidence very often demonstrates that the level of happiness is not necessarily higher for wealthy people in comparison to the poor. This holds within specific populations of a country, and in macro terms by comparison between the happiness of populations with low and high GDP_{ppp} per capita. Different research studies have used other economic and social explanatory variables for determining consumer happiness within countries. The present paper adds the new factor of income inequality that affects happiness. It is empirically proved that at extreme values of inequality measured by the Gini index, the effect of happiness is negative regardless of GDP_{ppp} per capita. However, at the intermediate ranges of the Gini index the effect of changes in the index on happiness is ambiguous. These results are found regardless of the actual values of GDP_{ppp} per capita.

(Tavor, T. et al., 2017)

Essay Prompts

Level I: Analysis-Response

1. See the Tabor, T. et al. article abstract that appears in the paragraph "Translation" exercise above, or look up the article abstract using the unit bibliography. Once you understand the abstract (be sure to look up all unfamiliar terms), analyze the basic arguments contained in the abstract then, in a separate paragraph(s), respond to these arguments.

2. Considering Gilbert's description of the psychological immune system, analyze and reflect upon a moment in your life when your own psychological immune system may have kicked into gear in order to help you to avoid despair. Maybe you even ended up synthesizing happiness out of a potentially depressing situation. In the chapter that follows "Paradise Glossed" in his book, *Stumbling on Happiness*, entitled "Immune to Reality," Gilbert clarifies that the psychological immune system does not kick in with small annoyances but only responds to major traumatic events. (Let's also bear in mind that Gilbert argues that there is no distinction between so-called "organic" happiness and "synthetic" happiness.) Be sure to focus on explaining the purpose and the operation of the psychological immune system. This prompt is not calling solely for a personal meditation; you also want to understand, explain, and explore the psychological mechanisms that Gilbert describes.

3. Analyze one or more valid sources in order to draw a distinction between short-term and long-term happiness. Define these concepts. Analyze what factors might bring about each. Respond on a personal level as to how you may have experienced some form of short-term and/or long-term happiness in your own life.

Level II: Making Connections

1. Explore the common biological processes involved in feelings of romance and feelings of happiness. This assignment can be expanded into a research topic but need not be. Even at Level II, you must be careful to define your terms and narrow the scope of your explorations.

2. Explain the operations of the psychological immune system as a function of neuroplasticity.

3. To what extent can you correlate participation in social media platforms with feelings of personal happiness? You can approach this topic at the Level I, Level II, or Level III phase. Obviously, the parameters of the assignment change based on the essay level which you choose to pursue (or which you are assigned).

4. Draw a connection between brain plasticity and happiness studies. Find significant and meaningful connections between the human capacity for neuroplasticity, revised neural mapping, and the human pursuit of happiness. As always, be careful to define your terms and narrow your topic.

5. Explore generational differences in the concept of happiness. Are there significant differences in the pursuit of happiness among, say, baby boomers and Gen Z? If there are no significant distinctions to be discovered, then this is not a good topic. On the other hand, you may be able to uncover significant distinctions in what produces happiness among different generations of Americans.

6. What are the most significant connections between a person's level of happiness and a person's chosen career, profession, or job? Moreover, how should a young person approach college studies, career decisions, and considerations of long-term contentment while understanding the possible effects of artificial intelligence and robotics on America's twenty-first century work force?

7. Love is supposed to provide us happiness. Why then, does "love" so frequently cause the opposite of happiness? Using the work of Helen Fisher in her lectures and publications and/or other authorities, connect romance studies with happiness studies. How or why can "love" so frequently cause pain and misery? Focus on psychological, neurological, biological and/or biochemical processes. Or at least start there.

Level III: Research

1. *Several of the Level II topics above can be expanded or transformed into Level III research topics.*

2. Explore the common biological processes involved in feelings of romance and feelings of happiness. What are the most important biological drivers of *eros* or romance? What appear to be the biological drivers or mechanisms behind feelings of pleasure, contentment, or other distinct forms of happiness? To what extent do the biological functions of happiness resemble the biological functions of any distinct type of love other than romantic or erotic love (friendship, spiritual love, love of family, or another distinct form of love)? Clearly, your task must involve narrowing your topic to specific terms as you develop your major research question.

3. *Money can't buy you happiness.* This is a common conceit. Analyze the phrase scientifically, using valid source materials. To what extent does wealth create or not create a sense of fulfillment and/or happiness in a person's life? Don't rely on your own guesswork, ambitions, or instincts; rely on credible scientific evidence.

4. From the ancient world to the modern world, are there common refrains regarding what actually constitutes *happiness* and what actually creates happiness in an individual? Has the concept of happiness changed over time, or does it essentially remain the same? What, then, are the keys to happiness, according to the most credible ancient and modern sources? Do not neglect the science of happiness as you explore the philosophy of happiness.

5. Produce a science-oriented research paper on the topic of happiness. What does the latest science in fields such as psychology, medicine, health sciences, or biology have to tell us regarding sustainable happiness?

6. Possibly related to the topic above, produce a science-oriented paper that explores the connections between health and happiness.

7. Research the connection between happiness and the practice of meditation (and/or the practice of prayer). Rely mainly on scientific data. Explain why there is a connection between certain cognitive practices and a sense of happiness. Clarify the biological and neurological processes involved in meditation and/or prayer.

Further Inquiry

"Aristotle." History of Happiness, *The Pursuit of Happiness,* 2018, https://www.pursuit-of-happiness.org/history-of-happiness/aristotle/.

Barker, Eric. "Neuroscience Reveals 4 Rituals That Will Make You Happy." *The Week,* 28 Feb. 2016, https://theweek.com/articles/601157/neuroscience-reveals-4-rituals-that-make-happy.

Bergeisen, Michael. "The Neuroscience of Happiness." *Greater Good Magazine,* 22 Sept. 2010, https://greatergood.berkeley.edu/article/item/the_neuroscience_of_happiness.

Bergland, Christopher. "The Neurochemicals of Happiness." *Psychology Today,* 29 Nov. 2012, https://www.psychologytoday.com/us/blog/the-athletes-way/201211/the-neurochemicals-happiness.

Brooks, David. *The Second Mountain: The Quest for a Moral Life.* Random House, 2019.

Carlisle, Clare. "What Philosophy Tells Us About the Happiness Index." *The Guardian,* 15 Nov. 2010, https://www.theguardian.com/commentisfree/2010/nov/15/happiness-index-philosophy.

Cave, Stephen. "There's No Such Thing as Free Will." *The Atlantic,* June 2016, https://www.theatlantic.com/magazine/archive/2016/06/theres-no-such-thing-as-free-will/480750/.

Corcoran, Kevin. "Happiness on the Brain: The Neuroscience of Happiness, Part 1." Biola University Center for Christian Thought, 21 Oct 2015, https://cct.biola.edu/happiness-on-the-brain-neuroscience-happiness-part-1/.

Craig, Heather. "The Psychology, Theory, and Science of Happiness." Positive Psychology Program, 14 Feb. 2019, https://positivepsychologyprogram.com/psychology-of-happiness/.

Deresiewicz, William. *Excellent Sheep: The Miseducation of the American Elite and the Way to a Meaningful Life.* Free Press, 2014.

Dunn, Elizabeth. "Helping Others Makes Us Happy--But It Matters How We Do It." TED Talk, 26 Apr. 2019, https://www.ted.com/talks/elizabeth_dunn_helping_others_makes_us_happier_but_it_matters_how_we_do_it.

Fredrickson, Barbara. "Positive Emotions Open Our Mind." Greater Good Science Center. *YouTube.com,* 21 June 2011, https://www.youtube.com/watch?v=Z7dFDHzV36g.

Gilbert, Daniel. *Stumbling on Happiness.* Alfred A. Knopf, 2006.

— "The Surprising Science of Happiness." TED Talk, Feb. 2004, https://www.ted.com/talks/dan_gilbert_the_surprising_science_of_happiness.

Hall, Edith. "Why Read Aristotle Today?" *Aeon,* 29 May 2018, edited by Nigel Warburton, https://aeon.co/essays/what-can-aristotle-teach-us-about-the-routes-to-happiness.

Haybron, Dan. "Happiness." Stanford Encyclopedia of Philosophy, 6 July 2011, updated 23 Sept. 2019, https://plato.stanford.edu/entries/happiness/.

Joshanloo, Mohsen. "Eastern Conceptualizations of Happiness: Fundamental Differences with Western Views." *Journal of Happiness Studies,* vol. 15. no. 2, 2014, DOI: 10.1007/s10902-013-9431-1, https://www.researchgate.net/publication/257589617_Eastern_Conceptualizations_of_Happiness_Fundamental_Differences_with_Western_Views.

Lyubomirsky, Sonja. "What Determines Happiness?" Greater Good Science Center. *YouTube.com,* July 8, 2010, https://www.youtube.com/watch?v=_URP3-V1sY4.

Nichols, Shaun. "Is Free Will an Illusion?" *Scientific American,* 1 Nov. 2011. https://www.scientificamerican.com/article/is-free-will-an-illusion/.

Park, Soyoung Q. et al. "A Neural Link Between Generosity and Happiness." *Nature,* 11 July 2017, https://www.nature.com/articles/ncomms15964.

Pianalto, Matthew. "Happiness, Virtue and Tyranny." *Philosophy Now,* 2008, https://philosophynow.org/issues/68/Happiness_Virtue_and_Tyranny.

Sapolsky, Robert. "To Understand Facebook, Study Capgras Syndrome: This Mental Disorder Gives Us a Unique Insight into the Digital Age." *Nautilus,* 16 Nov. 2016, http://nautil.us/issue/42/fakes/to-understand-facebook-study-capgras-syndrome.

Sharot, Tali. "The Optimism Bias." TED Talk, Feb. 2012. *YouTube.com,* https://www.ted.com/talks/tali_sharot_the_optimism_bias?language=en.

Socrates. "In Pursuit of (Philosophical) Happiness." *Classical Wisdom Weekly,* 2 Sept. 2014, https://classicalwisdom.com/philosophy/pursuit-philosophical-happiness/.

Tavor, T., et al. "The Effects of Income Levels and Income Inequalities on Happiness." *Journal of Happiness Studies*, vol. 19, no. 7, pp. 2115-2137 (2018), 18 Aug. 2017, https://doi.org/10.1007/s10902-017-9911-9, https://link.springer.com/article/10.1007/s10902-017-9911-9.

Taylor, Steve. "Benjamin Libet and The Denial of Free Will." *Psychology Today*, 7 Sept. 2017, https://www.psychologytoday.com/us/blog/out-the-darkness/201709/benjamin-libet-and-the-denial-free-will.

Thijssen, Johannes M.M.H., and David R. Loy. "Happiness and Invulnerability from Chance: Western and Eastern Perspectives." *The Challenge of Chance*, editors Landsman K., and E. van Wolde. The Frontiers Collection, 2016, https://link.springer.com/chapter/10.1007/978-3-319-26300-7_8.

Twenge, Jean M. and W. Keith Campbell. *The Narcissism Epidemic: Living in the Age of Entitlement.* Free Press, 2009.

Warren, Rick. *The Purpose Driven Life.* Zondervan, 2002.

"What Is Happiness? And the Neuroscience Behind It." *BrilliantLivingHQ.com*, 2019, https://www.brilliantlivinghq.com/what-is-happiness-and-the-neuroscience-behind-it/.

UNIT NINE

Research in the Twenty-First Century

Identifying a Public Discourse

21st C. Literary * Social (Dis)Connection * Brain Plasticity * Love's Biology * Appropriation * AI + Robotics * Generation Studies * Happiness Studies

Finding Connections: In order to specify and narrow your topic and research scope, you may want to develop synthetic connections and areas of concern that span two discourse topics.

Identify a Discourse That Is Significant to You and Others

What concerns do experts express in regard to this discourse?

What concerns do you share in regard to this discourse?

What audiences are aware of these concerns?

What audiences exist who would be interested but are not yet aware of these concerns?

What do these audiences know or not know in regard to these concerns? What would they want to find out? What problems require examination, contemplation, or solutions? What specific questions would interest your readers?

Develop a Major Research Question

The Research Process

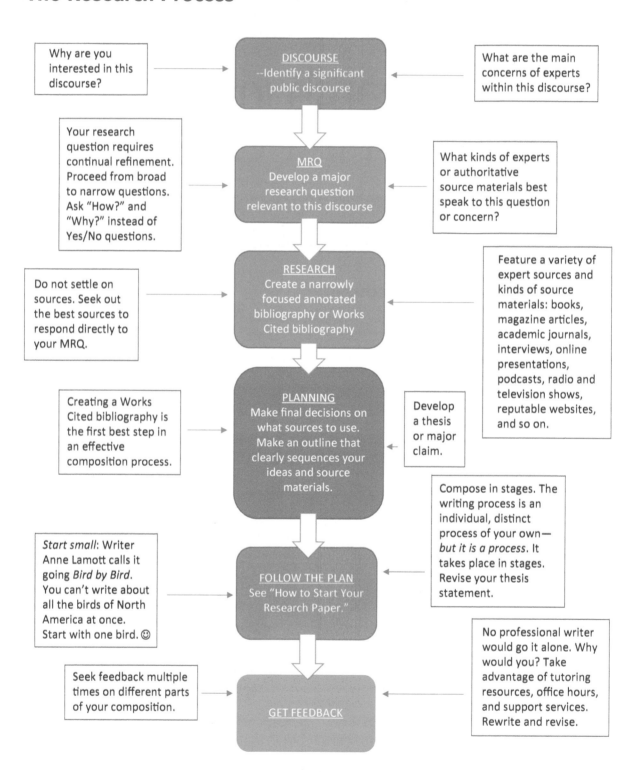

Why are you interested in this discourse?

DISCOURSE
--Identify a significant public discourse

What are the main concerns of experts within this discourse?

Your research question requires continual refinement. Proceed from broad to narrow questions. Ask "How?" and "Why?" instead of Yes/No questions.

MRQ
Develop a major research question relevant to this discourse

What kinds of experts or authoritative source materials best speak to this question or concern?

Do not settle on sources. Seek out the best sources to respond directly to your MRQ.

RESEARCH
Create a narrowly focused annotated bibliography or Works Cited bibliography

Feature a variety of expert sources and kinds of source materials: books, magazine articles, academic journals, interviews, online presentations, podcasts, radio and television shows, reputable websites, and so on.

Creating a Works Cited bibliography is the first best step in an effective composition process.

PLANNING
Make final decisions on what sources to use. Make an outline that clearly sequences your ideas and source materials.

Develop a thesis or major claim.

Compose in stages. The writing process is an individual, distinct process of your own— *but it is a process.* It takes place in stages. Revise your thesis statement.

Start small: Writer Anne Lamott calls it going *Bird by Bird.* You can't write about all the birds of North America at once. Start with one bird. ☺

FOLLOW THE PLAN
See "How to Start Your Research Paper."

No professional writer would go it alone. Why would you? Take advantage of tutoring resources, office hours, and support services. Rewrite and revise.

Seek feedback multiple times on different parts of your composition.

GET FEEDBACK

Your Major Research Question

The Major Research Question (MRQ) is a key prompt for a good research paper.
This question guides you in the development of an engaging, focused topic.

One of the *Engaging Discourse 2.0* units will inspire you to develop a "major research question."

- Ideally, the "answer" to your MRQ becomes your **thesis** or **major claim**. Remember that your purpose is more than informational. You want to present an argument or a position rather than simply to convey facts and information.

Once you have chosen a general discourse topic, here are some essential concerns when it comes to **drafting** and **developing** an **MRQ, or major research question**:

- An adequate major research question can *never* be answered "Yes" or "No."
- A good major research question is likely to begin with "How" or "Why."
- Your major research question should not already be answered by the article that inspires your topic.
  - The idea is to expand beyond the boundaries of the article that you have read. Make synthetic connections with other articles to inspire your research.
- If someone could write an entire book based on the answer to your major research question, then your question needs improvement. We are writing one research paper of modest length. Make sure your MRQ fits the scope of a single research paper.
- In almost every instance, your draft MRQ will need to be narrowed. We all start out with *broad* questions. It's only practical, however, to answer *narrow* questions. The good news is that it is *much easier* to answer narrow questions, so it is *much easier* to write research papers that have a narrow focus.
- **Develop your MRQ in stages: draft and revise.** A clear, narrow MRQ leads to clear, narrow research. Broad research questions become overwhelming and sometimes prove counterproductive.

Considering the pointers above, understand why these are

FAULTY Major Research Questions:

- Is technology good to use in the classroom? (A *Yes/No* question leaves you with nothing left to research.)
- Does AI affect me? (Again, this is binary, i.e. *Yes/No*. "How does AI affect me?" is a much better starting point for your major research question.)
- When did the self-esteem curriculum emerge in U.S. schools? (If one of our experts has already answered this query, then you need to revise. "Why" might produce a better question.)
- When did smartphones become a significant part of American life? (Hasn't one of our experts already answered this question?)
- How does the psychological immune system operate? (To what extent does Gilbert already answer this question in his article? What other questions and concerns, on the other hand, does he leave unanswered? Revise and narrow: *What is the role of the psychological immune system in dealing with grief or heartache resulting from a failed romantic relationship?*)

Designating A Public Discourse

Your feature article or research paper guides your reader through your topic or public discourse. By public discourse, we mean "significant public conversation that concerns a wide array of people." In some instances, you will address a specific audience or a narrow discourse community. In general, we address research topics that concern a wide range of people.

In order to define your discourse, think about the article that inspired your topic. This published article is part of a larger public discourse. In fact, it is most likely part of several larger public discourses. You must define the specific discourse which you wish to engage. Consider the relevant topic or subject matter. Ask yourself, "Who cares about this conversation? Why do they care about it? Why is it a significant conversation?" Answers to these questions will help to define your discourse and to identify your own true areas of interest.

What "public discourse" is important to your audience, or to the (sometimes imaginary) readers who will engage your article? Designating a public discourse provides a *framework* for your writing. Operating within a defined framework makes your job a little bit easier. Experts have already staked out the territory. You don't have to invent anything. You can instead focus on making a significant, meaningful contribution to the ongoing conversation.

Getting Started

Start with a clear topic sentence (a sentence that opens a paragraph). Use simple syntax. An easy-to-follow first sentence draws the reader into your paragraph.

Designating a Public Discourse

Complete the following brainstorming exercises in order to generate ideas and language that will allow you to define a specific discourse. The terms "topic," "conversation," and "discourse" may be replaced with specific language. For example, "this topic" can become "brain plasticity" or "cultural appropriation."

We ought to care about this topic because _____.

_____ are the people who care most about this topic because _____ _____.

Experts who are concerned with this topic include _____.

The history of this significant discourse stems back to _____.

This discourse is timely and significant because _____.

One of the most important experts who is concerned with this topic is _____.

The importance of this topic became clear to _____ on the day when _____.

One of the most important aspects of this conversation that often gets overlooked involves _____ _____.

The moment when this topic became widely known was _____.

Annotated Bibliography

Research Tip: Create an Annotated Bibliography

One of the most useful things that you can do in order to write a good research paper is to organize your research and source materials into a single document. Research typically takes place *before* you begin your composition. Of course, writing a section of your paper may inspire you to reach out to find new or different source materials (let's stay flexible and adaptable), but ideally you will complete your research prior to drafting and revising.

Creating an annotated bibliography or a comprehensive bibliography of potential source materials is one of the most useful things that you can do to make your job as a writer easier.

Understand what an annotated bibliography is.

It is a list of citations. A note follows each citation. The purpose of this annotation (note) will be either to summarize, assess, or reflect upon the source material indicated in the citation. The length of each annotation can vary depending on your purpose and your instructor's assignment instructions. Notes can typically range from 30 to 100 words (more significant sources usually have lengthier notes). However, detailed annotations can run several hundred words each.

You can also visit:

https://owl.purdue.edu/owl/general_writing/common_writing_assignments/annotated_bibliographies/index.html

SAMPLE Annotated Bibliography Assignment

- Following extensive research, list 12 valid sources in MLA (or APA) format. The annotated bibliography represents a "road map" of your final feature article.
- Feature a *specific title* that lists a narrow topic of interest.

EXAMPLE of a Focused Title:
Annotated Bibliography on Neurochemical Reactions of the Fight-or-Flight Response

Alphabetize your list in accordance with MLA format.

The purpose of your brief annotation (note) will be either to *summarize*, *assess*, or *reflect upon* the source material in question, depending on the source, your own judgment, and the required level of detail. The length of each annotation can vary from 30 to 100 words (more significant sources are followed by lengthier notes).

List the following *minimums*, 12 sources total:

- two articles from different unit discourses, or two from the same unit
- two articles from the Further Inquiry bibliographies
- two peer-reviewed scholarly articles

- two popular interest magazine or newspaper articles
- one podcast
- one TED Talk or another video lecture
- two library database articles *with the database correctly listed in the citation*
- two audio/visual programs of academic merit, such as TV programs or interviews from websites such as YouTube, PBS.org, or like sites
- one book or one book chapter
- Note that a single source may cover more than one category.

Remember that your annotated bibliography (a comprehensive list with notes) and your Works Cited page (the sources that you actually cite in your paper) are not the same document.

Avoid encyclopedic articles and the like. You may list these articles *in addition to* the required sources mentioned above, but they do not count toward your source total. You can often find acceptable source material in the footnotes or citations sections of a Wikipedia or other encyclopedic article. Listing superficial, unfocused or non-academic sources instead of valid sources does not fulfill the assignment requirements. Match your source materials to your *purpose* and your *audience*. If you are unclear on either purpose or audience, consult your instructor.

Sample Evaluation Criteria for an Annotated Bibliography Assignment

Assignment turned in on deadline with appropriate title	10%
Appropriate variety and quality of research materials—moreover, sources appear to have a similar limited focus on a particular aspect of the stated topic • high quality sources and types clearly listed (100%) • minimum quantity or type not quite met, or unclear (75%) • questionable quality, falls short of quantity/type, or unclear (50%)	60%
Evidence of reading completion and comprehension • annotations consistently assess and reflect (100%) • annotations unclear and/or mainly offer superficial summary (50%) • annotations convey little or no information or comprehension (0%)	20%
Formatting: Clear, correct MLA, APA, or other standard formatting, as directed • documentation incudes all required citation elements (100%) • student leaves out required citation elements (0%)	10%

How to Start Your Research Paper

The real start of your feature article or research paper is the **research**. Spend 2x or even 3x as long researching as writing. Start by creating a Works Cited bibliography which serves as a de facto guideline for your paper. Your instructor may ask you to produce an **annotated bibliography**.

Plan ahead:

- **outline**
- **sequence source materials**
- **plan out transitions from source to source**
- **develop a thesis statement or major claim**
- **rely on evidence, data, and expert opinion**
- **draft, revise, edit**

HINT: Remember that you can draft paragraphs and pages "out of order." Start in the middle. Draft a text introduction of important source material. Transition to another important source. Always keep in mind: What is your purpose? What is your focus and your contribution to the discourse? Stake out your own position. Make sure that paragraphs start and end with your own prose. Your voice shapes the discourse.

Drafting Your Introduction

When you are ready to draft your introductory paragraph(s), consider these options:

- Anecdote/Story
  - Relate an anecdote that embodies a main theme you wish to convey.
- Profile
  - Profile an important individual (an expert in the field, for example) in order to introduce your subject matter.
- Brief History
  - Offer your audience a brief summary of necessary background information that the audience needs to know in order to understand your topic, or narrate an intriguing episode that embodies or contextualizes the topic at hand.

- Big Questions/Big Ideas
  - Hook your audience by asking big questions that are relevant to your subject matter, or propose a big idea that will grab the attention of an educated, engaged audience.
- Establish a Public Discourse
  - Outline a current controversy, public debate, or significant public discourse that is relevant to your topic.
- If All Else Fails, Introduce Source Material

Embrace the role of *author.*

By the time your research is completed, you possess some *authority* on your topic. You are not an expert, but you have synthesized the views of leading experts so that you are in a position to present an argument or major claim to your readers. Clarify the discourse for them. They haven't done the research. You have. Share your knowledge.

Start Playing Games

Using a Fictional Scenario to "Make It Real"

The Timely Topics *game provides a touch of "real world" context to your research project.* Check with your instructor, who may not wish to play!

The Scenario

In this game, pretend that the instructor is actually the editor of a prestigious national journal called *Timely Topics.* The journal's audience is a highly engaged, highly educated group of 250,000 readers from all corners of the country. The audience includes a broad range of thinkers and academics, including professors and scientists from a broad range of disciplines who expect to read insightful articles. The journal's audience is 50/50 male/female. Ages range from ambitious undergraduate and graduate students in their 20s through (mostly) career professionals 30-60 with some retirees in their 70s and 80s. So, articles must engage a general readership. *Engaging Discourse 2.0* contains many such general interest articles that you may or may not want to use as models. *Timely Topics* engages its readership with significant, current public discourse.

Write the Editor a Pitch Letter

The Timely Topics Research Prospectus

The editor of the *Timely Topics* journal (yes, this is your instructor, but *shh*) has a problem: one of his/her most reliable freelance writers has fallen in love and gone on an around-the-world cruise with her new husband. She has vowed not to do any work for one full year. (We did say this was a fantasy scenario, right?) The editor relies on this freelancer for a yearly feature research article. Now there is a hole in the publishing schedule.

Good news, though. This is *your* opportunity to publish a major article in a prominent national publication. Lucky you! Now all you have to do is get the job.

You need to write the editor a "pitch letter" or **research prospectus** to capture the editor's interest in your proposed feature article. Your letter/prospectus touches on several important points: *What public discourse will you engage? Why will readers be interested? What is your major research question? What are the parameters of the writing assignment, and will you be able to meet the research and composition requirements on deadline?*

See the "pitch letter" research prospectus assignment sheet below.

Write a business letter to the editor of Timely Topics **in which you address the questions listed above and described in each paragraph below. Your assignment instructions appear in business letter format:**

Your name
123 Oak St.
Anytown, CA 94621

April 21, 2021

Bradley Summerhill
Editor, *Timely Topics*
7000 Dandini Blvd. #300
New York, NY 10010

Dear Mr. Summerhill:

Offer a "hook." What interests you about your proposed topic? Why would the *Timely Topics* audience be interested? Define your discourse. Identify an article or major source that has inspired you to become interested in this topic. Offer a few telling details to capture the editor's interest. What important scientific facts or principles stand out?

Identify the major research question that will guide you in your research. (Please note: It shouldn't be a yes/no question. If you feel that already know the answer to the question you are asking, then you are not asking a good question.) Study up on "major research question." In some cases, your so-called MRQ might appear as a series of questions.

Reiterate: Why is this a significant topic? What important issues will you explore? You don't know exactly what your thesis or major claim is at this point, but you probably have some ideas as to the general position that you will stake out. Ideally, the answer to your major research question will become your thesis or major claim. Identify who would be most interested in this discourse. Who would want to know this information? Who ought to know this information? Who ought to be concerned with this topic?

Acknowledge the parameters of the writing assignment. You and your "editor" must be on the same page here. How long is the assignment? What's the word count? How many sources are required? What formal style will you use to cite and document source materials? When is the research deadline? When is the first draft deadline? What resources will you use for revision and copyediting? When is the final deadline? Sum up your plan in detail.

Sincerely,
Jane Doe

Basic Business Letter Format

Search for "basic business letter format" in an online search engine in order to find business letter examples and templates.

Purpose and Audience

The two most important concerns when composing anything—from a grocery list to a blog to a research paper—are **purpose** *and* **audience**.

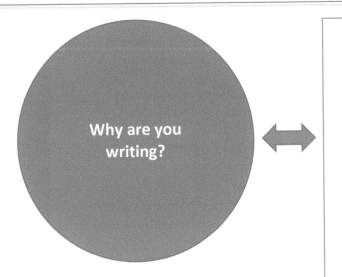

Why are you writing?

> Is your purpose informational or persuasive?
> Is your purpose argumentative? Do you need to make a claim or develop a thesis?
> Considering your purpose, what sorts of source materials will you need?
> What are the best ways to proceed with an argument, claim, or thesis? Will you rely on your own insights, or will you rely on expert insights?

> What communities understand this discourse?
> What communities could benefit from engaging in this discourse?
> Does the discussion require specialized terminology or vocabulary?
> What terms or language must be clarified, explored, or explained to your audience? What essential terms must be defined?
> What terms are common to this conversation? Do all readers share common understandings of these terms?
> What sorts of source materials will your audience most value?
> What are the needs or wants of your audience?

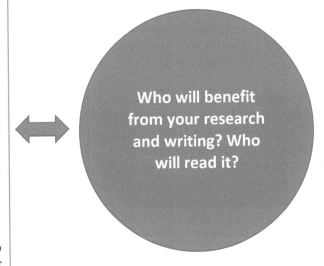

Who will benefit from your research and writing? Who will read it?

Incorporating a Contrary Viewpoint

Offer a Contrary Viewpoint as an Effective Rhetorical Strategy

Allow the skeptics to have a say. Allowing space for a contradictory viewpoint in your composition validates your own viewpoint. Think about it. Wouldn't you yourself instinctively trust a source that implies, *Let's take a spectrum of views into consideration* rather than, *There is only one viewpoint worth considering on this matter?*

Often, **acknowledging an alternate perspective** can be accomplished in a single paragraph. Begin this paragraph with a **topic sentence** along the lines of one of the following:

Some people may doubt my interpretation of the situation by objecting that _____
_____.

Other experts find this interpretation unconvincing. They contend that _____
_____.

_____ may wish to point out that _____.

- Example: Ethicists may wish to point out that a person's behavior is the final measure of character.

Critics of social psychologist Stanley Milgram take the contrary view that _____.

It is important that you represent alternate, skeptical views with fairness and respect.
The whole idea here (from the standpoint of rhetorical or argumentative strategy) is to gain the trust of the audience and thereby become more persuasive in your own analysis. If you appear to disrespect or dismiss (or leave out) a credible alternate viewpoint or naysayer, then you harm your own cause.

If you cannot conceive of a credible alternate viewpoint to your own, then you have a big problem. Most likely, either 1) you don't really have a major claim or thesis of your own for someone else to oppose, 2) you are failing to imagine how someone else might approach the topic, or 3) you have not done sufficient research. If you are dealing with a significant topic, then adequate research will reveal more than one credible perspective on the issue.

Why not simply leave out all dissent?
Why not present only one viewpoint? First of all, presenting only one viewpoint may appear to your audience as a flaw on your part, a failure of imagination. It is entirely possible that your audience is already forming the same doubts that you can anticipate by allowing opposing critics or skeptics to have a say. By acknowledging doubt, you validate your audience and yourself. Using Aristotle's terms, you have increased your *ethos*, the audience's sense that you are a trustworthy source of analysis. Including a skeptical view is also a sound method of *logos* or logical argument when you clarify the reasons why you do not embrace this other viewpoint.

- Understand opposing viewpoints and sympathize with them.
- Understand why a reasonable person would hold a position or viewpoint contrary to your own.
- Part of being persuasive is being empathetic to other people's perspectives.

Web Resources

Look up "Rogerian Argument" online. On top of effective rhetorical strategy, there are emotional and psychological reasons to offer a contrary viewpoint in a fair, respectful manner.

Presenting Your Argument or Major Claim

Investigate the Toulmin Method, Rogerian Method, and Classical Method of Argument

Refutation Paragraph

Check out this practical advice on how to incorporate a contrary viewpoint: *https://www.mesacc.edu/~paoih30491/Refutationpgphs.html*

Drafting Pages

- Consider starting in the middle. Draft some of the most important text introductions and text analysis paragraphs that will appear in the heart of your paper.
- Write with a plan and a purpose. Do more than simply inform. Stake out a position and claim a viewpoint.

Self-Check Workshop

One of the best things that you can do is to get feedback *along the way from trusted tutors or mentors. At some point, you will need to review your own work for "publication quality" before you turn in the work to your "editor" or instructor. Check off these boxes:*

- **Sources**
  Why are these valid sources? Do my sources speak to a common topic or discourse? Why will my audience value and appreciate the source materials that I have selected?
- **Major Research Question**
  How can you narrow and focus your main research query in order to 1) make your job as writer easier and 2) create a sharper sense of urgency and interest in your readers?
- **Terms**
  Which terms require definitions? What language, that is common to this discourse, must I incorporate?
- **Major Claim**
  What is my purpose in writing this article? Does each paragraph consistently pursue my overall purpose and major claim? Is my thesis or major claim clear and easy to understand? Am I staking out a distinct position?
- **Voice**
  Do I compose in an appropriate tone? Are my sentences simple and clear in structure and meaning? Improving grammar and word choice clarifies your critical analysis.

Examining Your Draft Essay: Tips for Editing and Revision

Look for the following:

- **Pronouns** like "this," "it," "these" and "which" **must refer to specific nouns**. Clarify or replace vague pronouns. Be wary of sentences that begin "This is…" or "It is…." Can you specify? This *what?* Whenever "this" or "it" appear in a sentence, determine if they are pronouns that require concrete antecedents. Avoid starting sentences with "which."
  - For example, "this" becomes "this proposition." *This is why scientists decided to research… becomes This problem is why scientists decided to research ….*
- **Replace weak verbs** such as "is" or "talks about."
  - Use dynamic verbs to expand the analytical process. For example, *The article is a study of the biology of love* becomes *The article examines the biology of love.* Or, *The author talks about the biology of love* becomes *The author explores the biology of love.*
- **Favor simple sentence structures** and **attribute ideas and actions to an author**: "She argues" and "Smith claims," for example, are reliable ways to start a sentence. *It is seen that people will convince themselves that traumatic situations turn out for the best* becomes *Gilbert demonstrates that people convince themselves that traumatic situations turn out for the best.*
- **Keep your subject and verb together** at the beginning of your sentence: *Twenge, who is a psychologist and studies matters of self-esteem, observes changes in the curriculum…* becomes *Twenge observes changes in the curriculum….*
- **Keep clauses and modifying phrases short**: *Twenge, who is a widely published author known for her work on generation studies and her examination of the self-esteem curriculum, observes changes…* becomes *Widely published psychologist Jean Twenge observes changes….*
- **Periods are your friends**. **Long sentences are your enemies**. Turn lengthy and complicated modifying phrases into new, distinct, separate sentences.
- **Cut wordy phrases**. Mercilessly slash and **delete unnecessary words**.
- Use **transition words and phrases** to demonstrate **logical connections** between ideas, sentences, and source materials. Oftentimes, you can start a sentence with a transition word or phrase, placing a comma directly after the transition word or phrase.
  - Common transition words and phrases to indicate *a continuation of an idea* include:

    Furthermore,

    In fact,

    Besides,

    In addition,

    Moreover,

    In other words,

    [*and, too, also,* and *as well* also indicate continuation]
  - Common transition words and phrases to indicate *a contrasting concept* include:

    However,

    Nonetheless,

    On the other hand,

On the contrary,

Despite this fact,

By contrast,

[*although..., even though..., but, whereas* and *regardless* also indicate contrast]

- Common transition words and phrases to indicate *cause and effect* include:

Therefore,

As a result,

Accordingly,

Consequently,

[*then, thus,* and *so* also indicate cause and effect]

- Common transition words and phrases to indicate *examples* include:

For example,

For instance,

To illustrate the point,

After all,

- Common transition words and phrases to indicate *conclusion* include:

As a result,

In conclusion,

To sum up,

In short,

Therefore,

- Common transition words to indicate *comparison* include:

Similarly,

Likewise,

- Common transition words to *concede a point* or *expand the discourse* include:

Of course,

Naturally,

Ideally,

Granted,

Sample Edit:

Original:

This connects to the evidence used by Fredrickson who tells that functional magnetic resonance images (fMRIs) are used to prove the neurological synchrony of two brains that physically display a connection that is made.

Improved:
Fredrickson validates this concept. Functional magnetic resonance images (fMRIs) demonstrate neurological synchrony between two brains as physical contact occurs.

Read It Aloud

Did you know that people used to always read aloud? That's how it was done in the ancient world. There was no punctuation back then, so it was necessary to read aloud to get a sense of the text's meaning. Punctuation is a relatively modern invention that allows for silent reading. When punctuation is faulty, the writer's meaning gets lost.

Read your paper aloud to yourself. If it does not sound "right" to you as you read it aloud, then there is probably room for improvement. Clear, efficient prose is the goal.

Offer a Context for the Benefit of Your Audience

Typically, an **"outside audience"** must be able to understand your final essay draft. Discuss the issue of *audience* with your instructor. Unless you are addressing **a specific discourse community** (an audience of psychologists, biologists, or *Star Trek* junkies, for example), your final essay draft must be understood by an "outside audience," that is, a group of readers who are not intimately familiar with your source articles or topic. Your instructor may want you to address **a specific audience** or to engage **specialized terminology or language**. Or you may be addressing a **general interest readership**. Check whether your instructor has any advice regarding *audience*.

Outside readers can only understand synthetic connections between texts if you explain these connections in clear terms. Start at the start. Make sure your writing is clear and direct. **Define terms** when necessary. **Put sources in context**. Consider the rhetorical situation of each source. See "The Rhetorical Situation" in unit five Resources. Is it important to mention the text's original publication context? Is it important to mention an author's expertise or credentials? Use an author's own words to explain his or her ideas. **Clarify the author's methods, reasoning, and evidence**.

Greater Implications

Give your readers **a reason to care**. Address a reader's possible objection of "Why should I care?" or "Why should anyone care?" Who does care about your topic or discourse? Why do they care? Who doesn't know about this discourse and, in your view, ought to know about it? Why is this topic or discourse **significant** or meaningful? Who thinks so? Why do *you* care about this discourse and the major claim you are presenting?

See Unit Eight Resources, Model Student Paper

We did not include this paper because it is the best student paper ever written. We do not think it's a shoddy paper either. Look over this model student paper and evaluate its effectiveness for yourself.

Research in the Twenty-First Century

It's as simple as Googling a string of words, right?
The short answer is, Um, no.

Let me ask you this: Can you tell me what Google is and how it delivers information to you? Can you tell me how to distinguish "real" news from "fake" news? Do you have the capacity to assess the reliability of source materials?

Search engines like Google have made information access easier than at any point in human history. You have been born into an age that represents one of the fundamental shifts in the history of humankind. Scholars have likened the significance of the advent of the Internet age to the prehistorical shift from a hunter-gatherer to an agriculture-based society. The fundamental importance of the Internet has been compared to the development of the movable type printing press. The economic shift, we are told, is as significant as the impact of the Industrial Revolution. We now live in a "post-industrial" economy in which the flow of digital data is as important as the flow of goods and services.

When it comes to easy information access and data sharing, what many early observers of the Internet failed to recognize was that "information" does not always mean "valid" or "reliable" information. We recognize now that there is plenty of "bad" or "unreliable" information out there on the Internet. At times, unreliable and even malicious information seems to have as much impact on our public discourse as valid, reliable information has. Moreover, on the Internet, information is often instantly "politicized" or distorted in a manner which, in my view, has a corrosive effect on our national discourse. When two people can't even agree on a common set of facts, how can they proceed with any kind of meaningful discourse?

As teachers, we sometimes focus on these negatives for fear that our students will become prey to propaganda and manipulation. It is important to acknowledge as well that we live in an age of marvels and wonders. Not in my wildest boyhood imagination could I have come up with the realities that we take for granted in the twenty-first century. If I were to write this textbook in the 1980s (when I was much too young to write a textbook, by the way), I might have spent an entire day at the library researching a few "fair use" court decisions; nowadays, I can look up the information in a matter of minutes. I can instantly text, phone, or video link with my editor who lives a thousand miles away. And I can do it while I sip an Americano at Josef's, my favorite local café. I can play chess in real time with a friend who lives halfway around the world. (The 1980s version of this chess game took months or years and involved the actual licking of stamps.) Via social media, I can engage in public discourse with likeminded citizens or with people who don't share my worldview.

This is the point when I tell my students, *You have more computing power in your smartphone than NASA had on its Apollo 11 mission when it sent men to walk on the moon. And what do you do with all of this magnificent power? That's right. You play Candy Crush.*

Look, I like cat videos too. Actually, I'm more of a dog person.
But you get the point.
So how does all this relate to research?

News You Cannot Use

A 2018 study from the Massachusetts Institute of Technology (MIT) demonstrates that false news stories are 70 percent more likely to be shared on Twitter than actual news stories. To put it another way, "fake" news travels six times faster than "real" news. The computer scientists who authored the study speculate that emotions of "surprise" and "disgust" account for the drastically increased likelihood that fake news will be forwarded and shared. If fake news spreads like wildfire on Twitter, it is safe to assume, it seems to me, that fake news spreads in a similar fashion on other online and social media platforms.

After all, real news stories—which tend to take well-considered, moderate stances on the issues—are not nearly as exciting as Internet posts that implicate U.S. presidential candidates in childhood slavery rings run out of pizza joints. Yes, that happened. In fact, an armed man fired off his AR-15 rifle in the pizzeria, convinced that employees were hiding kidnapped children in the restaurant. The controversial—and, I would add, unethical—website, *InfoWars.com*, and its radio show host have had to apologize and pay fines on multiple occasions, including an apology for promoting the false story that inspired the gunman to terrorize this pizzeria. Yet the website and its associated radio show plow forward, churning up dreck that some citizens mistake for actual news.

Some journalists are not comfortable with the term "fake news" because "news," according to traditional denotations, is never "fake." Nevertheless, the term entered public discourse following the 2016 U.S. presidential campaign. When you encounter the term "fake news," consider: *Who is using the term and why? Would the term "false information" serve as a better substitute?*

Social scientists are alarmed. In an essay published in *Science*, a group of 16 political scientists and legal scholars call for research into ways that we can reduce the spread of false information within our "news ecosystem."

When encountering various forms of media, including print and electronic sources, are people, even reasonable people, capable of distinguishing *fact* and *opinion* or *real* from *fake*?

No prior generation has ever been challenged with an information/propaganda dilemma of such widespread, massive proportions.

If, like me, you value America's history of free speech protection, and if, like me, you appreciate the role of an educated populace in a functioning representational democracy like the United States, then, like me, you may recognize that we face a problem with no quick or easy solution.

Data for Sale

As we go about our daily routines, we might forget that Google is a commercial entity peddling its for-profit service, funneling you toward advertisers who have paid top dollar to get your attention. The Internet encourages skimming, encourages emotional responses to flickering and flashing stimuli. It does not encourage calm, well-reasoned cognition. It does not, generally speaking, encourage reflection or the meditative assessment of source materials. Even your teachers, if they are honest with you, will admit that they too have been on the losing end of distracting advertisements and "fake news" stories from time to time.

This is why your teachers worry.

And this is why research in the twenty-first century remains as complex as ever. Although it may only take me ten or fifteen minutes to look up those "fair use" court cases on the Internet, the cognitive skills that are required to comprehend and assess the materials remain the same as in the 1980s when I needed an entire day to locate and review the materials. I could also, in that day of dedicated research, reflect upon my subject matter. I could ask the librarian a question or two. I could consult an information expert. I could learn along the way.

The twenty-first century has cut out the middleman and called into question the authority of the expert. The utopian promise of the Internet era involves accessing power—the power to go directly to an information source, for instance. And with great power comes … you guessed it … great responsibility.

Curated and Non-Curated Information

Problems surrounding the reliability of information are not new. In the 1860s, Mark Twain produced a great deal of "fake news" and "alternate facts" as he entertained newspaper readers of Virginia City's *Territorial Enterprise*. Charlatanism goes back to the very origins of English language journalism with Richard Steele's *The Tatler* and its successor *The Spectator*, co-founded by Steele and Joseph Addison in 1711. Their friend and literary companion Jonathan Swift confused and outraged the public in 1729 when his anonymous essay "A Modest Proposal" suggested that England could solve the problem of dealing with so many poor Irish babies by cooking and eating them like calves and suckling swine. Swift's political satire is evident to the knowledgeable reader: bad English policies of governance are starving and consuming the poor of Ireland. Yet, in 1729, some readers missed the satire entirely and believed that a madman was actually proposing a scheme to harvest and consume babies. Each fall in American colleges and universities, a few naïve college first-years continue to fall prey to Swift's satirical charade.

One point is clear: when assessing information, you need to understand an author's "context." I use the word "context" here to represent the need for a holistic understanding of an author's purpose and intent, his or her social or political motives, if any, and the historical or publication context in which the author's text can be better understood. For example, when reading Judy Brady's essay "Why I Want A Wife," it is helpful to know that she published the article in *Ms.* magazine, a publication with a clear social and political agenda (a second wave feminist agenda). Knowing this information doesn't invalidate the article's content; it simply enhances our understanding of the article's content.

If an editor or publisher reviews and approves an article for publication, that article might be said to be a "curated" source of information. *To curate* typically means "to organize an art exhibit." In this case, however, *to curate* means "to put together and/or to select for presentation." Mainstream news sources such as CBS, CNN, NBC, NPR, *The Economist*, *National Review*, *The Nation*, *The Washington Post*, or *The Wall Street Journal* presumably present "curated" information, meaning that an editor or a fact-checker has reviewed the writer's work prior to publication or broadcast.

So, when researching, is it a good thing to seek "curated" sources of information?

Generally speaking, yes. Oftentimes, you can avoid being duped by a false information feed simply by ignoring non-curated sources of information. If an appalling news story makes its way to you from a web site that you have never heard of, then maybe you would be better off deleting the story and moving on with your life.

"Curated" information implies that the information source represents more than one person's opinion. It may represent a consensus view, or it may represent an analysis of a situation that multiple people have reviewed. In some cases, the source may represent a single person's view that an editor, board, or publication believes worthy of public consideration.

"Curated" information does not always mean "correct" information, however. Editors and editorial boards make mistakes. In the 1990s, several prestigious publications, including *The New Republic* and *Rolling Stone*, were taken in by the fabrications of writer Stephen Glass, who concocted from imagination what were supposed to be nonfiction news stories. He quoted people who didn't exist. His editors loved the vivid, telling details he wove into his prose. No one bothered to check the facts. Later, it was determined that 27 of the 41 articles Glass wrote for *The New Republic* contained fabricated material.

I used to do this to my students: I would direct them into the password-protected confines of the college library's EBSCO database in order to find a story by Glass called "Hack Heaven." In the story, a teenaged hacker is rewarded for his crimes with an offer to become a security consultant for the company he hacked. The students and I would engage in a serious discussion of the issues. Was it OK for companies to hire teenaged criminals? Then, of course, I dropped the bomb: there was no hacker, there was no company. Glass had made it all up. Instead of being upset at Glass for his rotten journalistic ethics, the students, I got the feeling, were upset at me. Of course, I was trying to prove a point: even curated information can be false.

It's not often the case. I don't believe it is healthy or fair to engage in a cynicism that says, *You can't trust anything in this world!* Instead, let's take on a healthy mantle of skepticism by admitting, *We need to be careful about what sources of information we choose to trust.*

If the dynamics surrounding the reliability of information were important to understand in a pre-Internet world, then they seem critical to understand in the twenty-first century when data jumps at light speed from server to your computer. Don't forget that your phone too is a computer hooked up to those same servers and networks.

Clearly, if we must brandish skepticism with curated forms of information, then we must be even more careful with non-curated forms of information.

What non-curated forms of information do you see and hear every day?

How about Snapchat and Instagram? How about all manner of Internet advertisement, including political advertisement? How about Twitter and Facebook? What else?

Recently, many of these companies have come under public pressure to moderate or "curate" the enormous streams of information that their platforms present, yet the very notion of "curation" runs counter to the early ideals of Internet pioneers like John Perry Barlow, co-founder of the Electronic Freedom Foundation, who in his "A Declaration of the Independence of Cyberspace" (1996) wrote:

> We are creating a world that all may enter without privilege or prejudice accorded by race, economic power, military force, or station of birth. … We are creating a world where anyone, anywhere may express his or her beliefs, no matter how singular, without fear of being coerced into silence or conformity.

If these Internet companies wish to continue to abide by such foundational principles in the twenty-first century, how can they at the same time monitor and extinguish false information or "unacceptable" forms of speech, even hate speech?

Profound questions surrounding the distribution of non-curated forms of information are not entirely new in our country's history. State and federal governments have from time to time engaged in forms of censorship which were usually quickly overturned by the courts. More than any other nation on earth, America has offered legal protection to free speech, even to forms of speech that many citizens find offensive. In 1989 and 1990, for example, the U.S. Supreme Court upheld the First Amendment right of protestors to burn the U.S. flag. Most forms of speech and expression enjoy legal protection under U.S. law. Threats or speech deemed to cause imminent danger are examples of forms of expression that are not legally protected.

How will issues surrounding the distribution of non-curated forms of information on the Internet intersect or clash with the American legacy of free speech protection?

Are there any forms of non-curated information that might prove useful when you are conducting research? What about a blog, for instance? What about an amateur podcast? How can you determine if the author/producer of such forms of non-curated information is an expert whose knowledge is worthy of your consideration or a charlatan whose work must be disregarded?

See the list of "A Few Key Definitions" that follows. Why is it important to understand ".com" versus ".edu" versus ".org"? Will a "wiki" application tend to produce curated or non-curated information? And then there's this:

Doesn't everyone know you can't trust a "Wikipedia" article?

Wikipedia

"Can you trust a Wikipedia article?" I ask my composition students every semester. They do not hesitate with their response: "No."

It's clear to me that the formula "Wikipedia BAD" has been drilled into their heads. So, naturally, I have to mess with their assumptions:

"Why not?"

Typically, a moment of silence follows. Then, "Because anyone can contribute to it."

That's right. Wikipedia is an online encyclopedia run by a "wiki" application, meaning that anyone can offer up an article or a detail for publication. Anyone, too, can flag a suspicious article or detail. Anyone can cite a presumed fact as needing citation. The best Wikipedia articles are filled with citations. In other words, the collective authors of these articles have taken the time to verify their sources of information.

Wikipedia is an electronic encyclopedia. As such, its articles are supposed to be informative, not argumentative. If you were to see a Wikipedia article in which the author is making unfounded claims or offering opinionated analysis, you would want to flag that article as needing citations or ignore it completely. Obviously, you wouldn't trust information in an article that is offering up unsubstantiated opinion. This is one reason that it is so important to be able to distinguish *fact* from *opinion*.

So how is Wikipedia, launched in 2001, different from other encyclopedias?

I would say there are two main things: 1) it is electronic, and 2) its articles are either semi-curated or non-curated.

A traditional print encyclopedia typically features more rigorous editorial curation than Wikipedia. Yet, traditional encyclopedias can also contain falsehoods. My 1950 edition of *The Columbia Encyclopedia* identifies Pluto as a major planet discovered in 1930 which some scientists believe is bigger than Earth, while Wikipedia classifies it as a "dwarf planet" with five known moons, part of the Kuiper belt, the ring of more than a thousand "small bodies," a scientific designation distinct from the terms *planet*, *dwarf planet*, or *natural satellite*. All of the information is cited, and I can easily jump via hyperlinks from article to article to help broaden the horizon of my understanding.

So, at least in this single instance, Wikipedia is a far better source of information than my outdated print encyclopedia (which I love dearly and will not be trashing, thank you very much).

It is true that some "whacked" information has been published on the Wikipedia platform, especially in its early days. Teachers and professors hastened to warn off and even to forbid their students from reading Wikipedia articles. *Complex.com* offers a list of the "50 Craziest Lies in Wikipedia History," among them the slip-up (or intentional falsehood?) that Ernest Hemingway's *Death in the Afternoon*, a 1932 nonfiction book on bullfighting, concerns the "ceremony and traditions of Spanish whores." Could it have been an unfortunate typo, with the intended word being "mores," a noun from sociology meaning, according to Webster's, "folkways of central importance accepted without question and embodying the fundamental moral views of a group"? In any case, the sentence now reads "Spanish bullfighting." The list of "lies" that *Complex.com* attributes to Wikipedia articles consists mostly of pranks ("Bin Laden was a top bloke and a chronic masturbator") and digital forms of "throwing shade" more than it involves serious attempts to manipulate information or to impugn someone's character. In 2005, an American public figure was alarmed to learn that a Wikipedia page under his name listed him as a suspect in the assassination of both President Kennedy and his brother, Bobby Kennedy. No perpetrator for the libelous entry was ever identified. As is unfortunately true in other Internet venues, there exist politically motivated attacks as well, for example, identifying a politician as a vampire or an anti-Semite.

Facts or Ideas that Qualify as "Common Knowledge"

So why would I put any faith in Wikipedia at all?

Answer: If I'm doing deep research, I do not use Wikipedia or any encyclopedia as source material. Encyclopedias, whether print or electronic, are starting points. They are never end points. However, I will explore the citations listed at the bottom of a Wikipedia article. Why not? Often, I can find excellent source materials linked by way of Wikipedia citations, the same way that I find solid citations in a high-quality print encyclopedia.

Can I use Wikipedia to find "surface" information or to verify some item of "common knowledge"?

Answer: Absolutely. In the same way that I have to use a dictionary to remember how to spell a word from time to time, I can use Wikipedia to verify, for example, the capital of Missouri. (Jefferson City is the capital of Missouri. I just looked it up.) In this instance, I am not doing real research. I am verifying what is typically called "common knowledge." Even though I forgot the capital of Missouri, it is common knowledge that the capital of Missouri is Jefferson City. When a fact or idea qualifies as "common knowledge," then I don't have to cite my source of information.

What qualifies as "common knowledge"?

It's tricky. The basic idea is that information that most educated readers would know qualifies as "common knowledge." You don't need to cite common knowledge information.

- If you quote data or statistics provided by an author or website, it is not common knowledge and you must cite.
- If you paraphrase ideas that are new to you from a source with an author, it is not common knowledge and you must cite.
- If you don't know that the capital of Nevada is Carson City, you can look it up and assume that an average "educated reader" could know this fact, so you do not have to cite.
- There are certain scientific principles that a given audience might understand as common knowledge. For example, Pythagoras' theorem or Newton's first law of motion are common knowledge within a given community or audience. As such, these ideas require no citation.

Database vs. Search Engine

As a college student or career professional, you must understand the difference between a "database" and a "search engine."

A database is a curated collection of information, typically free from ads and other peripheral distractions. You will likely encounter a number of databases in your school, college, university, or public library. As a college student, you very likely have access to a number of specialized databases. Databases such as *EBSCO* or *JSTOR* provide access to a broad range of publications in the liberal arts and social sciences. *CQ Researcher* provides overviews of social and political topics. *ERIC* houses education-related resources. *Medline Plus* contains a medical encyclopedia and dictionary, a drug and disease database, and surgery videos. There are dozens of databases aiming to help college students in their efforts to find reliable source materials. In the professional world, there are hundreds of specialized databases curated for the benefit of professionals such as accountants, lawyers, and entrepreneurs. These databases typically charge an access fee. In fact, as a college student, it is likely that you are paying a fee for databases through student ... so you might as well get your money's worth and use them!

A "search engine" is "free" only in the sense that the money doesn't come out of the end-consumer's pocket directly. Search engines run on an advertising model or fee structure, that is, payment for traffic generated. Hence, unless you are very careful, almost all of what you find over a search engine comes to you with an invisible price tag attached to it, often in the form of a software "cookie" which tracks your Internet usage. Your habits and personal data have commercial value. Internet companies pay not only for the privilege to advertise to you; they pay to know what sites you visit, how long you spend there, whether a transaction is made, what hyperlinks you click on, and so forth.

Google, Bing, and Yahoo are examples of search engines.

Do I use these search engines? Yes, every day. I am also aware that I am constantly being sold something. This is the wearying price I pay for the use of a "free" search engine.

Is it possible to do deep research via a search engine?

The honest answer: it is difficult but not impossible.

Boolean Operators

Google Scholar (*scholar.google.com*) represents a combination of database and search engine. The site touts itself as "a simple way to broadly search for scholarly literature" across many disciplines. Thousands of relevant article abstracts and book previews are available. Some full-text articles are available. However, based on my somewhat limited experience, the site seems to push you toward commercial products. Clearly, Google profits from such commercial traffic. For example, a search of "e-learning in the twenty-first century" offers me an e-book of the same title as a top pick. When I follow the link for this e-book, I am provided a preview of the book with a prominent "Get this book in print" link where I can slide over to Amazon.com or other retailers to purchase the product. Software will track my route from Google to the retailer, and Google would almost certainly receive a fractional payment if I were to purchase the book. This may be good information, but it's not free information. Nor am I arguing, necessarily, that all information should be free. As a writer, I value intellectual property and copyright protections, and I believe that writers and publishers who put in the hard work to produce a product deserve capital reward. I am only arguing for full awareness and full disclosure.

On the other hand, if I search Google Scholar for "e-learning in the twenty-first century," I find that the second source is a complete PDF file, an authored article with endnote citations in case I want to pursue deep study. This is good information, and it is free information.

Frequently, your first attempt at a keyword search in either a database or a search engine will not yield good results or will yield too many results. Via *google.com*, a search for "e-learning in the twenty-first century" yields 5.32 million results in .62 seconds. The top returns, of course, are commercial in nature.

What are the chances that I will hunt through the first million results?

(Some rhetorical questions are so absurd that they deserve no response.)

"Boolean operators" can help us to control the information flow.

George Boole (1815–1864) was an English mathematician, educator, and philosopher who published several papers on the analysis of thought and logic. Today, his namesake "Boolean operators" are simple words—AND, OR, NOT, or AND NOT—used to combine or exclude keywords in a search engine or database search. Combining or excluding search terms can offer more focused and useful results.

In Google Scholar and many other web-based databases and search engines, you may have to look for an "Advanced Search" feature in order to take advantage of Boolean operators. Databases, on the other hand, will recognize Boolean operators, enhancing your capacity to more quickly find meaningful results.

- AND, OR, NOT, or AND NOT are Boolean operators used to combine or exclude terms in a database search
  - For example, weapons NOT guns

- Use quotation marks to create a "Boolean string" in order to search for a phrase instead of separate words
  - For example, "library resources" instead of *library resources* produces more focused results.
- Combine Boolean strings and Boolean operators to focus and enhance your results
  - For example, "nuclear weapon" AND submarine

Internet and Institutional Resources

One of the great privileges of being a college student is that, in most institutions, you will have instant access to a wide variety of curated databases such as *EBSCO*, *CQ Researcher*, *JSTOR*, and numerous other databases. As mentioned, you almost certainly help to fund database access by way of student fees, so take advantage!

Check with your instructor and your institution on what library and database resources are available to you.

Open Educational Resources (OER) and Open Movements

Increasingly, educational institutions are embracing what is known as OER, or Open Educational Resources. The website *OER Commons* defines itself as a "public digital library of open educational resources." The site offers online building tools for teachers of all levels.

More generally, open educational resources are any resources that are available online at little or no cost for the purpose of teaching, learning, or research. The idea of "open" resources stems most directly from the computer revolution of the late twentieth century in which some prominent digital pioneers emphasized the importance of "open source" software platforms built by a collective for the public good. Many educational institutions nationwide and globally have embraced the concept of developing free educational resource databases, including curated and peer-reviewed articles and full-text e-books. The hopeful idea of the Internet as a vast, free public library may come closer to fruition with such efforts.

For further information on open movements, see Unit Five Appropriation and specifically Finding Connections: Copyright Era and the Public Domain.

Skeptics like political scientist Langdon Winner rejected the utopian visions of early digital pioneers, and computer entrepreneurs like Microsoft co-founder Bill Gates built their fortunes on the outright rejection of the "open source software" or "shareware" mode of conducting business. Gates claimed patent and copyright protections for his software products and at various times in his career has been criticized for squelching competition and running monopolistic enterprises. To be clear, I am not endorsing or rejecting this view of Gates. I do think that the history of Microsoft embodies important developments in the history of the personal computer which should be understood by students today who probably take Internet "openness" for granted.

- An introduction to OER (Open Educational Resources) and a collection of open databases, advocacy organizations, and resources can be found under the "OER Resources" tab at *https://libguides.tmcc. edu/OpenEducationalResources.*

The "openness" of the Internet is something that we all take for granted, but as we see in the discussions above, the question of "openness" is a complicated one, made more complicated by issues of *copyright* and *public domain*. Be able to define "copyright" and "public domain." Look up exact definitions rather than muddling through with a vague, general ideas of what these terms mean.

See Unit Five Appropriation for information on copyright, public domain, and related issues.

The book that you are holding in your hand is, I hope, a bit of a hybrid between OER "open source materials" and copyright-protected source materials. Due to the legal protections of copyright, we must pay fees for our featured materials. I can't apologize for that because some things are worth paying for, and, as many a wise elder will remind you, there is no such thing as a free lunch. At the same time, we have attempted to provide you with a deep well of OER and Internet resources so that you can explore high quality materials free of charge. Unfortunately, a few of these "free" resources will come with blinking, distracting ads. These are examples of the "no free lunch" principle. Many of us simply cannot afford multiple publication subscriptions. The dynamic between "open source materials" and ad-based content is one of the significant conundrums surrounding general interest research in the twenty-first century.

Matching Your Research to Your Purpose and Audience

Understanding your *purpose* and *audience* are key concepts to keep at the forefront of your mind when writing and researching. Often, you can make important decisions on where to research, how to research, and which sources to select if you remain aware of purpose and audience.

For example, if you are writing for a specialized audience, your research sources will tend to be more specialized. If you are writing a paper for an upper-division biology course, then you might favor peer-reviewed studies published in academic journals. "Peer-reviewed" publication means that an original study or article has been reviewed by other professionals in the field. Peer-reviewed articles may be found in specialized databases, or sometimes online if, for example, a professional organization has a web site that is open to the public. Peer-reviewed articles are clear examples of "curated" sources of information.

"Specialized" audiences have their own vocabulary. Your anthropology instructor may want you to utilize the specialized vocabulary of this particular academic discipline. If your purpose involves communicating directly to a specialized audience, then your research will gravitate toward specialized databases and possibly even peer-reviewed primary source material—that is, original accounts and studies authored by the scientists themselves.

Many composition instructors ask you to address a general "outside" audience. (As always, check with your instructor.) Research assignments in a first-year composition course probably call for the writer to address a general outside audience. It is not always the case. For example, in a special topics composition course that I taught on "American Popular Music," I encouraged students to develop specialized vocabulary associated with music studies and criticism. Most of my composition courses require students to address a wide, general readership.

Primary and Secondary Sources

In different scholarly disciplines, "primary" and "secondary" source material can mean different things. In the field of history, a pioneer's nineteenth century diary entries can be considered "primary" source material, whereas a historian's overarching analytical account of such primary source materials can be called a "secondary" source. The scholar, in this case, summarizes the results of his or her analysis of historical documents.

In any given scientific field, a "primary" source could involve the published results of a scientist's experiment(s). Such a primary scientific source might feature jargon and mathematical symbols that would make it very difficult or even impossible for someone like me to follow. Although I am well educated, I simply don't have the background to be able to process a primary study in most scientific fields. In order to access this kind of information, I must rely on "secondary" source material. For example, a science writer may publish a journalistic account that summarizes the findings of an original study. I would find this secondary source much more useful. And, if I wanted to write an essay for publication on a scientific topic, I would have to track down and rely upon secondary sources.

In the humanities and in literary studies, there may be some confusion even among instructors regarding what constitutes a "primary" or a "secondary" source. Always check with your instructors. In a world literature class, a "primary" source is the author's original text, whereas an article that offers a contemporary reassessment of the author's literature may be called a "secondary" source. However, some instructors may call this latter article a primary source as well. It doesn't really matter (to me) if we call the scholarly article a primary or a secondary source, as long as we are all thinking in clear terms regarding our source materials.

Note that there is no *better* or *worse* when it comes to "primary" and "secondary" source material. Primary sources are not necessarily "better" than secondary sources. If the true primary source material in a world literature class was written in ancient Greek, for example, then we must rely on a secondary source, the English language interpretation of the original material, in order to access the information. Scholars who operate within a discipline on a very high level tend to deal with primary source material. These scholars generate secondary source materials that enable the rest of us to be able to engage in the pertinent discourse.

When you address a general audience, your sources will tend to be more general in nature. You would probably avoid, for instance, primary source materials aimed at a specialized audience which use field-specific jargon. Or, if you do use it, you will need to "translate" it for the benefit of your general audience. If you can't understand discipline-specific jargon in an article, should you be listing it on your Works Cited or References page?

Well-researched analytical secondary source materials that appear in general interest publications usually prove useful for you and for your audience. If I am writing an article on human efforts to manipulate genetics in the animal kingdom, am I better off using a cover story from *National Geographic* which offers a summary-analysis of recent developments, or am I better off using an original peer-reviewed study from the *Journal of Genetic Engineering and Biotechnology*?

The answer to this question, I believe, depends on two things: *purpose* and *audience*. If you are a graduate student studying genetic engineering, you must seek out specialized information for a specialized audience. If you are a first-year college student participating in an important public discourse, you are clearly better off integrating quotations from a well-respected general interest magazine.

A Few Key Definitions

How can we claim to be twenty-first century literate unless we can actually *define* the basic elements imbuing our everyday lives? Define the words and terms below, not with inexact phraseology (*it's sort like a thing that...*) but with an exact definition that an outside reader could comprehend. Write down these definitions in your notebook.

- What is a "search engine"? What is a "browser"?
- What is a "database"?
- What is the "Internet"?
- What is a "server"?
- What is a "domain"?

- What is the "cloud"?
- Define "cybersecurity" and "wireless."
- Can you distinguish between email, videoconferencing, blogs, chats, messaging, tweets, alerts, and podcasts? Describe each.
- What is a "wiki"? What is "UGC, or user-generated content"?
- What is a "user interface"?
- What is an "avatar"?
- What is an "IP address"?
- What is a "URL address"? What is "DOI"?
- What is "Google"?
- What are "http" and "https"?
- What do ".com," ".org," and ".edu" mean?
- What is "Wikipedia" or what is a "wiki" app? What is an "app"?
- What is "shareware"?
- What is "crowdsourcing"?
- What is a "course management system"?
- What is "concept mapping"?
- What are "tags"? What is "metadata"?
- Define "AI," "AGI," "deep learning" and "machine learning."
- What are "GIS" and "GPS"?

What other terms must we know in order to be information- or data-literate in the twenty-first century? (What about a "cookie"? Hint: you can't eat it.)

The National Council of Teachers of English (NCTE) Definition of Twenty-First Century Literacies

Updated February, 2013, Adopted by the NCTE Executive Committee, February 15, 2008

Literacy has always been a collection of cultural and communicative practices shared among members of particular groups. As society and technology change, so does literacy. Because technology has increased the intensity and complexity of literate environments, the twenty-first century demands that a literate person possess a wide range of abilities and competencies, many literacies. These literacies are multiple, dynamic, and malleable. As in the past, they are inextricably linked with particular histories, life possibilities, and social trajectories of individuals and groups. Active, successful participants in this twenty-first century global society must be able to:

- Develop proficiency and fluency with the tools of technology;
- Build intentional cross-cultural connections and relationships with others so [as] to pose and solve problems collaboratively and strengthen independent thought;
- Design and share information for global communities to meet a variety of purposes;
- Manage, analyze, and synthesize multiple streams of simultaneous information;
- Create, critique, analyze, and evaluate multimedia texts;
- Attend to the ethical responsibilities required by these complex environments.

This position statement may be printed, copied, and disseminated without permission from NCTE.
An updated NCTE statement entitled "Definition of Literacy in a Digital Age" (2019) can be found at https://ncte.org/statement/nctes-definition-literacy-digital-age/.

Further Inquiry

Coiro, Julie. "Predicting Reading Comprehension on the Internet: Contributions of Offline Reading Skills, Online Reading Skills, and Prior Knowledge." *Journal of Literary Research*, Vol. 43, No. 4 (2011), *doi: 10.1177/1086296X11421979.*

Coiro, Julie. "Talking About Reading as Thinking: Modeling the Hidden Complexities of Online Reading Comprehension." *Theory Into Practice*, Vol. 50, No. 2 (2011), pp. 107-115, *doi: 10.1080/00405841.2011.558435.*

Coiro, Julie and David W. Moore. "New Literacies and Adolescent Learners: An Interview With Julie Coiro." *Journal of Adolescent & Adult Literacy*, Vol. 55, No. 6 (Mar. 2012), pp. 551-553, *http://www.jstor.org/stable/41827858.*

Darnton, Robert. "The Research Library in the Digital Age." Harvard University Library, 2008, *http://hul.harvard.edu/publications/Darnton_ResearchLibraryDigitalAge.pdf.*

Davlashyan, Naira, and Irina Titova. Associated Press (AP). "Ex-Workers at Russian Troll Factory Say Mueller Indictments Are True." *Time.com*, 19 Feb. 2018, *http://time.com/5165805/russian-troll-factory-mueller-indictments/.*

Kang, Cecilia, and Adam Goldman. "In Washington Pizzeria Attack, Fake News Brought Real Guns." *The New York Times*, nytimes.com, 5 Dec. 2016, *https://www.nytimes.com/2016/12/05/business/media/comet-ping-pong-pizza-shooting-fake-news-consequences.html.*

Kleinman, Zoe. "Cambridge Analytica: The Story So Far." *BBC News*, Technology, 20 Mar. 2018. *http://www.bbc.com/news/technology-43465968.*

Knobel, Michele and Colin Lankshear. "Studying New Literacies." *Journal of Adolescent & Adult Literacy*, Vol. 58, No. 2 (Oct. 2014), pp. 97-101, *http://www.jstor.org/stable/24034699.*

Leu, Donald J. et al. "The New Literacies of Online Research and Comprehension: Rethinking the Reading Achievement Gap." *Reading Research Quarterly*, Vol. 50, No. 1 (Jan.-Mar. 2015), pp. 37–59, *doi: 10.1002/rrq.85.*

McCarthy, Tom. "Sherlock Holmes is public property ... But Steer Clear of Watson's Second Wife." *The Guardian*, 27 Dec. 2013, *https://www.theguardian.com/world/2013/dec/27/sherlock-holmes-copyright-ruling-public-domain.*

Meyer, Robinson. "The Grim Conclusions of the Largest-Ever Study of Fake News." *The Atlantic*, theatlantic.com, 8 Mar. 2018, *https://www.theatlantic.com/technology/archive/2018/03/largest-study-ever-fake-news-mit-twitter/555104/.*

Robinson, Lisa. "Why Chance the Rapper Makes Music for Free (and How He Actually Makes Money)." *Vanity Fair*, 9 Feb. 2017, *https://www.vanityfair.com/hollywood/2017/02/why-chance-the-rapper-music-is-free-and-how-he-makes-money.*

Rosenberg, Eli. "Alex Jones Apologizes for Promoting 'Pizzagate' Hoax." *The New York Times*, nytimes.com, 25 Mar. 2017, *https://www.nytimes.com/2017/03/25/business/alex-jones-pizzagate-apology-comet-ping-pong.html.*

Schultz, Colin. "'Sherlock Holmes' Is Now Officially Off Copyright and Open for Business." *Smithsonian.com*, 19 June 2014, *https://www.smithsonianmag.com/smart-news/sherlock-holmes-now-officially-copyright-and-open-business-180951794/.*

"To Our Readers." *New Republic*, vol. 218, no. 22, 1 June 1998, pp. 8-9. EBSCO*host*.

"What Is Common Knowledge?" *Academic Integrity at MIT: A Handbook for Students*. Massachusetts Institute of Technology, *integrity.mit.edu*, *https://integrity.mit.edu/handbook/citing-your-sources/what-common-knowledge.*

Plagiarism in the Internet Era

Ercegovac, Zorana and John V. Richardson. "Academic Dishonesty, Plagiarism Included, in the Digital Age: A Literature Review." *College & Research Libraries*, vol. 65, no. 5 (2004), doi: *https://doi.org/10.5860/crl.65.4.301.*

Gabriel, Trip. "Plagiarism Lines Blur for Students in the Digital Age." *The New York Times*, Education, 1 Aug. 2010, *https://www.nytimes.com/2010/08/02/education/02cheat.html.*

A Note on the Further Inquiry Sources

One of the goals of *Engaging Discourse 2.0* involves the development of independent critical thinking and the critical evaluation of source materials. Students must evaluate the authority and the validity of sources listed under the Further Inquiry unit bibliographies as they would other internet or library texts. Clearly, not all authors bear equal authority.

Unfortunately, students must sometimes evaluate a source's authority amidst blinking ads and other common Internet distractions. A teacher might avoid commercialized and monetized web pages, and the impulse to do so is the right one, in my view. Commercials belong in a classroom as much as they belong in a chapel, synagogue, or mosque. That's my not-so-hot take, anyway. Nonetheless, students need to learn to evaluate available resources and to filter annoying and pernicious distractions. They might also learn something about the value and cost of good information.

The Further Inquiry pages may in some instances call for a "teaching moment" regarding *.edu* and *.gov* sites, *.com* and *.org* sites, the distinctions of *library*, *database*, and *search engine,* and a host of other topics as covered in Unit Nine Research in the Twenty-First Century. Clearly, we can also draw connections to issues mentioned in Unit One Literacy in the Twenty-First Century and Unit Three Brain Plasticity (not to mention Generation Studies, Happiness Studies, and so on). Some of these sources and authors may have an agenda or a product to sell. In libraries as well as the free market we need to teach our students the meaning of *caveat emptor*, or "buyer beware." Beware, for example, of any product endorsements that sneak into these important discourses. Teachers may yet outdo AI if we can encourage curiosity and critical thinking while discouraging the simplistic cynicism of *believe nothing* that threatens our endeavors in an age of rampant misinformation and propaganda. To me, it's a timeless dynamic rather than a new paradigm. Some of these pages are selling ad space and collecting user data—a disturbing, seemingly unavoidable reality of American life in the Internet era, the most disturbing facet of which is that young people don't seem to understand why anyone would find data collection and tracking disturbing in the first place. Old-fashioned concepts about a right to privacy seem as quaint as the idealism of Internet pioneers and the belief that I shouldn't be forced to watch commercials in a movie theater before my movie starts. For that matter, it seems as antiquated as the notion that watching a film in a movie theater is somehow better than streaming it on a mobile device. What strange ideas the elders used to have!

Obviously, I cannot guarantee the reliability of each and every Further Inquiry source. I am not aware of any instances of bad or fake information residing in these pages, but it wouldn't shock me to discover that we had missed something. Google "Stephen Glass," whose made-up reports reside to this day in respectable library databases worldwide. Nor do I, and I hope this is obvious, endorse any thesis or major claim of any author who appears in *Engaging Discourse 2.0*.

Unit One Notes

Questions for Comprehension – Carr

1. False. Students who browsed the web performed worse on a subsequent test of lecture material.
2. There are no benefits to multitasking, according to this article. "Heavy multitaskers," researchers found, "weren't even good at multitasking."
3. b) perpetual mental locomotion. Clearly, Carr fears what constant mental locomotion does to the human brain. Meditation, contemplation, and introspection are not allowed to exist in such an environment, according to Carr.

Unit One Writing Assignments

Sentence Exercises

1. Note the necessary *comma* that comes after the introductory dependent phrase (the comma appears after "2010"). In introductory sentences, offer an interpretation of the author's thesis or main point, or the main point that is relevant to your discourse. You might mention the "rhetorical situation" of the text in question (see Unit Five Resources); in this case, we mention *The Wall Street Journal* (a publication with a particular audience and viewpoint) as well as the date of publication. See "Introducing Texts" in Unit One Resources.
2. We are *analyzing* content rather than *summarizing* content. You can look up the definitions of the verbs "analyze" and "summarize" instantly on *dictionary.com* or another web resource. This sentence template calls for a *contrast* in ideas from the first independent clause (in front of the semi-colon) to the second independent clause (after the semi-colon). The transition word "instead" indicates the logical relationship between these two independent clauses.
3. In a text analysis or expository assignment, you must explore the evidence that an author presents or the means by which the author attempts to convince the audience of a concept or viewpoint.

Unit Two Notes

Questions for Comprehension – Walton

1. It would seem that "true" is the best answer here. Experts believe that extensive use of Facebook (and possibly other platforms) can in fact cause feelings of social isolation. If we define "FOMO" as a symptom of anxiety or social isolation caused by social media use, then "true" is the best answer. A student might argue that "FOMO" does not qualify as the sort of overtly negative emotion that the article covers.

2. False. A research team undertook a study of 11 social media sites, "including Facebook, Twitter, Google+, YouTube, LinkedIn, Instagram, Pinterest, Tumblr, Vine, Snapchat and Reddit" and found an increase in a sense of social isolation corresponding to more time spent on these sites.

3. The article mentions studies that indicate that people who detach from social media undergo "a kind of withdrawal." The psychological effects of internet withdrawal are "accompanied by actual physiological changes." (These changes may or may not pertain to social media per se.) Another study speaks of "Facebook Addiction Disorder" which can include symptoms of "neglect of personal life, mental preoccupation, escapism, mood modifying experiences, tolerance and concealing the addictive behavior...." These and similar behaviors have long been associated with drug, alcohol, and other forms of addiction.

4. There is no link. One study asserts that "there seems to be a cap on the number of friends a person's brain can handle." More friends on social media doesn't necessarily imply a better social life.

Resources — Three Effective Ways to Integrate Quotations

Using a different original quotation, we can still integrate the language using these same three methods:
Original quotation from Margaret Atwood, "Pornography" (1988): "It would be naïve to think of violent pornography as just harmless entertainment. It's also an educational tool and a powerful propaganda device."

1. The **signal phrase** (with a comma):
   Atwood claims, "[Violent pornography] is an educational tool and a powerful propaganda device" (45).
   - "Atwood claims" is the signal phrase that must be set off with a comma. "Atwood writes" or "Atwood argues" are other examples of signal phrases. Note that we have replaced "It's also" in the original text with the bracketed phrase "Pornography is." The beginning of this quotation (which is a full sentence) requires a capital letter "P" on "Pornography." Avoid quoting faulty fragment sentences with the signal phrase method. With the signal phrase method, you want to quote or create a full sentence quotation.

2. The **whole sentence set up** (with a colon):
   Atwood claims that pornography has a profound capacity to sway its viewers: "It's also an educational tool and a powerful propaganda device" (45).
   - Note that we have set up the original quotation with *a complete sentence that is capable of standing on its own.* A colon [:] follows the complete sentence in order to set up the quotation. We use the colon to display the relationship between the set up and the quotation.

3. The **seamless transition** (no punctuation):
   Atwood writes that pornography is "an educational tool and a powerful propaganda device" (45).
   - There is *no comma* after "is." Other than the quotation marks, punctuate the sentence as you would a normal sentence of your own.

Sentence Exercise

Walton cites numerous negative effects that may result from overuse of social media, the most significant of which might be feelings of anxiety and depression.
[Obviously, other answers are possible.]

Paragraph Exercise

The main concept here is to determine whether you want to show addition or extension, contrast, *or con-clusion. See* Examining Your Draft Essay: Tips for Editing and Revision *in Unit Nine for a useful list of transition words and phrases.*

Experts disagree on whether Internet addiction is real. Nonetheless, studies do confirm that people may experience anxiety and other symptoms of withdrawal when separated from their digital devices. Moreover, feelings of social isolation are linked to social media use. As a consequence, we ought to use caution when engaging these powerful communication tools.

Or

Experts disagree on whether Internet addiction is real. However, studies do confirm that people may experience anxiety and other symptoms of withdrawal when separated from their digital devices. Additionally, feelings of social isolation are linked to social media use. Therefore, we ought to use caution when engaging these powerful communication tools.

Other combinations of transition words are possible. The blank spaces (where we fill in the transition words or phrases) must, in any case, serve the same or a similar logical purpose in all responses. Note, for example, that "Nonetheless" and "However" serve the same purpose (indicating contrast); "Moreover" and "Additionally" show expansion or continuation of an idea; and "As a consequence" and "Therefore" indicate a result or conclusion.

Unit Three Notes

Questions for Comprehension — Medeiros

1. "Neuroplasticity" means that 2) the brain is a mutable, adaptable organ whose very structure is capable of change at any point in life, according to Merzenich.
2. False. As Tallal and Merzenich illustrated, dyslexia results from the brain's inability to connect sounds and symbols (letters). As it turned out, this problem could be solved through so-called "brain training."
3. "On average, cognitive decline in humans starts when we're between 20 and 30."
4. Less accurate listening, narrowing of peripheral vision, faltering attention span and memory—these are the main symptoms of cognitive decline mentioned in the article. These physical symptoms are "usually accompanied by social withdrawal, egocentrism and a loss of confidence."
5. Gazzaley advocates "hardware and software as a form of medicine." He stresses that drugs won't work when it comes to brain health.

Finding Connections: The Aging and Plastic Brain

- What do you imagine are the best ways to carry out Merzenich's mantra of positive control of the plastic mind? *In fact, you may be doing one of the best things right now: fresh, continual learning throughout a lifetime. Other activities that encourage positive plasticity include walking, dancing, trying out a new recipe, learning a new language or musical instrument, flower arranging or other artistic activities. One's attitude is almost as important as the activity. On a neurological level, having an "open mind" means more than just being an accepting person. With muscles or with the mind, the slogan "use it or lose it" is equally valid. In general, avoid rote, repetitive activities.*
- What would you tell older relatives that they must do in order to remain on the positive side of cognition as they age? *Rote, repetitive activities do not help. See the list above.*
- In what crucial ways do the physical body and the thinking mind interact? *Whatever goes on with your body, internally or externally, also affects the mind. The mind and body are intimately connected. Taking care of the body with physical activity also takes care of the mind.*

Sentence Exercises

Obviously, there are many possible appropriate responses. The main ideas here are 1) to exhibit an understanding of the text, and 2) to be able to construct clear sentences. You may want to think of these as topic sentences to open a paragraph.

Merzenich believes that neuroplasticity allows a person to change throughout a lifetime.

Cognitive decline in humans can begin early and can cause hearing and vision impairment.

Neuroscientist Adam Gazzaley developed a video game in order to treat the symptoms of cognitive decline.

Paragraph Exercise

These are cognitive development exercises, puzzles as much as usage exercises. Fit together the appropriate parts of language to form coherent paragraphs.

Merzenich and other scientists believe that the human brain is plastic. Some of the most significant implications of neuroplasticity can be seen when children with dyslexia show dramatic improvements. As a result of these proven treatments, people who have suffered from dyslexia now find that they can learn to read and comprehend literary source materials.

OR

Merzenich and other scientists believe that the human brain is adaptable throughout a lifetime. Some of the most significant implications of this cognitive flexibility can be seen when an older person engages in brain training. As a result of new online training programs, people who have suffered from cognitive decline may now find that they are able to lead richer lives.

Making Connections Template Exercise

The "Making Connections" template exercises are cognitive puzzles. They also force students to consider prose syntax. (They do not necessarily produce the kind of clear, straightforward sentences valued by most general editors.) The following is one possible answer, not the only answer.

In the essay "Does the Internet Make You Dumber?" writer Nicholas Carr expresses concerns about our declining attention spans. Similarly, neuroscientist Michael Merzenich expresses concerns that the human brain can be remapped at any point in a person's lifetime.

Unit Four Notes

Questions for Comprehension – Fredrickson

1. False. The work of neuroscientist Uri Hasson reveals that brain coupling is "surprisingly widespread."
2. Oxytocin is nicknamed the "cuddle hormone" or "love hormone."
3. It increased the level of trust a person has in another person. The oxytocin nasal spray essentially doubled the level of trust that investors had in their trustees. As a side note, related research showed that the mere act of being entrusted with someone else's money raised the trustee's naturally occurring levels of oxytocin. The neuropeptide oxytocin shapes both trust and reciprocity.
4. *Calm-and-connect.*
5. "In May 2010, I had the immense honor of presenting the results of this experiment directly to His Holiness the Fourteenth Dalai Lama."

Making Connections Template Exercise

The "Making Connections Template Exercise" is a cognitive puzzle that encourages students to draw connections between unit topics. It also forces students to consider prose syntax. (These exercises do not necessarily produce the kind of clear, straightforward sentences valued by most general editors.) The following are possible answers, not the only answers.

Psychologists are increasingly aware of the connections between positive emotions and health. Therefore, policymakers ought to take practices that increase wellness into account when considering how to reform our health care systems.

OR

Educators are increasingly aware of the connections between positive emotions and health. Therefore, teachers ought to take mental wellness into account when considering their teaching strategies.

Unit Five Notes

Questions for Comprehension – Lethem

1. Anyone who looks at arts and culture with any level of real understanding will conclude that imitation, borrowing, and reference to other works is part and parcel of the creative act. (*Sine qua non* means "without which it does not exist.") To put it even more simply, there is no creativity without stealing from what's come before.

2. Shakespeare and Eliot are literary geniuses whose creativity sometimes leans on the work of others. It is not "cheating." There is nothing wrong with this sort of borrowing, Lethem claims. [Copy & paste-style plagiarism is cheating, it is wrong, and it is altogether different in spirit from the creative endeavors that Lethem cites.]*

3. False. Disney pulled almost all of its content for free from the public domain, mainly from European folktales. The images that Disney made from these tales were then copyrighted and monetized.

4. The public owns them. Have we lost the concept of "public ownership" and "public good" to such an extent that this has become a trick question?

5. These problems might be solved by surveying (reading) existing scientific literature. "Swanson showed that standing problems in medical research may be significantly addressed, perhaps even solved, simply by systematically surveying the scientific literature."

6. Clearly, there is not one correct answer here, although some answers may be "more correct" than others considering that the question requires the student to meditate on Lethem's meaning. "Originality" is a suspicious concept, many readers of Lethem's article could conclude. Picasso himself—inarguably one of the most "original" artists ever to have lived—is often quoted, "Good artists borrow, great artists steal." Whether he spoke these exact words is up for debate, but the sentiment itself is common among artists.

*An Additional Note on Plagiarism

See "Plagiarism" in the Unit Five introduction. Find further information in Unit Nine Research in the Twenty-First Century.

It is important to distinguish between the sort of "plagiarism" Lethem considers and simple cheating. Plagiarism is not always clear. Sometimes students fail to recognize when they are guilty of it.

From the artist's standpoint, T.S. Eliot writes in a 1920 essay:

Bad poets deface what they take, and good poets make it into something better, or at least something different. The good poet welds his theft into a whole of feeling which is unique, utterly different from that from which it was torn; the bad poet throws it into something which has no cohesion. A good poet will usually borrow from authors remote in time, or alien in language, or diverse in interest. (See Unit Five Further Inquiry bibliography for a citation.)

Students who are writing college essays, however, are not typically engaged in the writing process as artists. They are scholars, or maybe even journalists, who are ethically obligated to credit their sources.

Unit Six Notes

Questions for Comprehension – Tegmark

1. False. There is no general scientific agreement as to when (if ever) AGI will exist or be developed.
2. True. A heat-seeking missile has a goal. More germane to this discourse, AI or "superintelligent AI" can also have goals. For example, a computer program strives to win a game of chess or Go. Weather forecasting software culls data from the Internet with a goal of telling us if we need an umbrella or sunscreen.
3. AI has only a narrow scope of intelligence (for example, a chess playing program), while the possibilities for AGI are much wider. AGI would have *general* intelligence, or what we might call independent thinking. "Deep learning" or "machine learning" are related concepts. AGI would be able to independently work on problems beyond the typical narrow parameters of AI. What Tegmark calls Life 3.0 would be able to design its own "hardware" and "software." (Humans can only design our own "software" at the moment, although we are making progress at designing and integrating some "hardware" – bionics, artificial organs, etc.)

Unit Seven Notes

Questions for Comprehension – Twenge and Campbell

1. False. Actually, *two-thirds* of students in the survey said they should get special consideration if they explained they were trying hard, evidently missing the point that grades reflect performance, not effort.
2. D. entitled
3. "Unfortunately, wanting more money for doing less work is a fairly succinct definition of entitlement."
4. The very short answer would be, "gratitude." When we appreciate the things we have, when we are grateful for our food, our wealth, our family, and our friends, we not only dampen feelings of entitlement, we also tend to be more happy and healthy.
5. There are many possible thoughtful answers to this question. Understanding the context of the question and being thoughtful in one's response are the most important elements. Arguably, the idea that "illegals do the jobs that Americans are unwilling to do" points to a disturbing new attitude that "real" Americans are above manual and menial labor. This attitude reveals that Americans are not willing to start at the bottom and pay their dues, say these authors. On the other hand, educated Americans (who are often wealthy relative to world standards) may in fact have better job opportunities. Clearly, there is merit in the traditional paradigm of paying your dues and starting out in lowly positions. Too many young Americans, Twenge and Campbell say, feel that they are entitled to skip the lowly, humbling jobs that so frequently characterize the American experience of first or early employment. Working for minimum wage is not glamorous but it can build character.

Making Connections Template Exercise

The "Making Connections" exercises are cognitive puzzles. They also force students to consider prose syntax. (They do not necessarily produce the kind of clear, straightforward sentences valued by most general editors.) The following is one possible answer, not the only answer.

Kelleghan cites [or psychologists cite] research correlating frequent, lengthy use of social media with feelings of anxiety and social isolation. Moreover, Twenge claims [or psychologists claim] that teenagers are particularly vulnerable to feelings of depression resulting from overuse of social media.

Unit Eight Notes

Questions for Comprehension – Gilbert

1. The answer is "True," but we must emphasize that the happiness that results from the work of the psychological immune system is *real* happiness; it is not some sort of fake emotion. There is no distinction, in other words, between synthesized happiness and what we think of as "organic" or "real" happiness.

2. "The results showed that volunteers favored whichever technique [study] produced the conclusion that verified their own personal political ideologies." *Confirmation bias* is a phenomenon wherein people tend to accept facts or information that appear to confirm their own pre-existing beliefs. This is an especially important concept to consider in the twenty-first century, when the Internet and other forms of media overwhelm us with so many opinions, facts, and stories. Is it possible for humans to process any of this information in an objective fashion? Remaining "objective" is not a natural occurrence.

3. The explanation of this quotation involves a similar idea to the "confirmation bias" mentioned above in response 2. Gilbert draws a snarky (but accurate) conclusion that we don't need much to convince us of positive things that we already believe or would like to believe, but we need a great many facts and a great deal of information to convince us of negative things about ourselves or things we don't want to accept. Note that Gilbert uses the informal (and incorrect) "lotta" instead of the standard "lot of." This informality is a mark of his humorous tone and his personal voice. He is speaking to us as a scientist to a lay audience; he is not speaking scientist to scientist.

Paragraph "Translation" Exercise

Your instructor will be able to judge your level of success. The main idea here is to recognize and differentiate the needs of a scientific audience and the needs of a popular interest audience. Oftentimes, in college classrooms, we are wandering in gray zones between different modes of writing. Accuracy of the "translation" is paramount here. Instead of right and wrong, let's think in terms of *effective* or *ineffective*.

COURSE THEORY AND DESIGN

An Afterword for Faculty and Department Chairs

Whenever folks at a social gathering hear that I'm a college English teacher, an inevitable question follows: "Can college kids write these days?" Clearly, it is a rhetorical question to which I am supposed to respond, "No, they're awful! They don't even know how to use semicolons." Never mind that I'm speaking to a successful career professional who doesn't understand semicolons.

I surprise people by saying, "Of course they can write ... if they have something to write about. When they care about what they're writing, they write well."

A lot of people conceive of first year college composition as a mechanical how-to process: how to use semicolons, for example. What the course must be, though, is a keystone course that fosters the development of critical thinking.

The mechanical aspects of good composition are the byproducts of good critical reasoning. Grammar and syntactical problems seem to disappear, or at least become less egregious, once a student actually engages a given discourse. Once the student cares about what he or she is writing, that care translates into more clear prose. America's students, for the most part, come out of high school with the bare prose mechanics in place. My claims here do not stem from naivety. I've spent more of my career working with struggling students than with the academic elite. They do need to be better readers, of course. Our schools seem to have veered away from a devotion to reading. Good readers pick up the habits of good writing on a preconscious level. We comp teachers would have a lot less to do if they were all excellent readers.

Two-thirds of college-age kids in the twenty-first century will not get a four-year degree. At the same time, obtaining a college education has never been more critical for the personal or public good. When I tell my students that a college education is a matter of life and death, I inform them that I mean it *literally*. Then I explain what "literally" means and how no one uses it correctly—a real English teacher moment.

An unprecedented statistic emerged in the early 2000s. Americans in my basic demographic (white, male, middle aged) were, statistically speaking, leading shorter lives. With one exception. Those who are college educated are not experiencing the same shortening of life expectancy. First year college composition is one of the most important steps toward obtaining a degree. Obtaining a degree is one of the best things we can do for our personal and collective health and wealth. This course is a matter of life and death as far as I'm concerned.

If writing is a cognitive process, then first year composition seeks to develop critical thinking rather than mere skills development. Skills development, like sound grammar, is a byproduct of more significant goals. First-year college composition does not teach students *what* to think, but it must teach students *how* to think.

Quality Control

In the world of fast food, "quality control" means that every Big Mac and Chicken McNugget looks and tastes the same at each store nationwide. In the world of American higher education, I hope it means the opposite: that every student who completes first year college composition has taken a crucial step in becoming an *independent* critical thinker.

Engaging Discourse 2.0 aims for total academic success in first year composition.

The critical mission of first year composition is carried out more often by adjunct faculty and graduate students than by experienced, tenured faculty. So *Engaging Discourse 2.0* is user-friendly. The veteran instructor will find deep wells of source material on any of the unit topics, while a first semester graduate student finds an approachable, easy-to-manage textbook filled with student- and instructor-friendly resources. Hand this textbook to a tenured comp expert, a graduate student, or a part-time instructor one week before the semester begins and instead of panic and confusion, we have *quality control*: a textbook that offers simple guidance toward lofty objectives. Plus, these topics are interesting! Moreover, we honor academic freedom and individualism for both student and instructor.

Universal Objectives

In its "Framework for Success in Postsecondary Writing," the Council of Writing Program Administrators (CWPA), National Council of Teachers of English (NCTE), and the National Writing Project (NWP) enumerate the habits of mind that are critical to student success in college writing: curiosity, openness, engagement, creativity, persistence, responsibility, flexibility, and metacognition. *Engaging Discourse 2.0* fosters these habits of mind. Furthermore, it develops rhetorical knowledge, critical thinking, writing processes, knowledge of conventions, and the ability to compose in multiple environments in accordance with the joint CWPA, NCTE, and NWP guidelines.

Objectives for First Year College Composition

Engaging Discourse 2.0 encompasses a writing-intensive curriculum designed to strengthen college-level writing skills, with particular attention to persuasion, analysis, synthesis, and research. The general goal of the curriculum is to improve the reading, thinking, and writing processes associated with academic study.

- ✓ The course aims to develop and to reinforce literacy skills and communication skills, with special emphasis on the student's ability to communicate in clear, standard English language prose.
- ✓ The course aims to model and strengthen sound critical and analytical thinking.
- ✓ The course aims to explain, develop, and clarify methods for the evaluation of source materials.
- ✓ The course offers insights on twenty-first century research methodologies.
- ✓ The course introduces students to a sophisticated research and composition process that includes the production of an annotated bibliography and/or a detailed research paper or end-of-semester feature article. Many composition exercises are available to assist students. Many analysis-response and synthesis prompts are available to assist students and instructors.

Reading, Literacy, and Composition Standards

Many colleges and universities, following national composition standards, require students to produce 20–25 pages of formal prose per semester (circa 6,000 to 7,500 words) with multiple drafts leading to final essays formatted in MLA, APA, or another style as specified by the instructor.

Let's establish not only what we will do but why we will do it.

In 1996, the International Reading Association (IRA) and the National Council of Teachers of English (NCTE) set out a common purpose which can also stand in for our global objectives in first year college composition: "Our shared purpose is to ensure that all students are knowledgeable and proficient users of language so that they may succeed in school, participate in our democracy as informed citizens, find challenging and rewarding work, appreciate and contribute to our culture, and pursue their own goals and interests as independent learners throughout their lives."

Students, in order to fulfill their job and career potentials and in order to become contributing citizens, must learn to analyze the multi-various digital and print texts that are set before them in the twenty-first century. They must learn to engage these texts and the language presented within the texts (formal and informal, oral and written, explicit and implicit). That means they must be able to discuss and to write about these texts. They must learn how to engage in meaningful public discourse. They must learn how to engage in critical, independent thinking about the world in which they live. They must learn how to express that critical thinking in clear, standard prose so that a wide audience can participate in the discourse. These skills are essential for twenty-first century Americans who wish to lead fulfilling lives. These skills are essential for twenty-first century Americans who can contribute to our nation's economy and form of government.

More recently, NCTE has defined (2008) and updated (2013, 2019) its definitions of twenty-first century literacies. NCTE points out, "Literacy has always been a collection of cultural and communicative practices shared among members of particular groups. As society and technology change, so does literacy." The Committee on College Composition (CCCC) has also established (1989) and revised (2013, 2015) an insightful and useful set of guidelines in its "Principles for the Postsecondary Teaching of Writing." As college composition instructors, we must acknowledge the reality of the post-industrial internet society into which our students were born. That does not mean abandoning print texts. Study after study indicates the difficulties involved with the reading and processing of electronic texts. We cannot pretend, however, that twenty-first century students and citizens will procure most of their information from printed texts. Barring a societal shift of apocalyptic proportions, the internet is here to stay. People, for the most part, will visit a search engine before they visit a library or database. To me, this reality does not imply the inevitable death of the library, the database, or the printed book. Simple supply and demand economics tell us that if books become more rare, then they become more valuable. So as long as some of us value printed books over other forms, I believe they will persist. (I read and write on screen for work, but for pleasure and personal study I'll take a book every time.)

Engaging Discourse 2.0 has been designed to encourage the development of timeless literacy skills within the context of the twenty-first century. These discourses are, in fact, the most important conversations of our time.

Acknowledgements

Special thanks to my student James Wiltermood, who graciously allowed me to include his research paper in this volume. Once again, major shout-out to librarian extraordinaire Neil Siegel of Truckee Meadows Community College in Reno, Nevada, who spearheaded the unit bibliographies. Neil is as passionate about the gospel of information literacy as he is about the gospel of jazz. Keep spreading the good news, Neil!

Engaging Discourse 2.0 is the second volume in a series. *Engaging Discourse: A 21st Century Composition Reader & Curriculum (ISBN 978-1-5249-6906-6)* is also available from the Kendall Hunt Publishing Company, www.kendallhunt.com.

INDEX